FALCONS OF FRANCE

BY

CHARLES NORDHOFF

AND

JAMES NORMAN HALL

British Library Cataloguing-in-Publication Data
A catalogue record for this book is available from the
British Library

CONTENTS

Charles Nordhoff

Charles Bernard Nordhoff was born on 1 February 1887, in London, England. He was born to American parents; his father was Walter Nordhoff, a wealthy businessman and author of *The Journey of the Flame,* and his mother, Sarah Cope Whithall, was of Pennsylvania Quaker stock.

Nordhoff and his family returned to the United States in 1889, settling first in Pennsylvania, then Rhode Island, and finally moving to California in 1898. He demonstrated an early aptitude for writing, and had his first work (an article in an ornithological journal) published at the age of fifteen. Two years later, Nordhoff entered *Stanford University*, but transferred to *Harvard University* after only one year. He graduated in 1909, and worked for his father's business, spending two years in Mexico managing a sugar plantation. After this, Nordhoff spent four years as an executive of a tile and brick company in California. He resigned from this position in 1916 however, to join the ambulance corps, with whom he travelled to France. There, Nordhoff served as a pilot in the *Lafayette Escadrille* (a squadron of the French Air Service), and finished World War One as a lieutenant in the US Army Air Service.

After the war, Nordhoff remained in France, and published his first book, *The Fledgling* in 1919. It was during this period that he met James Norman Hall, another Lafayette pilot, but a man whom he never met during the war. Together, they wrote *The Lafayette Flying Corps* (1920) - a history of the unit, and thereafter travelled back to America. On a commission from *Harper's Magazine*, the men journeyed to Tahiti in order to write a series of travel articles. Nordhoff ended up staying on the island for twenty years, and their second book *Faery Lands of the South Seas*, was serialized in *Harper's* in 1920-21, and later published in book form.

Nordhoff married a Tahitan woman, Pepe Teara, with whom he had four daughters and two sons. He continued writing, on his own, as well as jointly with Hall for the remainder of his life. *The Derelict* (1928) is considered his finest solo effort, followed twelve years later by *In Yankee Windjammers* (1940); a retelling of the ships, sailors, and way of life about which his grandfather had written.

Nordhoff divorced his first wife in 1936, and left Tahiti a few years later. On his return to California, he met Laura Grainger Whiley, whom he married in 1941. The marriage was happy whilst it lasted, but sadly Nordhoff died eight years later. He died at his home in Montecito, California, on 10 April, 1947. The cause of death is uncertain, at the time it was reported as an 'apparent heart attack', but later sources indicate he had been drinking heavily, was depressed, and may have committed suicide.

Falconry

'Falconry' refers to the hunting of wild quarry in its natural state and habitat by means of a trained bird of prey. There are two traditional terms used to describe a person involved in falconry: a 'falconer' flies a falcon, and an 'austringer' (a term of German origin) flies a hawk or an eagle. Falconry has a long and distinguished history, and it has been suggested that it began in Mesopotamia, with the earliest accounts dating to approximately 2000 BC. It was probably introduced to Europe around 400 AD however, when the Huns and the Alans invaded from the East. Frederick II of Hohenstaufen (a member of the Swabian dynasty in the High Middle Ages who possessed huge amounts of territory across Europe) is generally acknowledged as the most significant wellspring of traditional falconry knowledge. He is believed to have obtained firsthand knowledge of Arabic falconry during wars in the region in 1228 and 1229, in which he participated in his role as Holy Roman Emperor. Frederick is best known for his falconry treatise, *De Arte Venandi Cum Avibus* (The Art of Hunting with Birds); the first comprehensive book on falconry, as well as a substantial contribution to ornithology and zoology. Historically, falconry has always been a popular sport of the upper classes and nobility, largely due to the prerequisites of time, money and space. However, within some societies, such as the Bedouin, falconry was not practiced for recreation, but for purely practical reasons of supplementing a very limited diet. In the UK, falconry reached its zenith in the seventeenth century, but faded reasonably rapidly due to the introduction of firearms for hunting in the eighteenth and nineteenth centuries. It did witness a revival in the late nineteenth and earlier twentieth centuries however, when several falconry books were published. Interestingly, in early English falconry literature, the word 'falcon' referred to a female falcon only, while the word 'hawk' referred to a female hawk. A male hawk or falcon was referred to as a 'tercel', as it was roughly one third less than the female in size. Whilst falconry is now practiced in many countries world wide, it is less common in areas such as Australasia. In Australia, although falconry is not specifically illegal, it is illegal to keep any type of bird of prey in captivity without the appropriate permits, and in New Zealand, falconry was legalised for one species only, the Swap/Australasian harrier, in 2011. There are currently only four practicing falconers in New Zealand. However, in countries such as the UK and US today, falconry is experiencing a boom. Its popularity, through lure flying displays at country houses and game fairs, has probably never been higher in the past 300 years.

It has also been the subject of a popular book *Falcon Fever,* written by Tim Gallagher in 2008. Falconry is also used for practical purposes in the modern day, the birds are taught to control other pest birds and animals in urban areas, landfills, commercial buildings, and even airports.

FALCONS OF FRANCE

I

A SOLDIER OF THE LEGION

TEN years have passed since we declared war on Germany, but the events of those days are etched indelibly on my mind. Like thousands of other young Americans, I thought of the war by day and dreamed of it by night; all the everyday interests of life had gone flat and stale, and their places in my mind were filled with day-dreams of trench warfare, heavy artillery, observation balloons, and aeroplanes. Particularly aeroplanes—small hornetlike ships manned by a single pilot, swooping down to spit machine-gun fire into the enemy's ranks, or manoeuvring high above the battlefield in duels to the death with German airmen.

My father, long past military age, but no less interested in the war than I, had subscribed to a great New York daily paper and a couple of illustrated English weeklies, read eagerly by every member of the family. When my turn came, I remember how I used to skip through the military and political news, on the lookout for less conspicuous paragraphs which told of the exploits of famous French and English fighting pilots. And when I read accounts of the American volunteers flying for

France in the Escadrille Lafayette, I read them twice or three times over, fascinated and in a mood of despairing envy.

Envy and despair are not pleasant words, and my state of mind in those days was not a pleasant one. I was seventeen; my eighteenth birthday was still some months ahead, and each month seemed longer than a peace-time year. The newly authorized volunteers would accept no man under eighteen, and I knew that the same limit would be set by the Selective Service Act, soon to become law. Those were great times, of great events, and I longed to play my little part in them as I have never longed for anything before or since. There seemed nothing to do but hang around my father's ranch, trying to keep my thoughts on the daily round of work, all through the summer and autumn, until I was old enough to pass the critical eyes of an examining board. The prospect was a depressing one; the admission makes me smile to-day, but many a time in that spring of 1917 I was conscious of a desperate fear that the war might be over before I could get to the front.

My father's only brother, my Uncle Harry, was a trader and planter in French Oceania, far off in the South Pacific. His schooner, which flew the French flag, had been sunk by a German raider the year before, and after a determined effort to join up in San Francisco, he had sailed south again, planning to build a new vessel in the South Seas. Neither the Army nor the Navy would have him, for Uncle Harry's eyes had been damaged by years of tropical sun. Toward the end of May I had a radio message from my uncle, asking me to run up to San Francisco to look after the shipment of a lot of material he had ordered—lumber, marine hardware, cordage, and an eighty horse-power Diesel engine. It proved to be a two-day job, for I had to cross the bay to Oakland, where the engine was built, and in the course of my work I had to call on M. Duval, the French consul, over some matter of shipbuilding material passing the French customs duty-free.

The consul was a great friend of my uncle's, and I had met him before. His secretary recognized me, and I was ushered into his office three minutes after I had presented my card.

M. Duval, a short stout man with gold-rimmed pince-nez, and the narrow red ribbon of the Legion of Honour in his buttonhole, seized my hand warmly and waved aside the sheaf of papers I held out to him.

"I know what it is," he said; "the new schooner, eh?" He turned to the secretary. "Take the papers and have the certificate made out; everything on the invoice is for shipbuilding, and there will be no duty to pay." He waved me toward a swivel chair. "Sit down, Charlie," he went on. "I'm not busy to-day and we'll have a chat while you wait. So you've had a wire from Harry. He's in Tahiti, then?"

"Yes," I said; "he wanted to get into the war, but they wouldn't have him—turned down on account of his eyes. He felt pretty badly about it. I think he's building this schooner partly to keep his thoughts off the war, for he told me he couldn't do much with labour as scarce as it is down there. All the able-bodied men have gone overseas." M. Duval nodded sympathetically.

"I know—I know. *Ce pauvre* Harry!"

The sympathy in his voice gave me an excuse to air my own small troubles, the full extent of which I had not made known even to my father. I wanted to talk.

"I'm in the same fix," I said mournfully. "I can't get into the Volunteers, and they won't even let me be conscripted till I'm eighteen! I'll have to wait for months—it makes me sick!"

The consul looked me up and down with an air of astonishment. "You're not yet eighteen? I would have guessed your age at twenty, at least!" He took off his glasses and wiped them carefully with a silk handkerchief before he spoke again. "What branch of the service would you like to join?" he asked. I smiled.

"Oh, I'm like every other young fellow," I told him.

"I'd like to fly, of course!"

"You'd like to fly, eh? Your parents would not object to your enlisting if the Army would take you now?"

"Not a bit."

He took from his desk an enormous pipe of cherry-wood, with a long curved stem, stuffed it carefully with coarse French tobacco, lit a match, and exhaled a cloud of smoke.

"How would you like to join the Lafayette Flying Corps?" he asked.

My heart seemed to skip a beat, and I caught my breath. "Do you think they'd take me? Would there be a chance?"

M. Duval smiled at the note of eagerness in my voice. "An excellent chance," he remarked. "But do you know what the Lafayette Flying Corps is?"

"I suppose you mean the Escadrille Lafayette—I've read about it in the papers."

"That's only a part of it—a single squadron composed of fifteen men. The Corps which was built up from this unit is a larger organization—a hundred or more young Americans, enlisted in the Foreign Legion for the duration of the war, transferred to the Aviation, and serving with many French squadrons at the front. Think it over, and if you decide seriously that you'd like to join the Corps, let me know. Dr. Gros, who looks after the volunteers as they arrive in Paris, is a very old friend of mine."

I sprang up nervously. "There's nothing to think over!" I said. "M. Duval, if you could get me into the Lafayette Corps I'd feel indebted to you all my life! I'd start to-morrow if I could!"

"You're sure—quite sure?"

"Yes, sir!"

"It's settled, then. There'll be a preliminary physical examination, but you're almost certain to pass. Let's see." He took up a pencil and tapped the desk softly as he reflected.

"First the doctor; can you take your examination this

afternoon if I make an appointment for you? Good! Then your passport; that will take time—three weeks, I'm. afraid. Make out your application to-day and let me forward it to Washington for you. Meanwhile you can be getting ready, and when your passport arrives, come straight to me. I'll give you a letter to our consul in New York, so there will be no trouble about a visa, and another letter to Dr. Gros. Call on him as soon as you reach Paris. You'll find him the kindest and most charming of men; it is mainly due to him that the Escadrille Lafayette has been enlarged into a Corps."

A moment later the secretary appeared with my uncle's papers. M. Duval stood up, so I judged that our interview was at an end.

"Thank you, sir, a thousand times!" I said. He gave my hand a friendly pressure.

"You're at the Palace, eh? I'll telephone you at lunch time to let you know where and when you're to take your examination. Odd to think of it, eh? In less than two months you'll be a soldier of France!"

At eight o'clock that night, when I boarded the southbound train, I had made out my passport application, and passed with entire success a searching physical examination administered by a French doctor to whom M. Duval sent me. He was an old resident of San Francisco, and when I had stripped and been questioned and stethoscoped, had my eyes tested, and hopped about blindfolded on one foot, he told me to put on my clothes.

"Sound as a dollar!" he said as he shook my hand. "You'll live to be a hundred if the Bosches don't get you. Good-bye and good luck!"

The summer night turned very hot an hour out of San Francisco, and as I lay half naked in my lower berth, my thoughts were too busy for sleep. To say that I was elated is to say nothing at all; I was half delirious with joy. M. Duval had spoken with such conviction that the prospect before me seemed assured. "No," I thought, "I'm not dreaming. Before many days I shall actually be on my way to France!" Hard experience teaches us all to distrust the prospect of great happiness, of realised hopes, but though I thought over my plans from every angle, I could see no serious danger of a hitch, nothing that might prevent my sailing for France. I smiled to myself, a little proudly, perhaps, as I thought of my parents. They would let me go; they were Spartans when it came to the matter of their country's defence in time of war. I winced a little at the thought of telling my mother that I was going to fight in the air, for in those days the older people considered flying itself a hazardous sport for crack-brains, and war flying fifty times worse.

Long before the early summer dawn, when the porter came to call me, rubbing the sleep from his eyes, he found me still awake. I was the only passenger to alight at San Isidro, and the little town was dark except for the cheerful light in its single restaurant. Two brothers, Spanish Californians and old friends of mine, were the proprietors. Tony acted as cook and waiter by day, and Porfirio ran the night shift. My sleepless night had given me a keen appetite.

It was good to be alive that morning. Meadow larks whistled their exultant little song on the fence posts bordering the road, and quail with broods of half-grown young scratched in the dust and whirred away in short flights across the fields. Stirred by a gentle ground swell, which undulated smoothly through the beds of kelp offshore, the Pacific stretched away like a vast blue desert to the horizon. Below the new state road were the dunes, the yellow beach, and the creamy line of the breakers. There was a salty perfume in the air, and as we mounted to the mesas I sniffed with relish the clean, wild scent of sage-brush, fresh with dew.

On arriving home I found my father by the back door, conferring with our stooping, leathery foreman, who turned away to mount his horse as I approached.

"Hello, son!" called my father as he touched a match to the first pipe of the day. "Did you get Harry's business settled?" he went on after a few puffs. "It must have taken longer than you reckoned."

"Yes, sir—it's all fixed up. The French consul got the papers ready in half an hour; he was very kind. I'd have been back yesterday if it hadn't been for the engine. I had to go to Oakland to see the manufacturers. Where's Mother? Is she up?"

"Yes; she's having her tea."

The moment seemed an auspicious one, and in any case I was so eager to tell my father of my hopes that the thought of delay was intolerable.

"I had quite a talk with M. Duval," I said. "We spoke of the war, and I told him they wouldn't let me enlist, and how hard it is for me to wait till I'm old enough. And it *is* hard, sir; I love the ranch, but I hate to hang around anywhere just now." My father nodded, smiling a little behind his beard.

"I don't blame you a bit," he remarked; "but it's the law, of course."

"I know, but M. Duval said if I wanted to, and you gave your permission, he could get me into the French Army. I told him I knew you wouldn't object, for you'd already said I could enlist if the Army would take me. It's the Lafayette Flying Corps—we were talking about it the other day. I was so sure you wouldn't mind that I passed the physical examination at a French doctor's, and sent my application for a passport to Washington."

The smile faded from my father's eyes, and he held up his hand.

"Hold on, son!" he exclaimed. "Hold on till I get this straight! You're taking all the wind out of my sails! You've passed a physical examination? You've applied for a passport? You're going to fly?"

"Yes, sir; I knew how you'd feel about it."

"That's right—though I wish you'd chosen a different job. But we Americans will have to forget this fool 'Safety First' slogan of ours—at any rate till the war's over. Yes, it's all right with me—it's your mother I'm thinking about. But she wouldn't want you to hold down some safe job in the rear. Yes, if you've a chance to go to France, go ahead. I'll talk to your mother—leave that to me."

There is no need of telling how, after what seemed an eternity of waiting, my passport came at last; how I crossed the continent and boarded the small French steamer *Rochambeau* on the first day of July. Our country was not at that time the great armed camp it became later in the year, but all the way from coast to coast I was aware of a vast stir and buzzing which made me think of a swarm of bees preparing to defend their hive.

The *Rochambeau* sailed at five o'clock of a hot, clear summer evening. I stood on the after deck while the strange skyline of New York dropped away astern; we passed through the Narrows, and presently the ship was heaving to the long Atlantic swell.

I was one of a little group of passengers by the rail, assembled to bid farewell to peaceful North America. The others were speaking French, and, as I listened half unconsciously, my schoolboy knowledge of that language enabled me to pick up a word of their conversation here and there. A tall, vigorous old man, with ruddy cheeks and an enormous white moustache, stood beside me. He carried an attaché case of pigskin, and there was a gardenia in his buttonhole. Just beyond him I saw a dark wiry chap of about my own age. The two were conversing in French, rapid and largely unintelligible to me, but something about the cut of his jib—as a sailor would say—convinced me that the younger man was an American. His smile, once or twice when the older man chuckled rumblingly at something that came up in the talk, attracted me, and I liked his thin, determined face, with its fine dark eyes. I liked him instinctively, in fact, and that evening, after a rather lonely dinner, I met him on deck.

"You're an American, aren't you?" he asked. "What do you say to a little walk?"

It was good to hear a compatriot's voice on this foreign ship, and I was in need of exercise. "I'm your man!" I said. "That's what I came on deck for."

"Same here. I've been cooped up in hotels for the last week. Lordy! How I hate cities!"

As we strode along, passing the crowded deck chairs, we exchanged confidences. My companion's name was Gordon Forbes, and I learned within ten minutes, that, like me, he was just under eighteen; that he too had made an unsuccessful attempt to enlist, and was now bound for the office of Dr. Gros in Paris, on the same errand as mine. It struck me as a strange coincidence, but I can see now that there must have been one or more Lafayette Corps recruits on nearly every French steamer sailing in those days.

"So the consul in San Francisco gave you the idea," Forbes remarked. "M. Hérault fixed things for me; he's an old friend of my father's. I saw you on deck before dinner; did you notice me? I was talking to an old man with a white moustache. That's M. Hérault; he's on his way home from a mission in America. You must meet him."

Before the evening was over I had learned a good deal about Gordon Forbes, and I felt that I had made a new friend who might turn out to be among my closest and best. It would be hard to find anywhere two youngsters whose lives had been lived so far apart as ours, but our tastes were remarkably congenial for all that. Forbes, who had lost his mother in early childhood, was the only son of a railroad builder and financier. His father, so far as I could judge, must have been a man of broad and varied tastes, and the bond between father and son exceptionally close. Mr. Forbes had never believed in schools, and had had the courage to put his theories into practice, bringing up Gordon in the Adirondacks and on the North Carolina coast, with a tutor and much of his father's companionship. There were guns and horses and dogs, and boats; long days in the open air, and evenings of study and talk. Then, when Mr. Forbes, unlike most middle-aged men of affairs, had had the good sense to retire, father and son crossed the Atlantic to spend three years in Europe, where

Gordon, a natural linguist, perfected his book knowledge of French. The war came early in their sojourn abroad, and Gordon's father, who had spent much time in France and loved that country only second to his own, plunged into the relief work which shortened his life. He had been dead only a few months when I met his son, now sole heir to interests which might have staggered an older man. And it seemed that his father's training, instilling as it had a love of nature, of the open air and simple basic things, had rendered the son as little fit as I to deal with the complexities of modern life. Disliking cities, hating the prospect of business and finance, Gordon would have made a first-class hunter, trapper, sailor, or explorer; but when it came to following the path his father's executors pointed out to him, he balked.

"This chance to get into the war," he remarked as we walked the deck, "is a life-saver for me! Of course I'm not of age yet, but they've been after me all the time, trying to make me understand my father's affairs. Lordy! Business poisons me! Don't you ever wish you'd been born back in the old days? I don't know what I'll do if I get through the war. There doesn't seem to be any place where a fellow can fit in."

I met M. Hérault next day. Like nearly all cultured Frenchmen he spoke English fluently, though with a strong accent. He and Forbes and I had a walk after breakfast, and the old gentleman, with the consideration of his race, kept to

English in his talk with us.

"Gordon tells me," he remarked, "that you too are crossing to enlist in the Foreign Legion, since your own Army will not accept volunteers under eighteen. With a hundred and twenty millions you can afford to pick and choose. Poor France—she's in harder straits and must take men where she can get them; she asks few questions of those willing to help her nowadays." He gave me a friendly clap on the back and turned to Gordon. "Here's a Californian for you! I know that country. There's something in the soil out there that grows big men."

"I know all about the Lafayette Flying Corps," he went on, after he had halted in a sheltered corner of the deck to light a cigar. "M. de Sillac, the President, and Dr. Gros, the Vice-President and Director for France, are friends of mine. They were the godfathers of the Escadrille Lafayette, and thanks to them the American squadron has been expanded to make the present Corps. I am more or less connected with Aviation, you see, for I am a member of the syndicate which manufactures his Hispano-Suiza motor. Perhaps you two have never heard of the Spad, the fastest single-seater fighting plane on the front to-day. Well, our motor made the Spad possible. Since both of you are going to fly, it may not bore you to hear something about the machines I hope you will use. No!" He smiled at our eager chorus of "No, sir!"

"Nearly a year ago, Guynemer, the greatest of our aces, took the first Spad over the lines, and his report on its performance caused a stir. It was equipped with the original model of our motor, of one hundred and forty horse-power, and the authorities were so impressed that they placed large orders at once. To meet this demand a syndicate of manufacturers was formed, each one pledging himself to turn out so many of the new motors in a given time. Then, by increasing the compression, without changing the dimensions of the motor in any way, its horse-power was raised to one hundred and eighty. The Spad, equipped with this newer model, has proved itself the most formidable fighting plane on the front. And there is no harm in telling you that our engineers, still without changing the bore or stroke, have once again raised the motor's horse-power, this time to two hundred and twenty, though this super-compressed type is still in an experimental stage. When your country declared war, the military authorities asked our syndicate to send someone to America to confer with your motor manufacturers as to the possibility of making the Hispano-Suiza in the United States. The task was allotted to me, and it has been a pleasant one. Your factories lack a little of our precision, perhaps, but we have much to learn from them. We know little of standardization or production in quantity."

I listened to M. Hérault's remarks without understanding all that he had to say, for I have never had taste for mechanical things. But Forbes was keenly interested, and I judged that in spite of his outdoor tastes he understood motors thoroughly.

The gunnery was what interested me.

"How does a single-seater pilot do his shooting?" I asked. "I've read in a newspaper somewhere that the bullets go through the course of the propeller. Is that true?"

"You will soon know a good deal more than I about aeroplanes," said M. Hérault, "but I can answer that question at least. Our early Nieuports mounted a Lewis gun on the upper plane, which shot over the propeller—an awkward arrangement in many ways. Then we captured a Fokker monoplane, of the kind used by the German ace, Immelmann, and found that it was equipped with a gun of the Vickers type, with an ingenious cam arrangement, so timed that it could shoot through the upper arc of the propeller, but could not discharge a bullet when one of the blades was opposite the muzzle. The Allied air forces adopted this idea at once. It permits the machine to be mounted rigidly, on the motor hood directly in front of the pilot, where it can be sighted most easily and cleared in case of a jam. To aim the gun, the pilot simply aims his plane, manoeuvring until the sights are in line with the mark."

The old gentleman sighed, and a shadow seemed to steal over his ruddy face. "America is like another planet," he went on slowly, half to himself. "Over there the war seems so far away, so unreal. But now, all the youth of the world . . . It's hard to realize. In another three or four months you two, who ought to be studying Latin and geometry, will be graduates of another kind of school. Well, you have an old man's best wishes for success at your new trade!"

I saw a great deal of Forbes and M. Hérault during our voyage, and when we docked at Bordeaux, early on a foggy summer morning, my companions seemed like old friends. The Frenchman, after he had dispatched some telegrams, insisted on hiring a motor car to show us the sights of the beautiful old town. It was the first time I had set foot on European soil, and I was young enough to feel keenly the strangeness of all I saw. I thought it likely that some of my own ancestors had enriched with their blood the fields outside the town, fighting with pike and halberd and crossbow in the old wars between France and England. America, after all, had been a wilderness only a few generations ago, and her background of history was the history of the Indian tribes. As for us, we are Europeans, thriving after a short transplantation in the New World, and every one of us who stops to think must experience a certain sense of home-coming as he lands for the first time in a European port. I felt this strongly on that summer morning, and I fancy that I express the feelings of many other Americans when I say that during all the time I spent in France I never once had the sense of being a stranger in a foreign land.

M. Hérault invited us to lunch at a restaurant. Our train for Paris left early in the afternoon, and as long as daylight lasted I sat by the window of our compartment, gazing at the panorama of French countryside, so different from my own corner of the world. I saw peace, order, and the beauty of a land long inhabited and mellowed by age; fields ploughed and planted by innumerable generations of men, and farmhouses that seemed natural outgrowths of the soil on which they stood. It was not easy to realize that I had come to this peaceful land to fight; that off to the north and east the great guns were booming day and night. Half dozing by the window, I came to my senses once or twice with a start, saying to myself, "You are in France—there *is* a war, and you're going to fight in it." And, looking out of the window once more, it struck me that if any people in the world had a country worth fighting for, it was the French.

The sun set and the long twilight faded to dusk. We were approaching the outskirts of Paris now; country was giving place to crowded houses, in which lights were beginning to twinkle as we flashed past. The sky was overcast, and as we entered the city a fine drizzling rain blurred the window-panes and glistened on the asphalt of the streets. Presently the train stopped; we got down in a great glass-roofed station, and Forbes and I followed M. Hérault to the taxicab a porter reserved for him. I accepted the old man's invitation to stop at his house.

In those days most of the motor cars in France were serving the Army, and the little old cab in which we crossed the city must have been unearthed—like an old reservist—from the last resting place of taxicabs and forced into reluctant service once more. The driver, a lean ancient with a fiery nose and thick grey stubble on his chin, seemed to fit his vehicle. The small one-cylinder engine chugged unsteadily as we rolled along the wet streets, and from time to time the chauffeur reached out to press the bulb of the horn, which emitted a shrill asthmatic honk. Blurred lights, glistening pavements, a fine unceasing rain, the smell of wet mouldering leather, and the shrill fitful sound of motor horns—such are the impressions that first drive through the streets of Paris left on my memory.

Our taxi stopped with a jerk before a high, old-fashioned house on a quiet street, M. Hérault's house on the Boulevard Malesherbes. A gate in the iron fence opened, and an elderly manservant, wearing an apron and an embroidered waistcoat over his shirt, came forward to greet his master. The manufacturer shook his old retainer's hand. "It's good to get home, eh Jules? You are well, old friend? And——"

At that moment a tall, smiling young woman, dressed in black, ran out of the gate, and before her father could tum, her arms were about his neck. Then she spied Forbes, and seized his hand without letting go her father's arm.

"Gordon! *Enchantée de te revoir!*"

M. Hérault presented me to his daughter, Mme. de Thouars. He had lost his wife many years before; his only son and his son-in-law—young officers in the same regiment of cavalry—

had given their lives for France, and now he lived alone with his daughter. United by deep affection and common loss, they faced life with the gay courage of their kind, and their household was anything but a gloomy one.

"I got your message," Mme. de Thouars was saying. "Come—we've a nice little dinner waiting for you. You must eat it before it grows cold!"

Their house was of a kind not common in Western America. It had three stories, and we went into a hall on the street level, where a broad flight of stairs led up to the living quarters of the family overhead. The tall windows of the drawing-room gave on the boulevard, the dining-room was behind, and old Jules showed me up still another flight of stairs to the room allotted to me. Ten minutes later I went down to the drawing-room, where Mme. de Thouars and Gordon were waiting. At my appearance she changed the conversation to English, which she spoke even better than her father.

"You must be starving, you two! Ah! here's father now." He stood in the doorway, smiling at us behind his great white moustache. A moment later Jules appeared, bowing with a napkin over his arm. "*Le diner est servi,*" he announced.

Our host, a friend of Dr. Gros, insisted that he had time next morning to accompany us when we presented our credentials to the Vice-President of the Lafayette Flying Corps. When I awoke, long before the others, the sun was up and sparrows were squabbling and twittering on the window sill. I bathed, dressed, and went downstairs, realizing that I was a kind of Western barbarian, unable to sleep after sunrise. But Jules was busy with broom and dustpan below. He gave me a smile and a good-morning in French, and I replied with a phrase carefully thought out and rehearsed in case I met one of the servants. "*A quelle heure déjeune-t-on?*" I asked, bashfully. The old man's smile grew broader, and after a diplomatic "*Monsieur parle français!*" he informed me that one breakfasted at eight o'clock. So I strolled out through the sunny court for a walk on the empty boulevard, consulting my watch at frequent intervals, and returned on the dot, with a keen appetite for coffee and rolls. A detail of that breakfast lingers in my mind: the saucer of saccharine tablets that took the place of sugar. The absence of sugar and the presence on the table of those tiny unpleasant pills brought home to me, somehow, the straits to which Europe was reduced.

Two hours later M. Hérault called for us in the large closed car his work for the Government forced him to keep. The stream of traffic was in full flow by now, and as we drove swiftly up the Champs-Elysées I had my first view of the Paris of those war-time years. Taxicabs, military automobiles, and ambulances, swept past us in a bewildering panorama, and the sidewalks were gay with parti-coloured uniforms—black, red, khaki, horizon blue. We reached the Etoile, passed the Arc de Triomphe, and turned into the Avenue du Bois de Boulogne.

The car stopped before No. 23, a house I was destined to visit many times, and one of pleasant memories to all pilots of the Lafayette Corps.

We were the only civilians in Dr. Gros's waiting room, in a little company that fascinated Forbes and me: half a dozen Americans in French uniform, and among them, aloof and regarded with a certain awe as he glanced through a morning paper, one veteran flying man with his left arm in a sling and ribbons on his breast. A moment later Dr. Gros appeared—a tall, handsome, dark-eyed man in early middle age—and shook hands warmly with M. Hérault. He received Gordon and me in a friendly way that put us at ease at once.

Only one other incident of that brief sojourn in Paris stands out in my mind—Forbes and I waiting naked in a corner of the Invalides where we signed our enlistment papers. With a score of other recruits for the Foreign Legion, we had been assigned numbers and ordered to strip and wait till our numbers were called. Our companions were a strange polyglot crowd—Swedes, Russians, a Mexican, a couple of outlandish negroes, and one small brown man I took for a Malay. They were all recruits for the infantry; Gordon and I were the only ones to be transferred to Aviation. At last the hard-faced sergeant shouted my number and beckoned me brusquely to an open door. Naked as a fish, I came to attention before a colonel and two captains seated at desks in a small-room. "Name Seldon Charles born in California 1899 American citizen unmarried no children desires to enlist in Foreign Legion for duration of war to be detached to the navigating personnel of the Aviation," read the sergeant monotonously, without a pause, and in three minutes I had been weighed, measured, stethoscoped, ears and eyes tested, and passed. The colonel looked at me coldly, without a smile. "An American, eh?" he remarked. "*Oui, mon colonel*," I ventured respectfully and at the sound of my halting French the ice melted, and he gave me a fatherly smile. "Good luck, my boy," he said, in English as good as my own.

II

SPROUTING WINGS

OUR orders instructed us to report within twenty-four hours at the great flying school of Avord, near Bourges, on the plains of Central France. Forbes and I were overjoyed, for this meant that we were to learn to fly on the Blériot—alone from start to finish. In the other schools, the pupil began in a two-seater plane, with an instructor and double controls, but it was believed in those days that the Blériot system produced finer pilots—entirely self-taught, on the tricky, unstable monoplane.

After our good-byes to M. Hérault and Mme. de Thouars, who were kind enough to insist that our leaves were to be spent with them, we boarded the train for the long journey to Bourges. We had lunch and a two-hour wait in that town, and a stroll past its beautiful cathedral; then a leisurely journey of ten or eleven miles, through a country flat as the sea and dotted with farmhouses and clumps of trees, brought us to Avord, a village smaller than my little home town in California. The École Militaire d'Aviation was three miles off, and as we stood on the station platform in our civilian clothes, looking a bit bewildered, no doubt, the driver of a big motor bus accosted us. "*Élèves pilotes?*" he inquired, and at Forbes's reply he sang out cheerily, "All aboard, then!" We shouldered our duffle bags and squeezed in among the soldiers and non-commissioned officers crowding the seats. They seemed to be all talking at once, in a jargon utterly unintelligible to me, but Forbes told me afterward they were conversing in the slang of the Aviation—a picturesque dialect I was destined to learn before long.

As we drew near the flying school, I began to get an idea of its enormous size. Dozens of planes were in the air, for the afternoon work had begun; there seemed to be square miles of aerodromes, scores of huge Bessonneau hangars, hundreds and hundreds of men. I learned afterward that more than three thousand men lived and worked within the confines of the school. Presently we drove through an arched gate, the bus stopped, and the driver pointed out the barrack assigned to the Americans.

The only occupant of the barrack at this busy hour was a rangy young man with the aquiline features of a Plains Indian, and blue eyes set in a weather-beaten face. There was a brown-paper cigarette between his lips, and he regarded us smilingly, leaning on a cane.

"Two more rookies, huh?" he remarked, coming forward to shake hands. "Wilding's my name, Jim Wilding. I get my mails in Holbrook, Arizona, when I'm home."

When we had introduced ourselves he volunteered to show us the ropes. "Come into our room," he said; "we can make a place for two more cots. Can you all *parlez français?*" Gordon nodded, but I shook my head. "One's enough," Wilding went on. "You'd better go right now and check in at the *bureau;* they'll give you slips there to take to the Quartermaster's stores where you'll get your uniforms and all that. I'd go along if I didn't have this game leg."

When we returned, half an hour later, carrying bundles that soon transformed us into two very raw recruits, Wilding was waiting for us, and chaffed us in his gentle drawl as we stuffed civilian clothes into our bags and donned with unaccustomed hands the horizon blue of France. Thanks to Gordon's fluent French and the good nature of the storekeeper our heavy boots of the kind called *godillots*, really fitted our feet, and our uniforms fitted as well as any French issue uniform ever fit any man. Wilding watched me trying to wind the blue spiral putties around my calves; finally he said, "Let me show you the trick. If I had a franc for every time I've wrapped these things around my legs I'd ask you fellows to dinner to-night at the Café des Aviateurs. Yeah—I was three years in the Legion before they'd let me try to fly."

I had observed with interest that Wilding wore two faded ribbons on his blouse and a wound stripe on one sleeve, now he caught my eye on the green and yellow ribbon of his Médaille Militaire. He was a man who took nothing very seriously, least of all himself.

"They gave me that," he explained dryly, "for letting a Heinie shoot me in the leg. They wanted to invalid me out of the Army because I couldn't march any more! Well, I fooled 'em by pointing out that a fellow doesn't fly with his legs, anyhow, so here I am! But I made a bum landing yesterday—turned the cuckoo over and twisted the old game knee."

"Were you flying a Blériot?" Gordon asked.

"Yes—I'm in the class they call Tour de Piste. You'll start on penguins to-morrow—little grass-cutters that can't fly, but are tricky cusses to run in a straight line. When you can run 'em straight at full speed with the tail up, they'll put you on the rollers: they can fly, but you're not supposed to let 'em do it. After that you'll try your hand in the *décoller* class. That's where you're first allowed to get into the air—just a few yards up and in a straight line. *Décoller*—pretty good, huh? You 'unglue' yourself from the ground in that class. And after that you'll be where I am now—in *tour de piste*. That means you fly round the field about two hundred metres up. After that you do a few spirals and an altitude flight, and then they send you across country for your brevet flights. When you've done those you can stick a couple of wings on your collar and call yourself an aviator. Then, if they think you're any good, they'll make a pursuit pilot out of you and send you down to Pau to do acrobatics; and if you get through without pushing up daisies or smashing too many machines, you'll be ready to try it out on Heinie. That's all." There was a short silence, and then Gordon said: "I'm going to end up on a Spad or bust!"

Wilding gave him a friendly smile. "That's the stuff!" he said approvingly. "That's the way we all feel!"

Our barrack was divided into three big rooms, giving on a narrow corridor, at one end of which were the shower baths. We spent the balance of the afternoon in setting up our cots and unpacking our duffle bags. Wilding, who had been lounging on his bed watching us, got up at last.

"You fellows got plenty of francs?" he asked abruptly. Gordon and I admitted that our purses were moderately full. "That's good," he went on. "Let's go up to the canteen and get some chow before the gang gets back. They'll work for another hour yet—as long as there's light enough to see. They hand out bread and soup and lentils at the mess—the *ordinaire*, they call it—but I don't recommend you to try it. I did—just once! As long as you've got any francs it's better to go to the canteen." He took up his cane and led the way to a building close by, where a stout, slatternly woman served passable meals and various things to drink. Wilding seemed to be a favourite of hers; and though she was well past fifty she giggled like a girl at his good-natured chaff, and bustled off to the kitchen to give his special instructions to the cook.

As we lingered over our meal, the place began to fill with an extraordinary crowd: men of every non-commissioned rank, from every branch of the most cosmopolitan army in the world. Through the hum of conversation in French, I caught snatches of talk in Spanish, English, and a language new to my ears, which I learned was Arabic. But though these men spoke in many languages, the subject of their talk was always the same—flying. Flying was an obsession with every one of them, from the moment when they woke in the morning till they lay down on their cots at night, and I was soon to learn that flying had even taken possession of their dreams. There were some infantrymen in the crowd, but the majority were sergeants and corporals of cavalry—Dragoons, Hussars, Spahis, Chasseurs d'Afrique. And the ribbons they wore showed that nearly every man of the lot had distinguished himself in action. The Americans, in fact, were the only men in the room who had not the air of veterans.

A group of Americans in flying clothes strolled in and took possession of a long table by the window; it gave me a little wave of homesickness to hear their cool, familiar, drawling speech. Then a stocky little chap, with thick red hair and a freckled face, appeared in the doorway.

"Hey, Bill!" called Wilding, at sight of the newcomer. "Come on over and eat with us!"

The red-haired man seemed to be known and liked by everyone in the canteen; as he saluted the company there were shouts of "Allo, Beel!" He sat down at our table, and Wilding introduced us. His name was O'Connor, and he hailed from Boston. He had been with the American Ambulance for a year, and did not neglect to wear the Croix de Guerre he had won at Verdun.

"John Boyle O'Reilly O'Connor, *à votre service*," he said, bowing in the best military fashion. Then, to Wilding, "Well, I've got the old altitude done, Jim! An hour above two thousand metres! Sounds easy, don't it? But wait till you try to get one of those worn-out Blériots up that high. I'm off for Châteauroux and Romorantin to-morrow; with a little luck I'll have my brevet two days from now!" He turned to Gordon. "You fellows get in to-day?"

"Yes."

"You're in luck! There's hardly anyone in the penguin class just now; they'll shoot you through in a day or two. I was struck three weeks on that field!"

That night I saw assembled under one roof all the Americans at Avord. They had one thing in common—youth—but they were from every part of the country and every walk of life. Some formed vociferous rings about three or four crap games that seemed to start in every moment of leisure, and I heard shouts of "Fever in the South! Big Dick from Boston! String of box cars! Fade you! Let her ride!" There were other groups clustered about some cot where a veteran who had actually taken a Blériot a few yards off the ground was explaining with great earnestness to recent graduates of the penguin class how it was done. Here and there, stretched on his cot and reading by the light of a candle stuck on the shelf above, I saw a man or two who for a few moments before bedtime was able to divorce his thoughts from flying.

I had had a long day, so packed with new experience that I felt ready for bed. So I turned in, and fell asleep at once.

Gordon's hand on my shoulder wakened me. It was half-past three and pitch-dark outside, but the barrack was aglare with electric light. All about me men were stirring and muttering as they rubbed the sleep from their eyes. I heard a shout: "Hey, Jim! How's the coffee this morning?" and, glancing toward the door, I saw a small native of Annam, whose grin disclosed betel-blackened teeth, entering with a heavy pail in his hand. "*Beaucoup bon!*" exclaimed the Annamite, chuckling. "*Beaucoup bon!*" These were the only words of French I ever heard him pronounce. Men reached for their tin cups and held them out, sniffing critically as Jim tilted his pail and poured out a stream of dark liquid, which had at least the virtue of being hot. I held out my own cup in turn and drank its contents gratefully, though it resembled coffee no more than it resembled tea. Five minutes later we were dressed for flying and out of the room.

I followed the crowd, safety helmet in hand, to the Bureau de Pilotage, under the wind-gauges and the great red balls that showed the passing side—right or left—for the day. All the flying personnel of the school was assembled there for roll call, and when that was over the instructor of the small class in which I found myself swung about to face us.

"Form fours!" he barked. "Forward march!"

He led us across the field and down a long white road that led toward the village of Farges. The sun had not yet appeared when we halted by a couple of small hangars, where sleepy mechanics were wheeling out our little penguins. They were tiny Blériots, with three-cylinder Anzani motors and short broad wings, incapable of flight. There were a dozen Frenchmen in the class, and Gordon and I were the only Americans. Our instructor was a big, blustering sergeant, who had been badly wounded while flying at Verdun. He hadn't a single word of English, but he liked Americans, fortunately for us. "*Allez! Roulez!*" he ordered brusquely, when the motors had been warmed up, and, glancing down at the paper in his hand, he called off four French names. The men took their places in the machines. Far off across the field I saw a brace of Annamites waiting to "turn tails" when and if the penguin pilots arrived at their destination. A laughable scene followed.

The task of the pupil—seemingly a simple one—was to open throttle, get the tail up, and run the little plane in a straight line five or six hundred yards across the field. Once there, the motor was allowed to idle while the waiting Annamite turned the tail till the plane was headed for the hangars once more. But the four men now under way were all beginners, confused by the rush of air from the whirling propellers and the operation of joy stick and rudder bar. Guided by inexperienced hands, the penguins rushed this way and that, with almost human perversity, spinning about suddenly, threatening to collide with their neighbours, and saved from turning over only by what seemed a series of miracles. Our instructor, reclining in a steamer chair, watched these evolutions contemptuously, without a smile, exclaiming from time to time, "*Oh, là là là! Les cochons! Ils veulent tout casser!*" After what seemed an interminable time they managed to return with their unruly mounts, and got down, crestfallen and red in the face. The instructor sprang out of his chair, called out three French names, and caught Gordon Forbes's eye.

"An American, eh? Your name? Forbes? All right, hop in! Your feet on the rudder bar to the steering—see?—just like a boat. Here's the throttle; when you open it, press forward gently on the joy stick to bring the tail up. Don't be afraid to give her the guns! All Americans are cowboys, *hein? Allez! Roulez!*"

Settling himself in the cockpit, Gordon opened the throttle wide. A blast of wind sent dust and bits of paper eddying behind the penguin; up came its rail, and it sped down the field straight for the waiting Annamite. A moment later it was rushing back at us at thirty miles an hour. The whirling of its propeller slowed, the tail skid came down, and the penguin stopped a few yards from where the instructor sat. He left his chair with a bound. "But you are an ace!" he exclaimed, slapping Gordon on the back. "Wait till those others get in, and if you can run her out and back a second time as well as you did this, I'll send you to the rollers this afternoon!"

Fifteen minutes later Gordon was walking back toward the barracks alone—a graduate of the penguin class. I shall not dwell on my own performance with those tricky flightless birds. However, three days later, I caught up with Gordon in the crowded roller class, where he had not thus far been aboard a plane.

It was obvious from the beginning that Gordon was born to be an airman. His landing of the Blériot was faultless, and only the overcrowded classes enabled me to keep up with him, through the rollers, the short straightaway flights a few yards above the ground, and the final great moments of actually flying around the field. I smashed a landing gear and broke a wing or two, but all through his training Forbes never broke so much as a wire.

Mechanical flight—so commonplace now—had still at that time the fascination of novelty, and I am tempted to try to set down the vivid impressions of those early days in the air. But I shall refrain, for the wonder of man's conquest of the skies is an old story nowadays—relegated to the past with Fulton's steamboat, and Stephenson's locomotive, and the motor car invented by so many men at once. But the altitude test which marked an epoch in my career in the air was an experience of such strangeness and beauty that I cannot pass it by.

We had done our right and left spirals the day before,

and half a dozen of us assembled that morning to do our altitudes—to spend an hour, that is, above two thousand metres. The sixty-horse-power Blériots were aligned before the hangar, but the sky was overcast with a sea of cloud, not more than four thousand feet up, and unless that broke there would be no altitudes that day. Somewhat depressed, we sat in the lee of the hangar—the six of us: three French non-commissioned officers, Gordon, an American named Slater, and I. Slater promptly made himself comfortable in the withered grass and went to sleep; the rest of us discussed the inevitable topic, flying.

Tommy Slater was certainly the strangest of all the Americans at Avord. He was a cadaverous boy of twenty, all bones and hollows, pale as an invalid and as hairless as a girl. He came from Philadelphia, I think, where he had been a choirboy in an Episcopal church. He rarely spoke, and when he did his voice was high-pitched and throaty. His life at Avord consisted of nothing but flying and sleep. He slept twice as much in barracks as any other man of our lot, and on the field he had the habit of dropping off to sleep at once, asking someone to waken him when his turn came. Add to this that he made no friends and seemed to want none, and that he was considered the finest natural airman who had ever passed through the school, and it will be understood why my memory of him is still fresh.

We others, in the lee of the hangar, had become so intent on our talk that we had lost track of the weather. The instructor's voice brought us back to realities.

"Slater!" he called. "Slater!"

I awakened him, and in an instant he was on his feet, clear-eyed and alert. "Present!" he shouted in his thin reedy voice. Glancing up at the sky, I saw that the clouds had broken overhead, leaving a blue hole through which a plane might climb.

"Take that plane, Slater," the instructor was ordering him, "and see if you can get up to two thousand. If you are not down in twenty minutes I shall send the others up. If you lose sight of the ground, take care to fly in circles, so as not to be lost when you come down through the clouds."

Slater took off beautifully, and a moment later the monoplane was high above the trees. Our instructor watched him approvingly.

"Born to the air, *ce garçon-là!*" he said, turning to one of the French sergeants. "He flies as a bird flies, without a thought, and he has no more nerves than a fish. Keep your eye on him. He will get his share of Boches!"

He glanced at his watch from time to time, and presently gave the word for two of us to start, I was the second to take off.

In ten minutes I was circling over the aerodrome at eleven hundred metres, higher than I had ever been allowed to fly before, and just above me I saw the blue hole Slater had climbed through. Up I went in narrowing circles, pulling back the joy stick till I felt the old monoplane lose speed and stagger once or twice. At sixteen hundred I burst through into the pure dazzling sunlight of the upper air. A sea of clouds stretched away beneath me to the horizon, and from the sea rose islands here and there, fantastic mountain ranges, foothills, divides, vast snowy peaks and dark gorges, widening, narrowing, deepening, streaming with thin grey mist. Twenty-two hundred metres—I glanced at the clock and at the sun before I began my first exploration of this strange and beautiful world of clouds. Gauging my position by the sun, I travelled in great circles, hoping that at the end of the hour, when I plunged down through the clouds to the grey everyday world beneath, I should find Avord in sight.

As I skirted the foothills of a cloudy mountain range, I saw far off to the north a moving speck, and knew that Slater was exploring this new cloud world astride his gaunt mechanical bird. The hands of my clock seemed to move inexorably, at twice their usual speed, and my hour was up long before I was ready to dive back to earth. But when the time came I shut off the motor reluctantly and went down in long easy glides. The clouds had closed up and the earth was nowhere visible. In an instant the sunlight was blotted out; cold grey mist streamed past me, and the monoplane pitched and staggered drunkenly. In the snap of a finger I had lost all sense of balance and direction. A fierce wind from one side screamed through the wires, and next moment I was out of the clouds and dropping like a stone in an almost vertical wing slip. I turned into it, giving her the motor as she straightened out; then I began to scan the earth nervously, fearing that I was lost. No—far away to the north I made out the hangars of one of the outlying fields. When I landed I found Gordon and two others still waiting in hopes that the clouds would break once more.

The first four or five days of that September were days of rain, and Gordon and I, ready and eager to do our cross-country flights, were forced to loaf about the hangars, damp, dispirited, and consumed with impatience. The instructor of the brevet class was a humorous little sergeant, scarcely five feet tall, who had as little respect for discipline as the wildest American in the school.

One afternoon, when we had marched out through a rain that had the air of lasting for a month, the sergeant lined us up just inside a hangar. "*Messieurs,*" he said,—the use of the civilian word was typical of him—"my orders are, in case flying is impossible to-day, to make you gather stones on that field, and deposit them in little heaps to be carted off by your fellow labourers from Annam. An excellent idea, no doubt. But listen carefully. I am planning to smoke my pipe in this hangar for precisely five minutes. At the end of that time I shall step outside and glance about. If I see any man making off, I shall have to report him, though I have singularly short sight.

And there will be *no* roll call before we march home." With a grin at all hands he seated himself on an empty gasoline tin and filled his pipe. In twenty seconds there was not a budding pilot within a hundred yards.

Most of the crowd went by inconspicuous paths to the Café des Aviateurs, which would be packed at this hour on a rainy day. No one was ever reported for going there, for it was out of bounds to every man in the school,—pupils and instructors alike—and a kind of unwritten armistice prevailed. But Gordon and I left the others and walked away on a secret path of our own, which led through the kitchen gardens of the artillery camp to an isolated farmhouse, where an old woman we knew could be prevailed on to serve cups of rich chocolate, fresh bread, and omelets seasoned with savory herbs. Wilding and O'Connor had finished at Avord and gone on to do their aerial acrobacy at Pau, in southern France, and the man we saw most of at this time was Harvey McKail, a slight, fair-haired chap from Illinois, who had arrived a fortnight after us, and whom we found particularly congenial. He and Gordon and I were the only habitués of the farm.

The old woman welcomed us at the door—red hands on her hips. "Yes, he is already here, your friend. He is reading, as usual. I think he likes his books better than my chocolate."

"May we have some chocolate, too?" asked Gordon. "We're frightfully hungry, *grand'mere*. How about a couple of omelets—four eggs each—with a lot of nice *fines herbes* chopped up in them?"

We found McKail installed at a table in a warm corner of the big old-fashioned kitchen. A steaming bowl of chocolate was before him, and he took a spoonful from time to time, without lifting his eyes from the book propped up to one side. It was Thoreau's *A Week on the Concord and Merrimac Rivers*, and when he became aware of our presence he held up a hand. "Listen to this, you fellows," he said, and read us the following:

"All around beneath me was spread for a hundred miles on every side, as far as the eye could reach, an undulating country of clouds . . . such a country as one might see in dreams with all the delights of paradise. There were immense snowy pastures, apparently smooth-shaven and firm, and shady vales between the vaporous mountains. It was a favour for which to be for ever silent to be shown this vision. The inhabitants of earth behold commonly but the dark shadowy side of heaven's pavement. How convey an impression of the gorgeous tapestry by which I was surrounded, such as men see faintly reflected afar off in the chambers of the east?"

McKail looked up. "He wrote that while sitting on the top of a mountain," he said.

"He puts it well," Gordon remarked. "I know he hated civilization and mechanical things, but I think he would have loved flying, all the same!"

Something in the remark made me think of my uncle, far away in French Oceania, and of a letter from him—the first since I'd been in France—which I was carrying in my pocket at that moment.

"I've got an uncle—I've told you about him, Gordon—who hates civilization too; he lives in the South Seas, where I've visited him twice. You fellows would love it down there! I've just had a long letter from him; would you like to read it?"

They nodded. I handed the typed letter to Gordon, who proceeded to read it aloud:

"Things are very dull just now, with all the able-bodied men away at the war. I've never really got over that trouble with my eyes, and so far I've not been able to visit Iriatai. They tell me the island is beginning to recover from the effects of the hurricane last year. The new schooner is framed and planked, but the work goes slowly with most of the shipwrights away. I'm building her here at my plantation and doing a lot of the work with my own hands. You'll like her, I think; she's more of a yacht than a trading schooner, and I'm hoping to use her as much for pleasure as for work. It's about time I retired, anyway.

"The thought of retiring brings me to something I want you to think over. Don't mention it in your letters home until you're quite sure of what you want to do, one way or the other. But I'll give you a little sketch of my castle in the air, and you can let me know how it strikes you. I live a rather lonely life, I'm not so young as I was, and I've got more business on my hands than I know what to do with; in other words, as I said before, I want to retire. I want to potter about my Tahiti place to my heart's content, and I want to make a trip or two out through the western islands—the Solomons and the New Hebrides. So much for me. Now you come into the scheme. If you get through the war you're going to find yourself at a bit of a loose end. You've had a taste of the South Seas, and you will have had an experience of the biggest show in the world's history. Will you be content to settle down to the life of a farmer? If you thought your father really needed you at the ranch I know you'd carry on, but now that Marion is married to young Gilmour and settled on the place with him, there's no question of needing you. Gilmour's a natural farmer—a better one than you or I could ever be. But if you don't go home when the war's over, what *are* you going to do?

"I asked myself a question like that many years ago, and though I don't want to brag, I've never had cause to regret the decision I made. We're put in the world to be happy, and the only way to be happy is to make full use of whatever equipment we're born with. A born sailor is wasting his time in a broker's office, no matter how rich he becomes, and the chances are ten to one that he won't get rich. And a born stockbroker would make a mistake to try his luck before the mast on a sailing vessel. A man is like a piece of machinery, designed and built to do a certain job.

"I have a fancy that I know you quite as well as you know yourself, and that is why I suggest this plan for our future. First of all, did you ever notice on the charts of this part of the world an island called Taiakau? Perhaps not; you've never seen the place, I know. It's a high island, quite a big one, and the last of its people died a month or two ago. She was an old woman, and, as all the Taiakau people were of one clan, she had a clear title to the whole island for a few months before she died. Well, I bought it from her. The old girl made me pay through the nose—I can't imagine what she wanted, or what she did, with all that money. There's nothing on Taiakau now,—it doesn't produce five tons of copra a year—but if a man could raise capital enough to clear the whole place and plant it, I reckon it would turn out about a thousand tons a year. Here's what I have in mind: supposing the idea appeals to you, we already have Iriatai, and we would borrow the money to clear and plant Taiakau. It would be a twelve- to fifteen-year pull to get it into bearing, but at the end of that time, as I said, it ought to produce a thousand tons. Iriatai, as you probably know, turns out about four hundred tons a year. At the end of about twelve years the two islands combined ought to bring in a net income, over and above all expenses, of about eighty thousand dollars a year.

"If I had children I might go ahead without you, but I'm too old to plant coconuts for my own benefit, and I haven't the energy I used to have. So I propose that you think over the idea of a partnership after the war. We should need a new schooner, much larger than the one I'm building now, and a lot of capital. That's where the rub comes in—money, as usual! But I think we could raise it, somehow. I wish you could see Taiakau before you decide. A wild, lovely island, overgrown with heavy jungle and running with clear mountain streams. The first job, after the money was in sight, would be a tour of the islands to get labour. There would be houses, a store, a church, and a school to build; a little world of our own, in fact, with everything in it to our taste. It's fun, that kind of work. You could run the schooner or take charge of Taiakau, as you liked; we'd have to pick up one first-class man in either case—the sort of man it isn't easy to find. As for me, I could look after the business end, here in Tahiti—selling copra, buying supplies, and all that.

"Think it over, old fellow, and let me know what you think. Don't let the fact that I've bought Taiakau influence you; I can always sell if for more than I paid. Chances to buy a whole rich island of that kind are very rare. Write when you feel in the mood, and tell me all about what you are doing. I won't say anything about the war. Odd to think how far apart we are just now—we couldn't separate much more unless one of us stepped off into space!"

As Gordon read, the book dropped unnoticed from McKail's

hand, and a rapt expression came into his blue eyes. "A South Sea Island!" he exclaimed. "I've always dreamed of living on one. A little grass hut under a breadfruit tree, a clear brook running into the lagoon close by, a long, comfortable steamer chair, and plenty of books. That's the life! I don't know what copra is, but it doesn't interest me. No buying or selling in a place like that!"

Gordon shook his head. "Not enough action in that kind of a life, Harvey. But I'd like to see the South Seas too. What do you say, Charlie? If the Boches don't get us, I wonder if your uncle would let me in on his scheme? He says you'd need money, and I've any amount of that."

There is no space in this story of war to tell how the weather cleared at last, and how on two successive days I made my two triangular cross-country flights of a hundred and fifty miles each—Avord, Châteauroux, Romorantin. I could not now describe the route I took, nor the aspect of those unimportant towns in Central France, but the beauty of their sonorous names still lingers in my mind. Nor is there space to tell of the friends I made among my countrymen at Avord—of whom I can only say that they were the cream of their generation, in the flush of youth, gay, high-spirited, and so keen on their work that more than once I saw a man in a neighbouring cot sitting bolt upright and sound asleep, while he performed aerial manoeuvres in his dreams. More than fifty of them lost their lives in combat over the lines, and they sleep together to-day in the quiet French countryside they loved, under the beautiful Lafayette Memorial Arch at Villeneuve l'Étang. The living are scattered far and wide—middle-aged men nowadays, with families, and financial worries, and greying hair. War friendships were warmer than those of peace-time—quickly made, more quickly severed. The friend of a fortnight, in training camp or billets, seemed like a lifelong chum. War brings men together as casually as it separates them; in many cases friends grow old and die without meeting again; and oftentimes, during the war, one heard with a shock of incredulity, "They got Bill yesterday—he went down in flames in the Saint-Mihiel Salient"; or "Harry's dead; crowned this morning on our side of the lines." One thought of Bill's amiable eccentricities, or of some human and lovable weakness of Harry's, and it was hard to realise that one's friend—the incongruous and picturesque bundle of qualities that made a human individual—was gone. One shook one's head in bewilderment, and banished such reflections by murmuring the sadly overworked phrase: "*C'est la guerre!*"

III

THE SCHOOL OF COMBAT

THE month of September, 1917, was a time of comparative quiet on the French front, and Gordon and I were allowed a seven days' leave before proceeding to Pau. We were full-fledged pilots now, with wings on our collars, and the little badges of aviators—wings and a wreath—to pin on our tunics. And from second-class soldiers of the Foreign Legion we had now risen to the rank of corporal. But I am sure that when we took our last glance at Avord and set out for Paris, where we were to spend our leave with the Héraults, we looked a great deal more imposing—with our stripes and wings and brand-new tailored uniforms—than we felt. Now that we had made the first faltering trials of our wings, we realised, as only fledgling airmen can, the difficulties ahead of us—the task of learning to fly really well.

After my life at Avord—with coarse food, irregular hours, and hard beds, the everyday civilian comforts of Monsieur Hérault's house struck me as almost Babylonian luxury. We saw little of our host during the daytime, but Mme. de Thouars was like an elder sister to Gordon and me. She encouraged us to sleep late in the morning, the greatest luxury of all after Avord. She took us to lunch at restaurants, and pointed out the celebrities of Paris round about. She insisted on our asking to her father's house the friends Gordon and I met nearly every day.

In my eyes, Paris will never again be the Paris of that autumn of 1917. The first contingent of Americans had arrived in France, and they were received with an enthusiasm that warmed my heart. And they were worthy of their welcome—splendid, trained fighting men of the Regular Establishment. Later on, when American soldiers swarmed all over France, and Paris was crowded to suffocation with non-combatant war workers—a good half of whom, it seemed to me, had crossed the Atlantic for a safe and somewhat distant glimpse of the war—it was inevitable that the feeling toward Americans should change. But during our seven days' leave Paris seemed all smiles and laughter and cheers.

Monsieur Hérault gave us two evenings, one to see *Carmen* at the Opéra Comique, and one for a round of the cafés with dinner at a great restaurant afterward. But another evening, which Gordon and Mme. de Thouars and I spent quietly at home, was the one I remember best. She knew a good many of the famous fighting pilots, and our conversation turned to their eccentricities and their exploits over the lines. Some were superstitious and never flew without odd mascots of different kinds; others had a horror of being taken prisoner, and never neglected to carry a toothbrush and a roll of hundred-franc bills. The September evening was chilly, and we were sitting before an open fire in the drawing-room.

"You two will soon be at the front," remarked Mme. de Thouars; "and who knows? One of you may be taken prisoner. In case that happens, what do you say to a little conspiracy in advance? I thought it all out last night. If you, Gordon, or you, Charlie, are forced to come down *chez Boche*, I shall soon learn of it, and it will be possible to send you packages through Switzerland—cigarettes, chocolate, clothing, soap, and tinned food." She paused for a moment to poke the fire, and then went on: "Now pay attention! I have a friend who owns a packing house where they put up very nice things to eat. If at any time I hear that either of you is a prisoner, I shall go to this factory and make certain arrangements there. They make a kind of potted meat called Pâté des Chasseurs. It comes in large round tins, and I want you both to remember its name! I'll enclose two tins of this pâté in every other package I send, and one of them will contain a pair of coiled-up little saw blades for cutting iron, a tiny compass, and maps of Germany and her frontiers, on oiled silk."

I suppose the thought of being captured was in the back of every man's mind in those days; I know I had some times thought of it, and wondered if it would be possible to escape. Although Mme. de Thouars's suggestion sounded far-fetched at the time, I knew it was good common sense, a wise precaution against an emergency that might easily arise. Gordon and I agreed to the plan and took pains to memorize the name of the tinned stuff which was to contain the contraband. And a day was to come when the sight of a tin of Pâté des Chasseurs would make me tremble with anxiety.

The seven days of our leave passed slowly, filled with the deep happiness of all war-time leaves, but I was so keen to get to Pau that I was not sorry when the time was up. We said good-bye to the Héraults, travelled south to Bordeaux, and from there to the School of Acrobatics and Combat, near Pau, in the Valley of the Gave, just under the Pyrenees.

The country was like my native California—the same remote skyline of mountains, with hills and broad valleys at their feet; the same cool clear autumn mornings, the same cloudless skies, flushing in the sunrise behind dark peaks. The school was a place far different from Avord. We lived, with a score of other Americans, like fighting cocks, in a barrack as clean, airy, and comfortable as a summer cottage at home. The food was wholesome and plentiful; the planes, all of the Nieuport type, seemed innumerable and in perfect condition. Instead of waiting for hours for a chance to fly, we were encouraged to spend every waking hour in the air. And it was very pleasant, after many a day of picking up stones at Avord, to be treated with almost unmilitary courtesy. The whole atmosphere and spirit of Pau might be expressed thus: "You are pilots now, in training to fight alone in the air. If you were not keen on the work you would not be here. Fly all you want—perfect yourselves—and we shall treat you as gentlemen."

On our first morning at Pau, Gordon and I were sent out to a distant field to do tight spirals in an eighteen-metre Nieuport. We travelled in a smart little Fiat, driven at breakneck speed along roads bordered with Lombardy poplars. Our chauffeur drew up beside a small hangar where a young officer, who had flown out from camp, awaited his class. Following the example of the French pilots with us, Gordon and I presented ourselves, saluting and mentioning our names when our turn came. The instructor glanced over his group of pupils.

"A little lecture first," he remarked. "Come into the hangar."

A Nieuport stood just inside, with motor and wings removed. The lieutenant climbed into the cockpit and took his place at the controls.

"This is the class of vertical spirals," he explained, "a manœuvre you are not supposed to have performed. Remember that when an aeroplane inclines laterally to over forty-five degrees, the controls become reversed; the elevator is then the rudder, and the rudder the elevator. In a vertical spiral, the farther back you pull the stick, the tighter the spiral becomes. You are at the same time dropping and whirling in short circles. When you can do five turns in losing three hundred metres I shall promote you to the next class. Now watch me. See—first, with the stick, I tilt the plane past forty-five; now I am going into my spiral, holding her nose up with the rudder—the elevator now. And I must pull back the stick—so—to prevent going into a wing slip. You understand?" He glanced down at a slip of paper in his hand—our notes, as the French called them—brief remarks on each man's performance at Avord. "Forbes!" he called. Gordon came forward.

"Take that plane yonder, go up to a thousand metres over those trees, and do me a tight spiral to the left. If you can do five turns in less than three hundred, stay up and have another try to the right. Your notes are good; show these chaps how it should be done."

Gordon took off beautifully, with a long rush and no foolish zoom near the ground. Precisely at the designated place and altitude, the Nieuport tilted and began to spin in spirals tight as a corkscrew. Then Gordon straightened out, regained the thousand feet he had lost and performed the same manœuvre to the right, with the ease and finish of an old hand. Straightening out once more, he came down in serpentine glides, and landed almost imperceptibly, tail skid an instant after the wheels. The lieutenant clapped him on the back as he climbed out of the cockpit. "Splendid!" he said. "There is nothing I can teach you about spirals!"

I took off in my turn without difficulty, and climbed to the required altitude, but the piloting of the unfamiliar little ship confused me, and when I went into my spiral I forgot to pull the stick well back, and came down in an appalling wing slip from which I managed to pull out j ust over the treetops. I had dropped twenty-five hundred feet in doing three quarters of a turn! The idea of having another try was not pleasant, but I went up again, doing my best to plan coolly the movements I must make to avoid another slip. At a thousand meters I flipped the little plane on her beam ends, gave her a touch of high rudder, and pulled the stick back into my belly, as we used to say. In what seemed an instant, the distant group of hangars I had chosen as a landmark had flashed past five times, as fast as one could count. I glanced at my altimeter as I straightened out, feeling a bit dizzy. I had lost just under three hundred metres. The right-hand spiral was harder—I do not know to this day why, whether from the torque of the propeller or because human beings are built that way—but I managed a fairly good one at the first attempt, and landed to receive the rating I deserved.

"*Là! Là! Là! Là!*" cried the lieutenant, shaking imaginary water from his fingers, in the odd gesture the French use at such times. "Go to the next class! I won't have you killed in mine! What's more, I'm sick of buying flowers to put on suicides' graves! Your two spirals were not bad. But I do not teach wing slips into forests on this field! I ought to give you ten days in the guardhouse—you didn't pay any attention to what I said about pulling back on the stick! But I'll promote you instead!"

Next day Gordon and I had our first flights on the fifteen-metre Nieuport, a real fighting single-seater, used on the front until replaced by the Spad. It was equipped with a Le Rhône rotary motor of one hundred and twenty horse-power, and I can still recall the sensations of limitless speed and power these little hornet ships gave me. They were immensely strong, could manœuvre like swallows, and seemed to go up or down with equal ease. We did spirals on them, learned to fly with others in formation, and spent many a happy hour at the sport of contour-chasing, skimming pastures a yard above the grass, leaping the poplar hedges, booming down the main streets of villages where the half-Spanish population rushed out to gape. At last we were ready for the class in acrobatics—the Haute École du Ciel.

This class, the final stage in the training of a pursuit pilot, was crowded just then, and we had to wait several days before our turn came. Tommy Slater, who had been through Avord with us, had stolen a seven days' march by refusing to take the leave offered him, and he had all but finished his acrobatics when we arrived on the field. His performance, in fact, was the talk of the school, and it was rumoured that the captain rated him the finest pilot who had ever passed through Pau.

In those days, when flying was not far from its infancy, the Haute École du Ciel was considered almost as dangerous as the front, and I fancy that the percentage of casualties justified the belief. It was the supreme test of nerves and stomachs, and of the soundness of one's training up to that time. The instructor was a celebrity among French flying men, a lieutenant dressed like a dandy, and rumoured never to remove the monocle from his eye. It was his custom to recline in a steamer chair, surrounded by assistants who stood about, gazing up through field glasses, and reporting from time to time that some fledgling pilot was about to perform a tail spin or an Immelmann turn. If the manœuvre was well done, the lieutenant murmured, "Not too bad," but any display of clumsiness or timidity brought a contemptuous grunt, or a muttered "Why do they send such men to me?" If, as frequently happened, some unfortunate with a dizzy head or a squeamish stomach plunged into the ground and killed himself, the lieutenant had his cure for the moment of depressed thoughtfulness that followed. He would rise languidly from his chair, hand his stick and gloves to an assistant, and climb into the cockpit of his own thirteen-metre Nieuport. Then he would give an exhibition of cold-blooded skill that made one's hair rise—loops, barrel turns, and spins, so close to the ground that the wheels of the little plane seemed to graze the turf as it straightened out, vertical banks between tall trees, so close together that the "Baby" Nieuport could have passed in no other position. It was done deliberately, of course, to keep the pilots "blown up"—*gonflé*, as the French used to say—full of courage and confidence and a spirit of emulation. But when Gordon and I arrived in his class the lieutenant had his arm in a sling and was unable to fly.

All the pilots in the school seem to have been jammed into this last class, and I saw at once that there would be no hope of my flying that day. There were a dozen Russians, officers of the Czarist régime, sent long before to be taught flying in France. Though full of courage, they did not take kindly to the air, and too frequently managed to kill themselves. Tommy Slater, alone as usual, had chosen a soft bit of turf and promptly fallen asleep. Our elegant instructor, seating himself in his steamer chair, beckoned to one of his assistants, who held out a slip of paper. His eyebrows went up. "Call him," he ordered his assistant; "or at least attempt to pronounce his name. But take care not to dislocate your jaw!" The assistant made a wry face as he called a name that sounded something like Chickerowski. "Present!" shouted one of the Russians eagerly. "Take up number nine, rise to twelve hundred metres, and do a tail spin."

The poor devil climbed joyfully into the cockpit, took off clumsily, and soon had his altitude. The plane lost speed, swayed for a moment, and plunged earthward, spinning. Down, down, down, the Russian came. Faces paled, mouths opened. Then—crash! The ground under our feet shook at the impact. It is enough to say of that ghastly fall that the grass where the ship struck was scarcely knee-high, and that nothing remained in sight above the grass. The ambulance, always in attendance, was under way twenty seconds after the Russian struck the earth, though every man on the field knew that it was a case for brooms and buckets.

"Slaterre!" the lieutenant called in his well-bred way. Tommy Slater jumped up, wide awake at once. With a wave of his uninjured hand, the officer indicated the rather horrified group of pilots standing about. "*Gonflez* this crowd," he said. "Take my plane and show them how to do a spin!"

Without any sign of emotion Slater crawled into the lieutenant's little thirteen-metre ship, and seemed to leave the ground like a bird, with scarcely any preliminary run over the ground. All eyes were on him, for, as I have said, he was already a small celebrity in the school. What followed was the most consummate exhibition of aerial acrobatics I have ever seen, performed within a few yards of the ground, and back and forth between hedges of tall trees where a single false movement or an instant's failure of the motor would have meant a ghastly smash. He zoomed almost vertically over the poplars at the far end of the field, turned in a beautiful Immelmann—half a loop, upside down, and a half barrel—came roaring back, nose-down, just over our heads, and did a loop from which he emerged with his wheels brushing the grass. His two spins, one right and one left, were done so close to the earth that they brought even the languid instructor to his feet, and each time, when he straightened out, the landing gear of the plane was no higher than a man's head. "Marvellous flying," I heard Gordon mutter nervously; "but he's mad—a lunatic!"

Slater's final manœuvre was the most spectacular of all. He

had risen to about a thousand feet, almost directly overhead. Suddenly he threw his plane into a vertical wing slip, and, just above the grass, turned into it, levelled off, and landed lightly straight into the wind, so that the machine came to a stop within ten yards of the lieutenant's chair.

The instructor removed his monocle, polished it with a dainty handkerchief, and touched his brow with the cambric before he screwed the glass back into place. "Not too bad," he murmured, "not too bad. *Sacré* Slaterre—wait till he gets to the front! Eh what? He ought to be able to *scare* the Bosches to death!"

Slater got his orders to leave Pau that same night—to report to the G. D. E., where all the flying personnel of the French Army awaited assignments to squadrons at the front. But Gordon and I were stuck for nearly a week without a chance to fly. Our turns came at last, and I recall vividly my nervousness when I went up to do my first tail spins.

I was flying a "Baby" Nieuport, a beautiful specimen of the most beautiful little plane produced in France during the war. These "Babies" had only thirteen square metres of supporting surface, and I fancy that no smaller practical plane has been made to this day. They were strong, very fast, and so sweet and delicate in manœuvre that the pilots of those days never tired of praising them, though their "low ceiling"—their range of altitude—owing to the small area of the wings, made them useless at the front.

I confess that I felt a decided sinking sensation as the little ship whizzed upward, high over the trees. The tail spin had a bad name in those days. Two turns of the field gave me my thirty-six hundred feet. With a strange empty feeling in the pit of the stomach, I slowed down the motor and pulled back little by little on the stick. The speed of the Nieuport slackened; she began to sway sickeningly. Gritting my teeth hard, I gave her full rudder and reverse stick, and pulled the stick all the way back. For an instant she seemed to hang motionless, then suddenly plunged, whirling downward. A great wind tore at my clothing and screamed through the wires. One hundred—two hundred—three hundred. Slowly and carefully I brought the rudder bar to the exact centre, centred the stick and pushed it forward, little by little. The whirling ceased, the wind abated; I glanced out to find myself in a steep glide, right side up. That moment, as I look back on it, was one of the greatest of my life. To any man in search of a new and glorious sensation, let me recommend a tail spin in a small single-seater pursuit plane!

The last week of September found Gordon and me aboard a train for Paris, where we had been granted forty-eight hours' leave before reporting at the G. D. E.

IV

AT THE G. D. E.

ON the morning of the first of October, Gordon and I left Paris for the G. D. E. at Plessis-Belleville. G. D. E. was an abbreviation for Groupe des Divisions d'Entrainement. It was the great clearing station through which all aviators in the French service were sent to the front: newly fledged birdmen like ourselves, pilots and observers being changed from one Aviation Group to another, veteran airmen, who, having recovered from injuries or battle wounds, were again ready to be assigned to squadrons, and so forth. Plessis, as everyone called the depot, is a small village like hundreds of others in Northern France, about thirty miles from Paris and perhaps thirty-five from the front at that time.

We were almost ridiculously happy that morning. At last we were on our way to the front—the next to the last lap—and Plessis was actually in the Zone des Armées. I could tell how inwardly excited Gordon was by the way he sat in our third-class compartment, his hands under his knees, rocking back and forth as he talked. And he talked of everything but flying. He asked me scores of questions about the South Seas in his cool, easy, interested way, but I knew well enough that he was thinking, as I was, of nothing but the adventures before us. It was Gordon's manner of keeping his eagerness and excitement in hand.

The train crept along with the deliberation of a heavy-duty truck, stopping at every little station, and squatting there as though it meant never to move again. We were nearly three quarters of an hour in reaching Dammartin, a station only a little more than half-way to Plessis. But from that point on there was no more talk, for the air was filled with planes: Voisins, Bréguets, Sopwiths, twin-motor Caudrons, huge three-passenger Letords, Morane Parasols, A-R's, Nieuports, Spads. Merely to mention the names of these old war craft gives me a thrill, although the war is now ten years past and I am writing this on the other side of the world. A flight of four *chasse* planes, contour-chasing almost on a level with the car windows, passed us so rapidly that we seemed to be moving backward rather than forward. The crisp autumn air was filled with the music of high-powered motors—it is music to an airman's ears—and, craning our necks out of the windows, we could see the sunlight glinting now and then from the underbodies of planes all but invisible in the depths of blue sky.

And then we got down at Plessis. Gordon sniffed hungrily. "Doesn't it smell good?" he said. I knew what he meant. The first thing we were aware of was the unmistakable, unforgettable fragrance of an aerodrome. How am I to define it or describe it? There are those who say that it is nothing but a compound of burnt gasoline and castor oil, but any old pilot knows better. Those smells were at the bottom of it, perhaps, but the odourless smell of clouds and windy skies was in it too, and the heady fragrance of a youngster's thoughts and moods as he flew high above the earth, trying to realize, trying to grasp the glorious truth that man had at last conquered the air.

But on that cloudless October morning I made no such analysis of "aerodrome perfume." Gordon and I merely drank it in, and what it meant to us then was "Here we are at home again!" For home, to an airman, is where-ever there are hangars, planes to fly, and a field to fly them from. Only three days had passed since we left Pau, but they had been such busy, pleasant days that it seemed more like three weeks since we had had our fingers on a joy stick. In those days we were never really happy unless we were a mile or two above the earth and could hear the struts and wires singing as they cut their way through the air.

There was an hotel, called the Hôtel de la Bonne Rencontre, near the station at Plessis. I suppose this may be translated "The Hotel of the Happy Meeting," and it was a place of happy meeting for us, for we found Bill O'Connor and Jim Wilding there. They had finished at Pau before us, and were still awaiting assignment to squadrons. Nearly all the Lafayette

Corps pilots stopped at the Bonne Rencontre while at the G. D. E.; and although it was a ramshackle place, with beds on three legs—and innumerable bugs on twenty or more—broken-down chairs, walls covered with hideous paper, and dust and grime over everything, I have an affection for it that amounts to love. And some day, when I return to France to relive the good old days, the Bonne Rencontre will be one of the first places I shall visit.

O'Connor and Wilding told us that three weeks was the average length of time at the G. D. E. before a pilot received his active-service orders. They were both sick of waiting; nevertheless they were having a thoroughly good time. Here the men were free from the somewhat irksome routine of the schools. The only duty was to fly, and never before, surely, had men obeyed the voice of duty more gladly than we did.

Mme. Rodel, the *patronne* of the hotel, assigned us a room where we dumped down our duffle bags; then the four of us went out to the flying field. Wilding and O'Connor were going up for practice in group flying; Gordon and I had the usual formalities for newly arrived pilots to go through with, and we set about them at once. We registered at the central bureau; then we were photographed as a preliminary to receiving the identification cards we should carry at the front; then we went to the Bureau de Pilotage to be assigned to our work at Plessis, the hours for flying, and so forth, for there were two or three hundred pilots waiting there and work had to be done on schedule.

At the Bureau de Pilotage we met Lieutenant de Gayic, the Chef de Piste at the G. D. E. We had heard of him long before our arrival: every airman in the French service knew him, and he was a warm friend of all Lafayette men. He had, I know, a secret sympathy with our undisciplined ways, and many a scrape he got us out of when we had done as we pleased rather than as Captain Hervé, commandant at Plessis, pleased. The commandant was a thorough soldier and had a soldier's respect—reverence, I should say—for the sanctity of orders. Most of us Americans thought the chief value of orders—I am speaking of unimportant ones—was in the pleasure one had in disobeying them, and we did disobey them right and left. So we were often in trouble, and Lieutenant de Gayic as often at *his* wit's end to devise means for getting us out of it. But he always did, somehow.

He was never too busy to do one a service, and on this first morning he went with Gordon and me to the Stores Department where we were to get our flying clothes. "You'll want things you can really *use* when you get to the front," he explained, "and Sergeant Marquettie has a faculty that amounts to genius for misfitting pilots. He'll hand out a four-foot combination for a six-foot man, and a pair of number-ten gloves for a number-seven hand. And he's as stubborn as the father of all mules—won't let you exchange a single article! However, I've known him a long time, and I'll see that you get a decent outfit."

And he did. He made old Marquettie paw over great mounds of equipment, and as a result Gordon and I each received a combination suit neither too large nor too small, excellent gloves and fur-lined boots, warm woollen helmets, and heavy bearskin overcoats which are not worn in the air, but only when milling around on the ground in winter weather. We didn't take the hard, ungainly leather helmets the French Government supplies its airmen. These are top-heavy, and we much preferred, as did all other pilots, the small close-fitting helmets of soft leather which we could buy in any outfitter's shop in Paris. Gordon and I were already provided with them, and we also had Meyrowitz goggles, by far the best airmen's goggles to be had at that time.

I now realize that those days at Plessis were the happiest of my life. I think that I realized this, subconsciously, even at the time; but then, of course, I lacked perspective for clear judgment, and we were so eager to get to the front that any delay seemed irksome. There were moments when we hated the G. D. E., and always we were haunted by the absurd fear, common to every young soldier, that the war would be over before we should have a chance to take an active part. Wilding and O'Connor received their orders to move three days after our arrival. Tommy Slater had gone the week before, to the squadron Spad 602, Groupe de Combat 31. O'Connor was assigned to the Escadrille Lafayette, at that time stationed on the Aisne front, flying from an aerodrome at Chaudun, a village not far from Soissons. He was to replace Sergeant Courtney Campbell, an American from Chicago, who had been killed in combat on the first of October, the day of our arrival at the G. D. E. We were envious of O'Connor, for nearly all Lafayette men hoped to be sent to the Lafayette Escadrille. That was impossible, of course, for there were too many of us to be contained in a single squadron. Wilding went to a French squadron, Spad 65, which was, however, in the same Combat Group with the Lafayette Squadron, occupying the same flying field. So they went off together, as happy as a pair of youngsters going to a circus.

Gordon and I were lonesome without them, but there was so much interesting work to be done that we soon forgot everything but our flying. We were in the air a good half of the time, group flying, stunting, or doing machine-gun practice with some old worn-out bus on the ground as a target. But most of our practice was in combat tactics—four or six or a dozen planes in one flight engaging another flight while Lieutenant de Gayic and his corps of instructors watched our manœuvres from below. They were great sport—these mimic battles—and they had their element of danger too. Four men were killed during our first week at Plessis, and all of them when practising battle stunts.

When the required flying for the day was over, those who

wanted to were at liberty to go up in groups of two or three for extra-practice flights of various kinds. Gordon and I took advantage of this privilege every fine afternoon to make a high patrol, on our own, over Paris. To be sure, we were forbidden to fly over Paris, but it was impossible for our officers on the ground to keep track of us in the air, and as long as we got safely back, no one was the wiser—no one, that is, but Lieutenant de Gayic. When he heard the faint hum of motors and saw two or three late birds flying fast and high, homeward through the gathering dusk, he would sniff the air critically. "H'm!" he would say with a faint smile. "I know where *they've* been! Those *coucous* smell of the grand boulevards!" But he knew what airmen were, and he didn't mind this disregard of a standing order. And we always flew high, never lower than twelve thousand feet when over the city, so that in case of motor trouble we could plane down to some aerodrome well outside the suburbs.

Gordon and I would make straight across country till we passed the great aerodrome at Le Bourget, then throttle down, just keeping flying speed, and make a leisurely circle over Paris, feasting our eyes on the magnificent panorama of palaces, theatres, churches, parks, and boulevards outspread below us in the hazy light of an autumn afternoon. The Bois de Boulogne was a beautiful sight from the air, and I thought I could identify the roof of Dr. Gros's house at 23 Avenue du Bois de Boulogne, as well as the Boulevard Malesherbes where the Héraults lived. I could see plainly the roof of the Invalides where we had enlisted as members of the Foreign Legion. That event seemed to have taken place years ago, so much had happened since then, so many interesting events crowded into the space of three short months.

To the westward we could see the great loops in the Seine, fragments of silver bands gleaming softly in the midst of parks and clumps of woodland, and innumerable country houses and suburbs and villages scattered far and wide. At such times I would forget that there was a war in progress; it would seem to me that the millennium had come, and that my part in it was merely to fly over a happy peaceful world, with no cares and no responsibilities other than to keep my spark plugs clean and my gas tank filled. I would think of the kite-flying days of boyhood, when I had lain out on some windy hill, lazily holding my kite string, and longing as only a boy can to be "up above the world so high," little dreaming of the changes a few short years were to bring. Then a thrill of delight would go through me at the realization of my good fortune, and I would look down again over the side of my little bus to reassure myself that all this was not a dream. At last we would turn reluctantly homeward, with throttles full open, listening critically and a little anxiously to the sound of our motors until the hangars at Plessis came into view.

But it was only on these flights that we were able to forget the war. On the ground there were reminders of it and to spare. Every morning on our way to the flying field we would stop at the bureau to examine the daily list of killed, wounded, and injured airmen in the French service. These lists were tacked on the bulletin board alongside the official communiqués and there was always a knot of sober-faced men before it. One found there, too often, the names of friends and acquaintances, of old comrades we had known at Avord, of men casually met in Paris, or whom we knew by repute. Jim Wilding's name was there ten days after we had said good-bye to him at the little railway station at Plessis. "Killed in combat near Chamomile, October 9." This was the first time, I'think,.that Gordon and I realized in our hearts—not merely in our minds—the seriousness of the work before us. It brought the war home to us as nothing else could have done. There was Jim's old bed at the Bonne Rencontre, the one I was now occupying, and on the bottom of the top drawer of the dilapidated chest of drawers that stood in the corner he had written his name and the date: "October 3, 1917," the day he left Plessis for the front. I had seen him write it there while he was hastily stuffing his clothes into his duffle bag that morning. "Some day, Charlie, a long time after the war, I'm coming back to Plessis, and that will be a little souvenir; it will bring back old times to see my name written here the day I went to the front." I could hear the very tones of his voice as he had said this, and could see him pounding first on one end of the drawer and then on the other to shut it again. For several days we kept hoping that there had been some mistake, but a note from Bill O'Connor gave us the facts. Wilding had been killed on his second patrol and had fallen five kilometres inside the German lines.

Gordon and I tried not to think of him, and fortunately there was so much to do that we had little time to brood. And our own near departure for the front gave us more than enough to think and talk about when not flying. Our dream was, of course, to be assigned to the same squadron; we wanted to go through the war together, from first to last, if possible, but the chances of doing this seemed very slim. Orders came from some mysterious headquarters in Paris, known as the Service d'Aéronautique Militaire, and how was some smart staff officer in charge of squadron assignments there to know or to care what happened to a brace of obscure Americans anxiously awaiting his orders at the G. D. E.?

"Now if this were the U.S.A.," Gordon said one evening as we were coming back from machine-gun practice at Ermenonville, "we might be able to pull a few wires; but here—no, old boy, I'm afraid there's small chance for us, not one chance in a hundred of our going out together. We may as well face that fact and make the best of it. But we'll both be on the western front, that's certain. Sometimes we may be within flying distance of each other's aerodromes, anyway."

That seemed to be all we could hope for—an occasional glimpse of each other, perhaps, at long intervals, with an exchange of letters at other times. We were both glum at the thought of an early separation, and to me, at least, the prospect was really painful. Up to the time I went to France I had lived a life rather lonelier than that of most American boys, and had little opportunity for forming close friendships. When I met Gordon, on the steamer crossing to France, I liked him at once, and knew that he was my kind of a man. I hated to lose sight of him so soon.

That evening we were having supper at the Bonne Rencontre when Lieutenant de Gayic came in. He nodded pleasantly, sat down at a near-by table, and, when he had finished his meal, asked us to join him for coffee.

"You two look rather mournful," he said. "What's the bad news? Something gone wrong to-day?"

Gordon shook his head. "No, everything here is all right, Lieutenant. But we're thinking about the future. I suppose we'll be getting our orders soon?"

"You mean you'll be sorry for that?"

"Of course not! The sooner they come, the better pleased we'll be; but we had rather hoped to be sent to the same squadron, and we're afraid there's no chance of it. We'd like to keep on together if we could."

Lieutenant de Gayic lighted a cigarette and leaned back in his chair, regarding us thoughtfully.

"Well," he said, "I've heard of such things happening."

"Do you think it could be arranged?" I broke in eagerly. He

didn't reply for a moment; then he said, "What would you like to do, you two, when you get to the front? Do you want to see some action, straight off, or would you prefer going to a quiet sector until you've learned the ropes? Wait a minute! One at a time! Selden, what do you say?"

What I said—and I knew that I spoke for both of us—was that we greatly preferred going to an active sector, one like Verdun.

"Verdun. Just so. It's lively enough there at all times. But let me warn you: it's not a healthy spot for young pilots just out of schools. You have the Boches coming in from two sides, the north and the east; furthermore, it's a favourite hunting ground for the Richtofen crowd. That's where one of your L. F. C. men was shot down not three weeks ago, and he was no novice, either; he'd been on the front since June. Let me see, what was his name? MacMonagle—Douglas MacMonagle. Fine chap and a first-rate airman." We both knew MacMonagle slightly, a Californian who had joined the Lafayette Corps after his service in the American Ambulance. He was before our time in the schools, but we had met him in Paris just after our enlistment as we were starting for Avord.

Lieutenant de Gayic crushed out the light of his cigarette in the saucer of his coffee cup and rose abruptly. "Good night," he said, "I must be going."

"But, Lieutenant! Will you see what you can do?"

"Of course—why not? Mind you, though, I don't promise

anything. But I'm always having recommendations to make—it's part of my work here. Verdun, did you say? Well, squadron commanders are needing new pilots in pairs up there, sometimes three or four at a time." Whereupon he left us to sleep on that somewhat sinister statement.

Several days later we went as usual, early in the morning, to look over the lists of active-service orders, and the first thing to strike my eye was "Caporal Forbes, Gordon . . . Escadrille de Chasse, Spad 602, Groupe de Combat 31."

Anxiously, hastily, my eye ran down the list, then a second time and a third. My own name was not there. I tried to take the disappointment philosophically, but for all that it was a bitter one. Gordon was as sympathetic as possible under the circumstances.

"It's too bad, Charlie. Well, it can't be helped. We'll see each other sometime or other now and then. Spad 602—by Jove! That's the outfit Tommy Slater was sent to!"

The following week was the lonesomest, I think, that I have ever spent, and the longest. But curiously enough I enjoyed every minute of it. That was the strange thing about life in the war-time Air Service: one was often mournful and happy at the same time; one's emotions got horribly mixed and there wasn't time to sort them out. I missed Gordon more than I would admit, even secretly, to myself, but the sense of loneliness was submerged in the feeling of elation I had in the mere fact of flying. For all that, it was a long week, but it came to the happiest possible conclusion. On October 21, I read on the assignment list: "Caporal Selden, Charles, . . . Escadrille de Chasse, Spad 597, Groupe de Combat 31."

Groupe de Combat 31! Gordon's Group, and Tommy Slater's! That meant that, although I should not be in the same squadron with them, I should, nevertheless, be flying from the same aerodrome, occupying the same flying field. Two hours later I was on my way to Paris and the front.

V

TO THE FRONT

I HAD four hours to spend in Paris before the departure of the five-o'clock train for Châlons. That was my destination according to the service order I had been given at Plessis. I wandered around alone till train time, avoiding Henry's and the Chatham and the other favourite meeting places for airmen in Paris. I wanted to gloat over my good fortune in solitude; so I strolled up and down the boulevards, watching the crowds.

I was at the Gare de l'Est a good three quarters of an hour before train time. The train was already made up and waiting, so I climbed aboard and found a seat by the window opposite the corridor in a second-class compartment. It filled rapidly, as did all the other compartments save the first-class ones, which were reserved for officers. Twenty minutes before we were due to leave there wasn't a seat to be had anywhere, and the corridor was jammed with soldiers sitting on their pack sacks on the floor. They were nearly all Frenchmen—seasoned, bearded campaigners; many of them looked almost old enough to have been my father. Even the younger ones had a serious, mature look, as though they had been soldiers from boyhood, which most of them had, in fact. I was proud to be in that company. No more schools; no more practice flights; no more mock combats. Now came the real thing! Well, it couldn't come any too soon for me. I felt a deep thrill of joy as the train got under way.

I had been so interested watching the crowds on the station platform that I had not noticed an airman in French uniform sitting opposite me. He was a man of twenty-five or so, with a fresh ruddy complexion, light hair, and blue eyes. Somehow, he didn't look like a Frenchman; then I noticed a little silver Indian head, about the size of a dime, on the lapel of his tunic, and knew at once that he was a pilot from the Lafayette Squadron. He saw me furtively scrutinizing him, nodded his head, and smiled.

"*Alors! Ca gaze?*" he said.

He was a chap named Robert Soubiran, from New York, who had been in the war since August 1914, first as an infantryman in the Foreign Legion, and, since February 1916, as an aviator with the Lafayette Flying Corps. He had been flying at the front for more than a year and was now returning from a three days' leave. He told me that the Lafayette Squadron was still at Chaudun, on the Aisne. He was to leave the train at Château-Thierry, where he would be met by a motor car from the squadron aerodrome.

Soubiran had been on patrol at the time Jim Wilding was

killed. There were four of them, he said: himself, a chap named Bridgman, from Illinois, Henry Jones, from Pennsylvania, and Bill O'Connor. They met Wilding's crowd from the Spad 65 over the lines, and the two patrols engaged a couple of Boche formations. Soubiran thought Wilding must have been killed at once, for his Spad fell out of control all the way and disappeared in a small wood well inside the German lines. The next day a German aviator dropped a message on our side saying that Wilding had been killed and giving the number of his plane, so that there was no doubt of the pilot's identity.

I was surprised to learn of this instance of war-time courtesy. Soubiran told me that it was a common one in the Air Service. When a German airman fell inside the French lines, a note was dropped on the German side, as close as possible to where they thought his squadron was located, giving the airman's name, the number of his plane, and information as to whether he had been killed or wounded. The note was attached to a stone with a long white streamer so that it could be plainly seen falling by those on the ground. The Germans were as courteous when the unfortunate aviator happened to be French. I was glad to hear this; it was good to know that one branch of war service retained an element, at least, of old-fashioned decency.

Soubiran asked where I was going. I told him that my *ordre de service* read "Châlons," and that was as much as I knew of the general whereabouts of my squadron.

"What outfit are you with? Spad 597? That's the Thirty-first Combat Group, isn't it? Well, I can tell you where you're going—to Sénard, at the foot of the Argonne Forest. Our Group, Thirteen, was there in August and September; it was only three weeks ago that we flew up to the Aisne front. You'll be patrolling the Verdun sector, from the east side of the Argonne, around the Salient as far south as St.-Mihiel. Wow! That's a hot shop for a green pilot—or an old one, for that matter. I didn't mourn any when we left it for the Aisne. We've been busy enough over the Chemin des Dames, but it's as quiet as Sunday after Verdun.

"You'll have to watch your step, Selden, and limber up your neck so that you can keep a lookout in three directions at once when you're in the air. The early morning patrols are the worst, when you're flying out to the east side of the Salient. You have the sun right in your eyes, and often you won't see the Boches till they're right on top of you. That's what happened when MacMonagle was killed: a flock of Albatros had the good luck to come down on us with the sun directly behind them. They should have gotten the lot of us instead of only one. I had twelve bullet holes in my Spad as a result of that mix-up. Lufbery had six, and Luf is as wary as they make them. It isn't often that a Boche has a chance to spray his bus."

I asked him to tell me something about Lufbery. I had heard a great deal about him, of course, in the schools; every Lafayette man knew Bill Thaw and Raoul Lufbery, by report, at least. They had both been with the Lafayette Squadron since it was first sent to the front, in April 1916. Thaw had been wounded once, in the forearm, but Lufbery, who had shot down more planes than any other Lafayette man, had never been so much as scratched by a bullet. He seemed to bear a charmed life, but Soubiran said it wasn't luck so much as good judgment and marvellous flying ability that kept Luf from stopping any lead.

"When he's leading a patrol, you can be sure that when you mix it with a crowd of Boches you'll have the odds if there are any odds to be had. He's as wary as an old fox. He'll keep his patrol waiting round until you begin to think he hasn't spotted the Germans; but the moment conditions are as favourable as he can make them, he waggles his wings to let us know and goes in. Luf thinks it's just as well to use the old bean when you're fighting Germans. They use theirs, I can promise you I It's only green pilots and plain damn fools who go at the first enemy ship they see without looking round to see Whether there are any others overhead. Luf got his eleventh German about two weeks ago. If the war lasts another year, and he lives, he'll have at least fifty to his credit."

We talked of one thing and another while the train made its way slowly along, and the autumn light faded from the sky. We stopped frequently at little stations where women in the uniform of the Croix Rouge passed along the train, shaking the coins in their collection boxes. What a familiar sound that was at every railway station in war-time France! If ever I were to find my recollection of the war growing dim, and wished to recall vividly my own state of mind in those days and the precise shades of emotion I used to feel, I should need only to put a few coins in a tin box and shake them up and down for a moment. Immediately time would be rolled back, and I should find myself again in the France of 1917, in a train filled with soldiers in horizon blue. And I should see again, as plainly as ever, the faces of the women who used to pass along the trains rattling their coin boxes. Most of them had the gracious manner and the fine sensitive faces of great ladies of France. It did one's heart good merely to look at them. They said nothing about one's duty or the splendour of military glory. They merely passed along station platforms and turned toward one for a moment their kindly, intelligent faces. That was enough. You felt that these were the women who represented the France that was fighting for its life. They gave the war a meaning and a purpose beyond anything the politicians were able to convey by their florid speeches.

It was dark long before we reached Château-Thierry. Soubiran left me there.

"Good luck, old son!" he said. "Remember what I said about keeping your head on a swivel at Verdun! The first two weeks are the hardest. If you get through them you'll probably live till Christmas!"

The train went even more slowly between Château-Thierry and Epernay, and on the last leg of the journey we seemed hardly to be moving. There were several long halts in the open country, when the dim lights were turned off and we sat in black darkness. We were not long in learning the reason for this deliberation. The Germans were again bombarding Châlons. It was a clear starlit night and very still. Most of us got out of the train at the last halt, to see what was happening; we stood by the track, listening. No one spoke. At first I heard nothing but the brisk cheery chirping of the crickets in near-by fields. Presently a soldier standing beside me touched my arm. "*Écoutes!*" he said. I listened more intently, and then heard a sound so faint and far away that for a moment I thought it was imagined sound, or perhaps the beating of the blood in my ears; but soon there was no mistaking it—a deep, resonant, snarling sound with an odd rhythm of its own; *Raum-m*, *raum-m*, *raum-m*, *raum-m*, growing louder every moment. My blood beat faster as I listened.

"Gothas!" my companion said.

"Do you think they are?" I asked.

"Think! I know! Do you mean to say you haven't heard Gothas before? You must be new to the front."

I told him that I was on my way up for the first time, adding, "And this is the first time I've heard the sound of a German motor."

"Well," he said, "it won't be the last. The Gotha is a twin-motored machine; that's why the engine makes that chiming sound. *Les salauds!* I wish they would play their music somewhere else!"

The music, such as it was, was soon drowned by the sound of the Châlons anti-aircraft defences. The guns were firing at a tremendous rate, and at intervals we could see the bright flashes and hear the faint "plop" of shells exploding high in air. Presently there were a dozen or more tremendous explosions; we could feel the ground quiver and the train windows rattling. Gradually the firing died away and ceased altogether, and once more we heard the sound of motors growing fainter now as they made their way homeward. From somewhere forward came a clear call: "*En voiture!*" We clambered aboard again and made our way slowly into Châlons.

The station was in darkness when we arrived, but soon three or four dimly burning lanterns were lit and hung in the various waiting rooms. They seemed to intensify rather than lighten the gloom. The platform was crowded with soldiers, those who were leaving the train here and others going farther along the front, to Vitry-le-François, or Bar-le-Duc. The station had not been hit by any of the bombs, but somewhere in the distance a house was burning fiercely, the glare in the sky growing brighter every moment. If there had been another flock of Gothas coming over just then they would have found Châlons beautifully lighted for them. Luckily, nothing of the sort happened. A company of soldiers had been commandeered to fight the fire, and within an hour's time had it well under control. I was surprised to see how little confusion the air raid caused; but Châlons, of course, was frequently visited by bombers. Both civilians and soldiers were used to them, and, while familiarity had by no means bred contempt, it had taught the people how to act under such visitations.

At one end of the station platform was a small wooden barrack, the headquarters of the military police. Not knowing where else to go, I reported there to the sergeant in charge, a fatherly-looking man wearing steel-rimmed spectacles pushed up on his forehead. He knew at once, of course, that my French was not all it might have been. I had no more than started to speak when he interrupted me with "*Mais tu n'est pas français!*" looking at me in a surprised manner. I explained that I was an American, a member of the Lafayette Flying Corps, and was being sent out to a French squadron.

"*Tiens! Un Américain! C'est très bien!*"

He glanced up from my papers, regarding me with a benevolent expression. "But how does this happen?" he went on. "I've heard of the Escadrille Américain, of course; but I thought it was only one squadron of Americans. Are there others?"

I told him that the Corps had grown so fast that there was no longer room for us all in one squadron, and that as we finished our training we were being sent in one's and two's to

French squadrons all along the front.

We had a very pleasant chat, and in the midst of it a sawed-off, dapper little man entered briskly. He had a snub nose, black eyebrows, and a tiny black moustache, nothing like so heavy as his eyebrows. His tunic was of dark blue with the yellow Aviation tabs on the collar and the number 2, which meant that he was attached to the Second Aviation Group. Corduroy breeches, a *béret,* and high laced boots completed his uniform. He greeted the sergeant familiarly.

"Evening, Sergeant! You haven't by any chance got a spare aviator here, have you? An American named—" Then his eyes rested on me, "*Le voila!*" he said. "If you're not the man, then I don't know an American when I see one. Am I right, Sergeant?"

The sergeant smiled and nodded. "Yes, he's your man." The chauffeur, for that is what he was, grasped my hand warmly. "Flingot," he said, introducing himself; "Jules Flingot." Then, with a broad grin, "Pursuit pilot, flying a Fiat truck I Had a blow-out at Auve; held up in a traffic jam at Tilloy—they're moving the whole French army up the road I came down; and when I heard those Gothas I decided to wait outside Châlons till they had dropped their eggs; that's why I'm late. I'm too valuable a man to France to be killed foolishly by a bomb. Where's your dunnage? Well, how do you like the Air Service, what you've seen of it? Have you decided to be an ace? Are you going to get a Boche on your first patrol over the lines?

That's what your friend did—what's his name? Forbes? He's a marvel! Think of that—a German his first time over!"

He kept up a steady fire of conversation, all in French, of course, interspersed with all sorts of aviation *argot*, much of which I didn't understand. I didn't have a chance to get in a word, but when he told me that Gordon had won a victory in his first combat, I grabbed him by the arm.

"What! Do you mean so say that Forbes——"

"*Mais oui! Mais oui!* And that other chap, that American—how do you call him?"

"Slater? Tommy Slater?"

"*C'est ça!* That's the man! The one that sleeps eighteen hours a day. Say! What's wrong with him, anyway? Has he got the sleeping sickness, or something like that? You'd think he hadn't slept since he was a baby and was trying to catch up! But when he's *not* asleep!" He kissed the tips of his fingers and flung them out in the familiar Gallic gesture that means so many inexpressible things. "Do you know what he did, day before yesterday? Well, he went up alone, on his own, and he had the good luck to meet up with a Boche two-seater crossing the Salient from St.-Mihiel. That little runt Slater—you'd think he wouldn't say boo to a goose—headed her off and knocked her down not five miles from Sénard aerodrome! He's a regular hound in the air!"

All this seemed incredible to me, and I may as well say now that it was an unusual performance for two young and inexperienced pilots. Such things happened, of course, but they were not common. Forbes and Slater however, were by no means men of average ability. Both, as I have said, had made brilliant records in the schools; they were born fliers, and I had more than once heard Lieutenant de Gayic predict great things for Slater when he got to the front.

While we were talking—or rather, while Flingot was talking—we had found my duffle bag and put it into the Fiat camionnette. Flingot asked whether I had had anything to eat. I said no—not since leaving Paris.

"*Bon!* You must be hungry as a prisoner of war. We'll have some supper. I know a place where we can get something. Hop in."

He released the clutch and stepped on the gas; the little Fiat leaped into action, throwing my head back with a jerk. We flew down the empty street, whizzed round a couple of turns, and drew up with a screaming of brakes before a dark, deserted-looking house with its windows boarded over. Flingot pushed open a heavy door and we found ourselves in a room hazy with tobacco smoke and filled with soldiers eating and drinking. Flingot nodded cordially to a fat old woman who sat on a very high chair at the cashier's desk, and we found seats at a table in the rear of the room. A few minutes later we were tucking in two huge omelets beautifully framed in borders of French-fried potatoes. Flingot ordered a quart of red wine, and when the decrepit old waiter placed the bottle on the table he poured a little into his glass, took a sip, rolled it around on his tongue, and made a wry face.

"*Mot de Cambronne!*" he said, looking at the waiter. "What do you think we are—house painters? I asked for *pinard*, not essence of turpentine!"

The old *garçon* shrugged his shoulders in a deprecatory manner and shuffled away. Flingot took another sip, a larger one this time, smacking his lips as he did so.

"Try it," he said. "It improves a little on acquaintance. Let me pour you out just a drop. Maybe you won't like it."

He decanted about a quarter of an inch into the bottom of my glass and waited expectantly while I tried it. It tasted as sour as vinegar to me. "Thanks," I said. "I'll drink water." His face lighted up in the most comical way, and I could see that he was relieved to know that he didn't have to share the bottle.

"You're right. Don't defile your stomach with any such stuff as this. But I've been at the front three years. What are we to do? All the good wine goes to the *embusqués* in Paris. We drink what we can get up here."

I couldn't see that Flingot suffered greatly in polishing off this particular bottle. Before he had finished it he ordered another six-egg omelet and ate it with enormous relish, whittling off large chunks of bread, washing everything down with *pinard*, which he diluted slightly with water. Then we had some black coffee, in bowls, and were ready to go. As we were about to leave, Flingot gave a start, clapped his hand to his forehead, and then slapped his pockets, one after the other.

"*Sacré nom d'une touque d'essence!* I forgot to bring my pocketbook! Wait a minute! Perhaps——"

He fished with two fingers in the little watch pocket of his breeches, and finally brought forth three sous, which he laid gently on the table, looking at me apologetically.

"Selden," he said; "have you any money on you? It was careless of me. I——"

"Sure thing, Flingot!" I replied. "I'll pay for the supper, Let this be my treat."

He grinned. "For that," he said, "I'll get you up to Sénard in an hour."

The sky had clouded over before we left Châlons a little after midnight, and the night was now pitch-dark. Flingot drove without lights, as all chauffeurs did in the front-line areas. The roads, after three years of war usage, were naturally in a bad state of repair, full of holes and bumps and ridges; but Flingot drove as though it were broad day and we were bowling along a California state road. There was any amount of heavy traffic going in the opposite direction; strings of huge camions coming down for supplies loomed out of the darkness directly ahead of us, and Flingot missed axles by what seemed to be the thickness of a cigarette paper, and, with no perceptible slackening of speed, would bump along the side of the road, turning his head now and then to let out a string of imprecations yelled at drivers who failed to give him every inch of right of way he was entitled to, and more, I held on to my seat with both hands, and it is well that I did, or I should have bashed my head through the roof a score of times. Presently we came to a halt, so abruptly that I nearly went through the windshield, and I could dimly make out a crossroad, filled with infantry, before us.

"*Mot de Cambronne!*" said Flingot disgustedly. "Now we're caught! We may have to wait here for half an hour!"

I wasn't at all sorry, for I was beginning to feel sore in every muscle. I passed Flingot my cigarette case, "How far to go now?" Tasked.

"About twenty miles. This is the main road from Bar to Rheims. I'm always getting held up here. Tell you what Selden: why don't you bunk down behind and have a nap the rest of the way up? Don't you feel sleepy?"

"Thanks, Flingot. I guess I can manage to keep awake till we reach Sénard. You were right when you said you flew your Fiat. Do you always travel like this?"

"What! Do you call this travelling? We've only been crawling! You ought to see me when I've got a little room to move in!"

He puffed silently at his cigarette. When he had finished it he hunched down in his seat and a moment later was sound asleep.

I've never forgotten that wait at the crossroads. A drizzling rain had started to fall, and I could feel rather than see the dank lonely fields stretching away around us. The only near-by sound was the steady, monotonous shuffling of feet, I could tell how tired those poor soldiers were by the way their feet dragged; they made not even a pretence of keeping in step. Occasionally I heard the faint rattle of a bayonet scabbard, or the clink of a tin cup against a belt buckle, but not a word was spoken; the column moved silently and slowly on, as though it had neither beginning nor end, as though it were made up of all the war-worn, utterly weary soldiers in the world. We were not three paces from their line of march, and I could dimly make out the figures as they emerged out of thicker darkness and vanished again in wet gloom.

Far away to the north, along one wide strip of the horizon, I could see the low sky suffused with flashes of dull red fire, and hear the mutter of guns that must have been behind the enemy lines. But "mutter" is not the word, for that low, sullen sound of heavy gun fire. What word is there, in what language, that can describe it adequately? I know of none, just as I can think of no way to describe the emotions of a young soldier when first he heard it, clearly, unmistakably. I listened soberly and, I realize now, with a kind of despair at my heart. I didn't try to analyze my feelings then, but I think that what I was vaguely conscious of was the unutterable sadness of war—its inconceivable folly and futility. It was as though the guns themselves were conversing in Gargantuan accents, in some language of their own, saying, "These presumptuous midgets called men! They think they have intelligence! They flatter themselves that they can manage *us!* Doom—doom—doom to them! Let us destroy them utterly and desolate their world!"

Away in the darkness somewhere a shrill whistle was blown. The shuffling of feet stopped instantly. Sharp commands were repeated down the line: "Fall out! Near-by shadowy figures dropped in their tracks and lay still. I shook Flingot by the shoulder. "Flingot! Get moving! The road's clear!" I felt his muscles harden under my grasp. He straightened up at once, the little Fiat quivered as it sprang forward, and we were on our way again.

It was nearly two in the morning before we reached the Sénard aerodrome. I could see nothing in the darkness until Flingot drew up in front of the barracks.

"Here you are!" he said. "This is where Spad 597 hangs out." He pushed open the door of one of those typical Adrian barracks, seen everywhere back of the trenches, and we entered a long low room with a mess table in the middle of it, a small stove at one end, and benches and chairs scattered here and there. It was lighted by an oil lamp swung from a rafter over the table. In one corner was an army cot on which someone was sleeping, huddled under a blanket.

"That's old Felix, your orderly," said Flingot. He went over and shook him by the shoulder. "Felix! Wake up, Papa Noël!

What do you mean, snoring like that! They ought to put a clothespin on your nose!"

A shining bald head emerged from the blanket; then a beard began to appear as the old man raised himself on his elbows and sat up. The blanket slipped down gradually, revealing more and more beard. Many elderly French soldiers wore beards, but I have never seen one that could compare, for length and luxuriance, with that of old Felix. It nearly hid his face; nothing was visible but the little patches of chapped skin over his cheek bones and a pair of mild, kindly blue eyes blinking at us uncomprehendingly. He was an old soldier of the regular army—had been in it since boyhood, but was now too old for the trenches. Being a lonely old man with no family and no home except the army, he had been made a squadron orderly.

"Ah, it's you, Flingot," he said in a low voice, throwing his blanket aside. "Sh-h-h! Don't speak so loud! They've had a hard day to-day, and we must be careful not to wake them."

Flingot introduced me and then went off to his own barracks. Felix lighted a candle, and, tiptoeing across the room, motioned me to follow him. He opened a door on the inner side of the messroom, leading to a narrow passageway running down the length of the rest of the barrack. The doors of the rooms of the various non-commissioned pilots led off from this. The captain and the other commissioned officers of the squadron had their own barrack and mess. Felix stopped before the door of one of the corner rooms and handed me the candle.

"You're to be in here, Corporal," he whispered, "with Sergeant Laguesse."

It was a tiny room, lined with tar paper and just large enough for two cots and an ingenious little washstand made out of the boards of packing cases. I could see only the tip of my roommate's nose sticking out from under his blankets. Felix returned with my duffle bag, which he set down very gently, without making the least noise. "Good night, Corporal. You must be very tired after that long journey. I hope you sleep well."

I got into pyjamas as quickly as I could, crawled under my blankets, and lay awake for some time, too excited for sleep.

"Perhaps to-morrow," I thought, "I shall be making my first patrol!"

VI

SPAD 597

IT seemed to me that I had no more than closed my eyes when I was groused by a joyous whoop from somewhere near at hand. I sat up in bed, rubbing my eyes. It was still quite dark in our room, but the open window framed a square of ashy light, barely perceptible against the surrounding blackness. Then a drowsy voice from one of the pilot's sleeping rooms said, "Who's making all that row? Is it you, Golasse?" and another voice said, "What's the weather like, Golasse?" "Glorious!" a third voice answered. "It's raining as though it never meant to stop! We can all go to sleep again!" Immediately there was a chorus of contented grunts and mumblings, followed by silence, broken only by an occasional snore and the steady patter of rain on the tar-paper roof.

That was the first I had heard of what all airmen in the French Service called *temps aéronautique*—flying weather. A beautiful day to an old war pilot meant one pouring with rain, or a day of thick fog, when it was impossible to fly and one could lie comfortably in bed instead of getting up in the cold light of dawn for an early patrol. Before I had been at the front many weeks, I too would breathe a sigh of relief when I heard that joyous early-morning shout: "*Vous pouvez roupiller! Il fait un temps superbe!*" ("You can pound your ears! It's glorious weather!") But on that first morning at the squadron I was bitterly disappointed as I looked out of the window over the wet fields glimmering faintly in the ashy light and saw the masses of heavy clouds hanging just over the tops of the trees. "No flying to-day," I thought; "that's certain."

I stuck my head out of the door and looked down the long dark passageway toward the messroom. No one was stirring. The air was raw and chilly, so I crawled under my blankets again. My roommate, Sergeant Laguesse, had not wakened, and I could see no more of him than I had by candlelight several hours before. I looked at my wrist watch: six o'clock. I had been asleep for about three hours. I was still sleepy, so I snuggled down, closed my eyes, and knew nothing more till someone wakened me. It was old Felix, who held a steaming pitcher in one hand and a plate of buttered toast in the other.

"Chocolate, Corporal. Excuse me for waking you, but it's nine o'clock, and I thought you might like a little refreshment. It's still raining; there'll be no patrols this morning."

He poured me out a bowl of hot chocolate and placed it on a box at the head of my cot, and another for Laguesse, whom he shook gently by the shoulder; then he went out to serve the other pilots.

A dark wiry chap, dressed in blue pyjamas, sat up in the cot opposite mine, rubbed his eyes, stretched, yawned prodigiously, and was about to take up his bowl of chocolate when he caught sight of me. He gave a start. "*Sacré*—Oh! Good morning! Lord, but you gave me a turn for a second! I thought you were de Guingon." He laughed nervously as he stretched out his hand. "Laguesse." I introduced myself and then asked, "Is de Guingon the man whose place I'm taking?"

"Yes. We've bunked together for four months, until last week. It's a hell of a war, isn't it? Here to-day and planted to-morrow. Well, that's the way it goes. He was a fine chap, de Guingon. You're an American, aren't you?"

We drank our chocolate and ate buttered toast, chatting as we ate. He was a man of twenty-two or twenty-three, and told me that he was in his first year at the Beaux Arts when war broke out. His hair was coal-black, brushed straight back from his forehead. His eyes too were black, and he had a thin nose and a determined-looking chin. I felt an instinctive liking and respect for him, and was not surprised to observe on the tunic hanging from the wall the ribbon of the Medaille Militaire and the green-and-red striped ribbon of the Croix de Guerre, with four diminutive palms fastened diagonally along it.

When we had shaved and dressed we went to the mess-room, which was also the squadron lounging room. None of the other pilots was stirring yet. "We usually sleep straight through to lunch time on rainy days," Laguesse explained. "There's nothing to get up for, and it's good to lie in bed after a long spell of work. This is the first break we've had in two weeks, and the Boches along this sector are a mordant lot. Our patrols haven't been what you would call promenades. Group 31 has lost eight pilots in the last three weeks, but replacements haven't all been on our side of the lines. Fritz has had his funeral parties. By the way, do you know Forbes and Slater? They're Americans too. Fly? First-class men both of them. And they've each got a Boche! Selden, you've got something to live up to! But let's go out to the hangars to see your new bus. She's a beauty!" he went on, as we were walking down the field. "I picked her out myself at Le Bourget; the test pilot there is an old friend of mine and he gave me my choice. I've got you a Hispano-Hispano, Spad-Spad—how's that?"

It may be well to explain that pursuit pilots at that period of the war were nearly all flying the Spad, equipped with a Hispano-Suiza motor of one hundred and eighty horse-power. Owing to the great demand, both the planes and the motors were being made for the government by various French factories, and the cream of all these planes were those made by the Spad factory, with motors made in the Hispano-Suiza shops. A bus of this sort was called the "Hispano-Hispano, Spad-Spad," and a pilot considered himself exceptionally fortunate who was able to secure one. I had done my Spad training at the G.

D. E., but not on one of these little superships. I felt grateful to Laguesse and told him so. "But did you have to make a special journey all the way to Le Bourget just to get my bus?"

"Of course! But you don't suppose I minded that? I had two days' leave in Paris, and flew out the third, wind under my tail all the way back. I made Sénard in an hour and a half."

It is curious how hazy my recollection is of the Sénard aerodrome. The reason is, I suppose, that during those early days at the front I was too excited, too elated to notice details of landscape. All that I remember clearly is a great level field of irregular shape, about three quarters of a mile long by perhaps half a mile in width, with Bessonneau canvas hangars bordering two sides of it. The hangars were camouflaged and set at some distance from each other in the little clumps of scrubby pines that formed so distinctive a feature in most of those aerodrome landscapes. The clumps of pines were supposed to conceal the hangars, and they did in a measure conceal them. For all that, enemy bombers had no difficulty in finding them when they wanted to; and, as a matter of fact, all aerodromes on both sides of the lines could easily be seen from the air.

There were four Pursuit Squadrons in Group 31—Spad 597, my own; Spad 602, Gordon's and Tommy Slater's; Spad 614; and Spad 609. There were no Lafayette men in either of these latter; we three were the only Americans in the Group at that time. Each squadron, at full strength, numbered fifteen pilots, both commissioned and non-commissioned officers, thirty mechanics, two for each plane, and a dozen chauffeurs for the various squadron trucks and camions. Beside these were the armourer sergeant and his assistants, cooks for the various messes, the clerks for the squadron bureau, squadron and officers' orderlies, and so forth. In all, the personnel of one squadron was in the neighbourhood of seventy men, so that the Group as a whole made quite a populous community.

And it was a busy one that morning—at least the mechanics' part of it. They were all at work indoors on account of the rain, at the never-ending task of tuning up motors, cleaning machine guns, tightening bracing wires—going over every part of the delicate mechanism of a little pursuit plane with the infinite patience and skill for which French Aviation mechanics were noted. They were singing and whistling at their work, exchanging banter back and forth, while the great canvas hangars billowed and flapped under the buffeting of the raw October wind. Laguesse stopped at the next to the last hangar on the short side of the field. "Here we are," he said.

The great canvas curtain had been drawn back, and there, just inside, was my Spad. Two mechanics were working on it, installing the Vickers machine gun which is mounted rigidly on the motor hood directly in front of the pilot's seat. They were standing on short step-ladders, one on either side of the machine. Laguesse seized one of them by the leg.

"Morning, Cartier. Well, how's the bus? Here's your

new pilot, Corporal Selden, *pilote américain*. Selden, this is Cartier, your chief mech., and that beardless youth over there is Vigneau, first assistant. What these two don't know about aeroplane motors, nobody knows."

The two men climbed down, grinning, and shook my hand warmly. Cartier was a very thin chap of about thirty. He couldn't have weighed more than one hundred and fifteen pounds. He had a pallid, pock-marked face in clear contrast to his sparkling black eyes. Vigneau was about my own age, with rosy cheeks and hair so blonde that it looked almost white. Cartier greeted me by my last name and used the familiar second person in speaking to me. I liked that; it put us on a friendly basis from the start. In fact, throughout the French Air Service, there was no standing on ceremony between pilots and mechanics. These latter considered their branch of war service as important as that of the flying men, and rightly so. It was not a very difficult matter to learn to fly, as thousands of men discovered during the war; but aeroplane mechanics had a much more exacting apprenticeship to go through. They were proud of their profession, with reason, for the success of war-time aviation depended upon their intelligence and highly specialized skill.

I remember many a thrill during the war, many a red-letter day when, to commemorate it,—not that it needed commemorating—I made an entry in red ink in my pocket diary; but there is none I recall more vividly, or with a greater glow of pleasure, than that dreary autumn morning when I stood with Laguesse, looking at my new one-eighty Spad. Up to that time I had flown only school machines that belonged to anybody and everybody; naturally I felt no sense of possessorship while flying them. But this superb little scout plane was my own, and had never belonged to anyone else. Neither of us had been over the front. We should make our first patrols together, be shelled together, fight our first battles together. I thought of it in an intimate personal way, as though it were alive—something that could receive and return loyalty and affection. And indeed it seemed to be a living thing, resting so lightly on the ground facing the open fields, as though eager to be off.

"What do you think of her? A beauty, isn't she?" said Laguesse. "And, man! How she travels! And she's got the sweetest-sounding motor you've ever heard! You know, there are some *coucous* you can trust from the start. This is one of them; she'll never let you down—I'm sure of it. What do you say, Cartier?"

"She'll do, she'll do," said Cartier. "I can't say I haven't seen better, but——"

"That's Cartier for you!" Laguesse interrupted. "He'll never admit that any bus is really A-1, and when he dies and goes to some Aviation heaven he'll still find something to grumble about. Now I'll tell you what, Selden: if I were you I'd go to report to Captain Clermont. He'll be up by this time. I'll go with you if you like. After that you might run over to see your friend Forbes."

Captain Raoul Clermont, who commanded Spad 597, was Norman-French, a light-haired, blue-eyed man of thirty who had been a cavalry officer at the outbreak of the war. As a result of trench warfare many cavalry regiments had been dismounted and converted into infantry units, and at that time scores of officers, who had a great distaste for foot-soldiering, had transferred to Aviation. Captain Clermont had been flying since 1915, and in command of Spad 597 for more than a year. We found him in his cosy little room being shaved by his orderly.

"Hello, Laguesse! Wonderful weather, eh? Hope it rains all day! How long is it since we've had a good loaf? I know—this must be our new pilot. Selden?"

He stretched out his hand cautiously, without moving his head, giving me a keen, appraising glance. "We're glad to have you here. What about his bus, Laguesse—ready?"

"The mechanics are mounting his Vickers this morning. They'll be finished in an hour or so."

"That's good. Better line up your sights as soon as they are finished, Selden. Who's your chief mechanic? Cartier? Good man. There'll be patrols this afternoon, of course, if it clears up, but from the look of the sky it isn't likely."

"A first-class C.O.," Laguesse said warmly as we were walking away, "and a keen pilot. He's not the sort who stays on the ground and lets his men do all the fighting. He's lost two brothers in the air. Naturally he doesn't love the Boches any too well. By the way, there's the barracks of Spad 602. You'll find Forbes there, very likely. Good chance to have a yarn with him if you want to. Cartier won't be ready for you for half an hour at least."

I lost no time in acting on this suggestion. There had scarcely been an hour since the day we had parted at Plessis that I had not thought of Gordon, and I could hardly credit my good fortune at being in the same Group with him. I went first to the hangars of his squadron, for, knowing Gordon, I was sure that he would be tinkering with his engine or his machine gun; and so he was. I found him seated on a gasoline case putting cartridges into his M.G. belt. He didn't see me till I laid a hand on his shoulder. He glanced up carelessly and it did me good to see his face light up.

"Charlie! For the Lord's sake! Why, what——"

"Didn't you know I was coming?"

"No! What luck! Have they sent you to 602?"

"Not quite such good luck as that. Spad 597."

"Oh, hell! Now why couldn't they—however, this is a heap better than we thought it was going to be, what? Man alive! What'll we do to celebrate?"

"I'll tell you what I have to do: line up my sights, and I don't know a thing about it."

"You don't? Boy, that's where I shine! I've gone through the whole business. Want some expert assistance? Just wait till I've finished filling this belt."

He had unloaded his machine-gun belt and was gauging every cartridge, rejecting those likely to cause jams. Every fifth bullet was a tracer which leaves a thin line of smoke in the air when fired, enabling a pilot to judge of the accuracy of his aim. We talked of scores of things while he worked, and the first chance I had I asked him about the Boche plane he had shot down.

Gordon made a wry face. "You know, Charlie, I don't like to think of it, somehow. Remember how we used to talk about our first victory when we were at Avord? We thought it would be a marvellous experience. Well, it's not, I can tell you that. Of course, you're glad you got your man instead of letting him get you; and when you see his bus falling, out of control, you do have a thrill. But it only lasts for a minute. Killing a man isn't such a joyous experience as I've heard some people say; anyway, I didn't find it so. It was really a fluke, my getting that German—pure luck. But I did get him—no doubt of that. I followed him down and saw him smash. It was a sight I'd like to forget if I could."

"What about Tommy Slater?"

"One thing you can be sure of, Charlie. If Tommy Slater lives, he's going to have a string of victories a yard long. Everyone in the Group predicts that, including Commandant Beaumont. He's as good a shot as he is a pilot. You've heard about the two-seater Roland he brought down near the field? Well, he fired only ten shots, and six of them went smack into his target. Both the pilot and his observer were killed by bullets—dead before they ever hit the ground. We went up to have a look at their bus, and let me tell you what Slater did. He stripped off the tunics and shirts of those poor devils so that he could see just where he had hit them. He examined each bullet wound as calmly as though he were looking at a map! Cold-blooded? He's hardly human! Everyone up here respects him for his abilities, but he's still as lonely as he was in the schools. He's a perpetual mystery to me. There he is now, by the way."

Slater was coming down the line of hangars, his hands in his trousers pockets, his head hunched down between his shoulders, the skirts of his raincoat flapping in the wind. He looked more than usually small and frail in that wide landscape. He smiled wanly when he saw me and held out his hand.

"Hello, Selden," he said in his thin shrill voice. "Have they sent you to our outfit?"

We chatted for a moment, and I found myself, as always when talking with Slater, both uncomfortable and puzzled. He had the nice manners of a well-bred child and looked like one, and at the same time he seemed a great deal older than either Gordon or I. He had a bored, weary way of speaking as though merely to move and breathe were a chore.

As soon as Gordon had finished loading his M.G. belt, he went with me to the hangars of Spad 597. Cartier and Vigneau had my gun mounted, and everything was ready for lining up the sights. Sergeant Durand, the squadron armourer, went with us to the far end of the field where the target was. Cartier taxied my Spad down; then I climbed in and the tail of my bus was lifted on to a wooden support so that the plane faced the target in line-of-flight position.

Two kinds of sights were used in the French squadrons of those days. One, a telescopic sight against which you screwed your eye while firing, was much the more accur-rate and was used by all the crack pilots. Gordon and Tommy Slater both used the telescopic sight, but after a quarter of an hour's experimenting I decided that it would be useless for me to have that kind; I couldn't have kept an enemy machine in sight for two seconds. So, against Gordon's advice, I chose an open sight, an arrangement of concentric rings much less difficult to use. It required half an hour's work to get it properly adjusted. Then with great care it was made fast. I fired several more bursts at the target to make sure that neither machine gun nor sights had been jolted out of alignment in the bolting process, but the bullets still centred well.

"*Voilà!*" said Cartier. "There's a good job done. Now, Selden, if you can shoot as well in the air as here on the ground, you'll be an ace in a week! What about your insignia? Might as well get that job under way."

Every squadron had its own insignia to distinguish it from the others in the Group. This was painted on both sides of the fuselage of each ship. Spad 602 had a black horse at full gallop; Spad 614 a red triangle; Spad 609 a rooster; and my own squadron a black cat with its back arching, spitting. In addition to this, every pilot had his own private insignia painted on the top wings of his plane. Gordon's was a red "F," and Tommy Slater's a pair of tombstones. I decided to have a coconut palm to remind me of old days in the South Seas.

Cartier threw up his hands. "A coconut palm! Never saw one. Can't you think of something easier? But what in the world do you want that for?"

I told him something of my life on my uncle's island. He listened with interest, and when I had finished, "Well," he said, "I don't wonder that you love that place. You're right—a coconut palm is just the thing for you. Could you make a little sketch of one, something for me to go by?"

I drew a rough, conventionalized sketch which Cartier tucked carefully away in his pocket. "All right," he said; "I'll see that you have your palm tree." And he did. Like all French mechanics, he was clever in more trades than one. Before the week was out he had painted on each of my upper planes a very recognizable coconut palm against a background of blue sea.

My first day at the squadron chanced to be one when all

the pilots were at mess together. In days of good weather we ate more or less irregularly, for patrols came first and meals afterward. There were twelve non-commissioned officers in our mess, a gay, hearty crowd who made me feel at home at once. Laguesse introduced me all round while Felix was putting the food on the table; then we sat down.

Sergeant Fontana, *chef de popote*, occupied the head of the table. He was a bluff ex-infantryman from Southern France, a man with an enormous appetite and what seemed to me a depraved love for garlic. Every day at lunch Felix placed beside his plate a huge spud of garlic, a gift sent to him regularly by his mother from their home in Aries.

On Fontana's right sat Marcantoni, a swarthy little Corsican whom everyone called "Napoleon." He bubbled over with good spirits and was popular with everyone, particularly with Fontana, who hung on every word he said and laughed at some of his witticisms till the tears rolled down his cheeks. "Did you hear what little Napoleon just said?" he would roar to the others at the end of the table. "Marc, after the war you've got to come to Aries; I'll never be able to live without you."

The other men nearest me were Adjutant Masson, Sergeant Volokoff, a Russian from the Foreign Legion, and Sergeant Golasse.

Golasse was the smallest man in the squadron, so short, in fact, that he had to have a special cushion made for the seat of his Spad so that his head could be brought up to the level of his windshield. He was a Parisian, arid very proud of the fact. He knew all the war-time songs of the boulevards, and his talk was so full of slang that at first I had difficulty in understanding him. Before the war he had been a taxicab driver. He had joined the squadron only two months before my arrival after three years in the infantry, and had already shot down two enemy planes. What a contrast he made to Volokoff, who was six feet three, an aristocratic, strikingly handsome man, and the only silent member of the mess. He had had the unusual distinction of winning the Legion of Honour in the infantry as a non-com. A good many commissioned officers have the decoration, but when one sees the red ribbon on the breast of a corporal or sergeant one can be sure that it is for some deed of exceptional merit—such a deed as wins the V.C. in the British Army or the Congressional Medal in the American Service. What Volokoff had done to win it none of the mess knew, for he never spoke of his past military service or of his past life. I think he was the most melancholy man, when sober, I have ever met. He drank a great deal of brandy, was a wonderful guitar player, and spoke English, French, and German with equal ease. The only times when he could be called talkative was when the conversation turned to Germany and her responsibility for the war. He hated Germans, individually and collectively, and it was the dream of his life to shoot down an enemy plane. He was recklessly brave, but such a poor flier and such a bad shot that he had had no luck thus far. He crashed more planes than all the other members of the squadron together, and his Spad was always getting riddled in the air.

Much of this, of course, I learned later. At my first meal with the non-coms, of Spad 597, I merely listened to the talk, making mental notes of my impressions of the various pilots. Scarcely a reference was made to flying or fighting. Rainy days were like schoolboys' holidays,—little breathing spells between periods of work,—and any one who mentioned work was immediately "sat on."

But the holiday of Spad 597 came to an abrupt end in the very middle of it. Felix had just brought the dessert—stewed pears and cake—and was going round filling the coffee cups when an orderly from Group Headquarters appeared. The moment he stuck in his head he was greeted with howls and execrations and bombarded with pieces of bread. Golasse and Marcantoni sprang up and danced around him, shooing him off with their napkins.

"*Va t'en! Va t'en!* Get out this minute! What are you doing here on a rainy day? Don't you dare tell us there's a patrol this afternoon! Man, it's impossible to fly! Look at the sky!"

The orderly leaned against the door jamb, folded his arms, and waited.

"Well, *look* at the sky," he said. "Then maybe you'll understand why I'm here. I didn't make the weather. If you must blame someone, blame *le bon Dieu*. All I know is that

Spad 597 has two patrols to furnish and you're to take off in twenty minutes." With that he went to the bulletin board, and tacked up the orders.

The messroom windows were fitted with ground glass like that used in factory windows at home. Not being able to see through them, we had not noticed that the rain had stopped and that the clouds were lifting a little. The pilots crowded around the bulletin board, gulping, their coffee as they read the orders. The squadron was to furnish two patrols, one of eight planes to fly below the clouds, covering the sector on the east side of the Salient as far south as St.-Mihiel. The order that set my pulse to beating faster read as follows:

High patrol—4,500 metres to 5,500 metres. Sector: Varennes-Étain. Sergeant Laguesse, Sergeant Volokoff, Corporal Selden.

Laguesse put his hand on my shoulder. "Good, Selden! I'm glad we're going out together for your first time over." He looked at his wrist watch. "One forty-five. We must be getting off."

VII

FIRST PATROL

THE hangars of Spad 597 were a five minutes' walk from our barracks. The flying field was soggy after the rain, and we squashed along in our wooden shoes, which all French pilots wore in such weather when going to and from the aerodrome. The sky was lightening perceptibly, and the cloud ceiling was now at about two thousand metres. Off to the north-east was a small patch of blue sky, the yellow sunlight streaming through it in a wide shaft.

"We'll go up through that hole, eh, Volokoff?" said Laguesse. "Chances are we won't even see the ground after we get up. It'll be a nice quiet promenade. Well, it will give Selden a chance to try out his *coucou*."

"Lucky dogs?" said Golasse, who was walking with us. "Now why couldn't I have been slated for high patrol to-day? Look at those clouds! Neither too high nor too low for the Archie gunners! We'll be right underneath, as plain as flies on a white ceiling. One thing's sure: the low patrol is going to be shelled to blazes!"

"*Sacré chameau!*" said Fontana. "What's the use of sending

us out merely to be shot at?"

"Listen to the ancient senator from Aries!" said Laguesse jubilantly. "My poor old garlic-eating friend, it's to make you agile in the air. You're too slow and leisurely in your movements—in other words, too fat. That old Spad of yours is getting fat too. Well, you'd better look sharp to-day when the one-hundred-and-fives are growling round you! Otherwise we'll be electing a new *chef de popote*. By the way, have you brought your garlic with you? There's none in Germany, you know, and what will you do in a German prison camp without your garlic?"

Our Spads were drawn up in beautiful alignment in front of the hangars. The mechanics already had the engines warmed up, and propellers were "idling over" at 350 revolutions. It was always a thrilling sound to me to hear the gentle rhythmical purring of powerful motors just before patrol time; it seemed to give a voice to one's own feeling of excitement at the moment when pilots were hastily jumping into their flying clothes, buttoning their combination suits, fastening the chin straps of their helmets, putting on their gloves. It was hard to realize at such times that a few moments later we should be miles distant from our quiet flying field seeking battle among the clouds or far in the depths of blue sky. Even at this distance of time and place, the mere thought of those days makes the pulses leap and brings a tightening to the muscles of the throat.

There was no dallying now, no further expressions of regret that there was work to be done. Everyone was eager to be off. One mechanic stood by each plane, ready to jerk the chocks from under the wheels the moment the signal was given. The pilots slid down into their tiny seats and armed their machine guns; the second mechanics mounted the steps to give a final polish to the windshield and to help fasten the buckles of the seat straps. The low patrol was to leave the field first. Captain Clermont was already in his bus. He tried out his controls, gave his motor full gas for a few seconds; the little plane quivered and pushed with all her strength against the chocks. Then he looked at his wrist watch and nodded to his mechanic. The chocks were jerked out; he taxied across the field and turned into the wind. The other pilots of his patrol followed in single file, and a moment later they were climbing swiftly toward their rendezvous over the village of Brizeaux, a few miles distant in the direction of Verdun.

The high patrol left immediately after, on the very stroke of two. Laguesse was leading, then Volokoff and I. We were to meet at a thousand metres over the field. I tried out my motor, pulling the throttle wide open while I watched the revolution-counter. The indicator leaped swiftly—1,500, 1,750, 1,800. It was glorious music the engine made, deep and powerful, sweet and clear, without a suspicion of a false note. Cartier clung to the side of the fuselage with both hands, bending his head against the blast of cold air from the propeller. When I reduced again he sprang on the step for a second and clapped me on the back.

"*Çà gaze*, eh?" he shouted in my ear. "Keep your eyes peeled! Good luck!"

I taxied out after Volokoff, swung round into the wind, and as I gave her free rein again my Spad lifted her tail, skimmed along the ground, and rose swiftly into the air. I had such confidence in her and was so elated to think that I was really off for my first patrol that I did a foolish thing—something that young and silly airmen were often doing. When not fifty feet from the ground I zoomed up in a steep climbing turn. My little bus responded beautifully. If she had not—well, there, very likely, would have been the end of both our careers. How many young airmen, I wonder, are sleeping in graves overseas merely because they wished to "show off" as they were leaving the ground—to do something "houndish," as we used to say? Scores of them, hundreds of them. One never saw an old and experienced pilot tempting fate needlessly. He waited until he was at a safe distance from old Mother Earth before trying any monkey tricks.

I climbed steadily for half a minute, then turned back toward the aerodrome. Off to the north-east the planes of the low patrol were taking height over Brizeaux; they looked like a tiny swarm of gnats. Below me I saw the mechanics standing in a group in front of the hangars. Each of them would be talking of the qualities of his particular Spad, and the faults and virtues of his particular pilot. They were a keenly critical lot, those French *mécanos*, connoisseurs of flying, and as outspoken as they were critical. To be highly praised by one's own mechanics was an experience to be remembered.

At a thousand metres a plane with a blue stripe running the length of the upper wings passed me, made a steep bank to the right, and headed north. That was Laguesse. Volokoff and I dropped in behind and we climbed toward the break in the clouds we had seen from below.

The opening seemed to have been made for our benefit, for it had considerably widened within a quarter of an hour; but the moment we had climbed through, it closed again, and we had below us an unbroken sea of clouds as far as the eye could reach in every direction. But now, overhead, was nothing but blue sky, a deep autumnal blue, and the air was so clear that it seemed to have washed the very sunlight from a rich gold to the palest yellow. It gave me a feeling of exhilaration to be flying in that lonely upper world, knowing that the earth was wrapped in grey gloom. One seemed no longer to belong to earth, to have no further concern with what might be taking place there.

For five minutes or more we flew steadily northward, skimming along just over the floor of cloud. It gave one the same sense of speed that flying close to the ground does. At times I could imagine that we were hanging motionless, and that it was the clouds that moved, streaming under us at a terrific rate. Here and there they billowed up in almost vertical columns of mist, dazzling white in the sunshine. Sometimes Laguesse, who was about a hundred metres in advance, would zoom over these—cloud-steeplechasing, we called it—and sometimes dash straight through, his propeller churning them up and ravelling them out in shreds of silky vapour; while Volokoff and I, following in his wake, would feel the cool moisture on our faces, beading our eyebrows and the little hairs on our cheek bones. Below us, and a little to the right, three lonely shadows of planes moved at incredible speed over a sea of foam.

For the moment I had quite forgotten that there was a war in progress; that there were such things as German aircraft—in fact, I had all but lost the sense of my own identity. I felt like a disembodied spirit that had escaped all the trials and tribulations of earthly existence and had nothing more to do for ever except to roam at will over limitless meadows of cloud. Of a sudden Laguesse brought me back—I can't say to earth, but to present consciousness—by rocking his plane horizontally. I knew what that meant. It was the patrol leader's signal: "Look out! Enemy planes!" Volokoff and I were flying wing to wing and not more than thirty yards apart. He waved and pointed upward to the right. I looked, but saw nothing. Laguesse made a bank to the left and started climbing The needle of my altimeter began to move slowly—2,500 metres, 2,800, 3,000, 3,200. I kept searching the sky, directly overhead, to the left and right, and to the rear, but still I saw only the great dome of blue, immaculate, lonely, seemingly empty. We turned northward again and held that course for a time. Soon we were at 5,000 metres, and the floor of cloud was farther below us than it had been above when we left the ground. Still no sign of a Boche. I was getting exasperated, and for a moment the suspicion crossed my mind that Laguesse and Volokoff were having a little game with me because I was a green pilot. But that was only for a moment. Of a sudden I saw that the air was filled with planes.

While in training in the schools I had often tried to imagine what my first air battle would be like. I haven't a very fertile imagination, and in my mental picture of such a battle I had seen planes approaching one another more or less deliberately, their guns spitting fire, then turning to spit again. That, in fact, is what happens, except that the approach is anything but deliberate once the engagement starts. But where I had been chiefly mistaken was in thinking of them fighting at a considerable distance from each other—two, or three, or even five hundred yards. The reality was far different. At the instant when I found myself surrounded with planes I heard unmistakably the crackle of machine-gun fire. It is curious how different this sounds in the air when one's ears are deafened by altitude, the rush of wind, and the roar of the motor. Even when quite close it is only a faint crackle, but very distinct, each explosion impinging sharply on the eardrums. I turned my head over my shoulder, to breathe the acrid smoke of tracer bullets, and just then—whang! crash!—my wind shield was shattered. I made a steep bank in time to see the black crosses of a silver-bellied Albatros turned up horizontally about twenty yards distant, as though the German pilot merely wanted to display them to convince me that he was really a German. Then, as I levelled off, glancing hastily to the right, I saw not ten metres below my altitude and flying in the same direction a craft that looked enormous, larger than three of mine. She had staggered wings, and there was no doubt about the insignia on the fishlike tail: that too was a black cross. It was a two-seater, and so close that I could clearly see the pilot and the gunner in the back seat. Body and wings were camouflaged, not in daubs after the French fashion, but in zigzag lines of brown and green. The observer, whose back was toward me, was aiming two guns mounted on a single swivel on the circular tract surrounding his cockpit. He crouched down, firing at a steep angle at someone overhead whom I could not see, his tracers stabbing through the air in thin clear lines. Apparently neither the pilot nor the rear gunner saw me. Then I had a blurred glimpse of the tricolour *cocardes* of a Spad that passed me like a flash, going in the opposite direction; and in that same instant I saw another Spad appear directly under the two-seater, nose up vertically, and seem to hang there as though suspended by an invisible wire.

What then happened is beyond the power of any words of

mine to describe. A sheet of intense flame shot up from the two-seater, lapping like water around the wings and blown back along the body of the plane. The observer dropped his guns, and I could all but see the expression of horror on his face as he turned. He ducked for a second with his arms around his head in an effort to protect himself; then without a moment's hesitation he climbed on his seat and threw himself off into space. The huge plane veered up on one side, turned nose down, and disappeared beneath me. Five seconds later I was alone. There wasn't another plane to be seen.

This, I realize, is a very sketchy account of my first air battle, but I am telling here, not all that happened, but merely what I saw. As for what I felt, I had time for only two sensations; first, astonishment at the sudden appearance of all those planes, and to find my windshield shattered; second, horror as I saw the German plane go down and the rear gunner hurl himself into the air; then another shock of surprise at finding myself alone.

The fight was over, of course, in much less time than it takes to tell of it. I don't believe twenty-five seconds elasped between the time when I first heard the crackle of machine-gun fire and the second when the two-seater vanished beneath me. I banked steeply to the right and left; I flew in circles, looking in every direction, mystified, completely at a loss to know what had happened to everyone. And I was ashamed too because of my air blindness. "Lord!" I thought. "I'll never make a pursuit pilot. I'll never find anything to pursue." What seemed most astonishing was that a huge German two-seater, wrapped in flame, could fall without my seeing how and where it fell. But I could still see, and smell too, the cloud of oily black smoke it had left behind, and the thin straight lines of smoke left by tracer bullets, criss-crossing in the air, now ravelling out in the wind. A sense of the unreality of the adventure came over me as I circled round them, looking at these faint vanishing evidences of combat. Had it happened? Shouldn't I wake up in a moment and find that I had dreamed it? Then for the first time I remembered my own machine gun. I hadn't fired a shot—I had not even thought of firing!

All this time I had been flying round and round, quite unconscious of direction or anything else except a feeling of bitter disappointment that I had been so helpless, so useless in my first air battle. No doubt many young airmen had similar experiences during their early days at the front. The trouble was, of course, that one's brain still functioned in the old leisurely way, and, when confronted with wholly new and strange conditions calling for immediate decisions and immediate action, all that it could do—in my case at any rate—was to register astonishment.

How strange these conditions were was brought home to me as I came out of my reverie with a start and looked at my clock. In every plane there was a small clock fastened to the instrument board in front of the pilot's seat among the other dials: the pressure gauge, altimeter, tachometer, gasoline gauge, and so forth. They were set by squadron time before every patrol. Looking at mine, I saw that it was twenty-three minutes after two. I didn't believe it, and looked again. Twenty-three minutes after two; and the clock was unquestionably running, the second hand making its leisurely sixty-beat circuit. It seemed impossible that only half an hour before I had been walking out to the hangars with Laguesse. We were to patrol the sector until four o'clock—an hour and a half to go. I didn't mind that, but I did mind having lost Laguesse and Volokoff and not knowing where I was. We were to cover the sector between Varenne and Étain, the north side of the Verdun Salient, but as to where they were—or Verdun, or Sénard, for that matter—I had only the vaguest of notions. Thinking back over the direction we had taken from the aerodrome, the turns we had made, and the length of time we had been flying, I decided that I must be somewhere over the Argonne, so I turned eastward. But I was a bit uneasy, knowing that my reckoning was probably wrong. If it was out and I was farther to the east, then I might be flying into Germany toward Diedenhofen or some such place. The floor of cloud still covered everything; not a break anywhere.

I throttled down my motor, just keeping flying speed, looking out sharply for Germans. But the sky was empty save for my little plane. I had just convinced myself of this when directly in front of me a Spad materialized out of thin air and passed over me diagonally, upside down in an Immelmann turn, as though it were being swept along by a wind blowing at hurricane speed. What a welcome sight those tricolour *cocardes* were! I turned at once to follow this airman and found that he was turning to have another look at me. We passed so close that I could see his plane insignia. On the side of the fuselage there was a red swastika and beside it the Indian-head insignia of the Lafayette Escadrille.

"What in the world is he doing at this part of the line?" I wondered. The Lafayette Squadron was at Chaudun on the Aisne, flying the Chemin des Dames sector, or had been when last I heard of them. For a moment I thought this pilot might be Bill O'Connor, flying down to Sénard to have a yarn with Gordon and me, but I immediately discarded this possibility. O'Connor, like myself, was an average pilot, and I knew that he couldn't fly as this man flew. I had never seen, except when Tommy Slater was in the air, more precise or beautiful manœuvring. After a leisurely examination of my Spad, he waved his hand as though in farewell and started off in a northerly direction.

But if he meant it to be farewell, I at least did not. I knew instinctively that he wasn't lost; the movements of his Spad convinced me that both of them knew what they were about. So I tagged along behind, very glad of company, and resolved to land wherever he did, even though it were somewhere on the Aisne front. He soon observed me following him and again waved his hand, as much as to say, "Coming along? All right; we'll finish the patrol together." We were flying at about 5,000 metres, but presently his bus began to rise swiftly, in the odd way which gives one behind the curious impression that his own plane is unaccountably sinking. He had started to climb, of course, so I climbed after him.

A first-class one-eighty Spad in perfect condition had a ceiling of 6,000 metres, and sometimes they could climb as high as 6,200. I was keenly interested to see what my little ship could do, so I followed my unknown companion, resolved to climb, or to try to climb, as long as he did. At 5,900 I passed him; then we both managed to reach 6,000; then I rose above him again by one hundred metres. He reached up a hand as though he meant to say, "Give me a lift, will you?" Six thousand was the best he could do, and 6,100 was the limit of my Spad, and she was very wobbly at that height. But I was more than satisfied. Never had I flown so high before. "Six thousand one hundred!" I thought. "Nearly twenty thousand feet!" Not many of the world's mountains were as high as that.

We came down again to five thousand and turned west, I still keeping about a hundred metres behind. I didn't worry much now about missing anything. I felt certain that if there was anything to be seen my companion would see it. It gave me a keen pleasure to watch him fly—he was so sure of every movement and seemed to make them as naturally as a fish swims. He loafed along, doing Immelmann turns, loops, and barrel turns, and I did clumsy imitations. I was glad he wasn't watching me. Nevertheless I was having a thoroughly good time, and it gave a zest to this patrol not to know where we were or where I should have supper that night.

We flew high for another hour in a lonely sky, eastward and then westward again, while the sun dropped toward the cloud floor. At last my companion tipped up and dove so steeply that I lost him for a moment; but I had my wits about me now and soon made him out, far below, descending in steep spirals. I followed, at first believing that he had sighted some Germans, but just before reaching the clouds he levelled out again and flew quietly on, winding here and there among deep ravines of mist now filled with blue and purple shadow in the light of the sinking sun. It was a glorious sight to see those clouds stained more and more deeply with colour, but I was prevented from thoroughly enjoying it because of the difficulty I had in keeping my companion in sight. Occasionally he would vanish; then, passing a great promontory, I would catch sight of him again banking steeply around a distant cloud castle, his Spad looking microscopic under those towering bastions, and I would speed after him, the roar of my motor reverberating faintly against walls of shining vapour. Suddenly he did a loop, and, instead of pulling up in line of flight, he went on down and disappeared in the clouds.

I followed, of course, and thought I should never reach clear air again. When I did, what a contrast to the sunny air above! It seemed almost dark on the ground, but my eyes soon became accustomed to the grey light, and I had the good fortune to find my patrol companion almost at once. He was circling round as though waiting for me, and the moment I joined him turned south, holding a steady course. Beneath us was a vast stretch of forest land, looking very gloomy in the fading light. I had lost all sense of direction above the clouds, and I thought it likely that this was the Forest of Villers-Cotterets on the Aisne front and that we should soon be landing at the aerodrome of the Escadrille Lafayette. Then I had another of my many surprises on this day. I found another Spad flying alongside me, and the insignia on the fuselage was that of a black cat, spitting. I made a climbing turn to pass over it, and the pilot's insignia was the long blue stripe of Laguesse. A moment later, looking down over the side, I saw the hangars of Sénard.

Years seemed to have elapsed since last I had seen that field. I felt as Columbus must have felt when he returned from his first voyage to the Indies. For mine too had been a voyage of discovery, with this difference in the circumstances, that I did all my discovering after the voyage was over. By good luck I made a beautiful landing and taxied up to the hangars feeling as proud as though I had gained a dozen victories. Cartier and Vigneau were waiting for me. I climbed down stiffly. Cartier was speaking, and for a moment I couldn't hear a word he said, my ears had been so deafened by changing altitudes; but after swallowing a few times and holding my nose, blowing through the ear passages, they were suddenly cleared. Then his voice sounded unusually distinct.

"*. . . comme un papillon!*" he was saying. "That's the way to land. I couldn't tell when your wheels touched the ground. Well, how's the little ship? Does she fly? Any trouble with——" He broke off abruptly, put his hands on his hips, and stood regarding me with pursed lips and a series of solemn nods. "One wound stripe for the old combination," he said. "Well, you've seen a Boche, that's sure; at any rate, he saw you."

Following his gaze, I saw that the left shoulder of my combination suit had been cut through as neatly as though it had been done with a knife. I was about to tell him about my shattered windshield when he mounted the step and discovered it for himself; and he found that another bullet had ripped the fabric on the side of the fuselage.

"That bird was after you, Selden! What did you do to *him*, if it's fair to ask?"

"Cartier, don't say a word! I didn't even see him till after he fired, and I was so surprised that I didn't remember I had a gun!"

A little knot of mechanics had gathered around my plane, and Vigneau was exhibiting the bullet marks as though they were valuable curiosities; for the French mechanics seemed almost as proud of their pilots when they brought home scars as when they brought victories.

Off to the west the clouds were breaking up, and the sun, very low, appeared through the trees, flooding the field with rosy light, casting long shadows over the wet smooth-shaven turf. The wind had died away and the wind sleeves on the hangars hung limp on their poles. A dozen or more Spads were circling over the aerodrome awaiting turns to land, for, beside the patrols of 597, formations had gone out from the other squadrons. The air was filled with the throbbing of motors and the whistling sound of planes coming down, and high overhead I saw three ships, their wings gleaming in the sunset light, losing altitude in spirals and serpentines. The aerodrome was always a scene of great animation when the last patrols for the day were coming in. Off-duty airmen strolled out from barracks to hear the news, and both pilots and mechanics gathered about the planes as they taxied up to the hangars. Here some birdman, usually a young one, would be sitting on the back of his ship, his goggles pushed up on his helmet, describing a combat with eloquent gestures; farther along another would be standing on his seat pounding his shoulders with his hands to get the blood into circulation after his long flight. Often the men were so numb with cold that they had difficulty in getting out of their flying clothes, and would stand stiffly, like tailors' dummies, while their mechanics unbuttoned them and removed their flying boots.

I was still talking with Cartier when someone slapped me

on the shoulder. It was Laguesse. "Now then," he said, "give an account of yourself! Where have *you* been all this while? You might give me a cigarette while you're explaining. You owe me at least one for pulling that Boche off your back."

"Did you do that?"

"Of course! Didn't you see me?"

I shook my head. I decided that I might as well make a clean breast of it and confess how very little I had seen.

Laguesse listened quietly until I had finished

"Well," he said, "I don't know what kind of *porte-bonheur* you carry, but whatever it is, keep it. It's a good one." Then he laughed. "But don't worry. You'll soon get your eye in. I was just as blind when I first joined the squadron, and just as bewildered, too, in my first scrap."

Then he told me what had happened. There were by no means so many planes in the fracas as I had imagined: only three German ships, in fact—the two-seater and two Albatros single-seaters; our own patrol of three, and a lone Spad that joined up from the other side at the moment of the fight.

"They were at five thousand when I first spotted them," he went on, "heading south-east across the Salient. They didn't seem to be in a hurry, and just after I signalled you they turned back north. That's why I turned west when we started to climb. Apparently they had not spotted us, and I wanted to keep in the sun. I don't believe they saw us until we were nearly on their level and about half a mile away; then they made straight for us. Whether they spotted that lone Spad coming down on them from the east, I don't know, but I think they must have. Pity for the two-seater he didn't know who was flying that *caucou*!"

"Was that the Spad with the Indian head and the swastika?"

"Yes. Didn't you see that?"

"I saw the plane, but I didn't have time then to examine his insignia."

"Neither did those Germans. Did you ever see prettier work? Luf came up from behind, stood on his tail for two seconds, and fired one burst. Good-bye, Fritz! Poor devils! A horrible sight, wasn't it? I saw the pilot fall over on his stick; he was evidently hit, but the observer wasn't. I take my hat off to that chap! It takes nerve to jump out of a plane at five thousand metres. Of course, it was certain death to stay—he would have been burned to a cinder—but just the same I doubt whether I should have had the courage to jump. By the way, that's Luf's thirteenth victory."

"Luf? You don't mean Raoul Lufbery, do you?"

"Now who else could I mean? How many Lufberys are there in the French Air Service?"

"Why, I've been flying with him! I met him after I lost you and Volokoff. I was with him all the rest of the patrol!"

"Well, that's nothing to your discredit. You couldn't have been with a better man, especially on your first patrol. Hello!

There's Luf now. He's a great friend of the Captain's. That's how he happened to be down our way to-day; he was coming over for a visit when we all had that happy meeting over the Argonne. Hey, Luf!"

The next moment he was introducing me, and I felt as proud as Lucifer. There would be a story for my grandchildren if ever I had any—my first patrol and my first battle in company with Lieutenant Lufbery, the best pilot in the Lafayette Flying Corps, and among the best in the entire French Air Service.

Lufbery smiled and held out his hand. "Selden? Oh, yes, I've heard your friend O'Connor speak of you. So it was you I was flying with, wasn't it?"

I thought that a very kind way to put it when the fact was so unquestionably the other way round. I had been flying with him, hanging on to his tail like a little lost boy to a kind policeman's hand. "But how in the world did you know where we were?" I asked. "Lord knows where I should have landed if I hadn't met you."

He laughed. "Oh, I had all the clouds marked. You must always do that when you can't see the ground. That is a fine little ship of yours. She can climb! By the way, Laguesse, what happened to that Albatros you prised loose from Selden's tail?"

"He dove just after you bagged the two-seater, and he must have gone down full motor. Never saw a ship fade so fast. I didn't float down by any means, but he was a good three hundred metres ahead when he ducked into the clouds. I ducked after him, but I couldn't find him again. Then I picked up a crowd from 614, and played round with them."

"What became of Volokoff?" I asked.

Laguesse laughed nervously. "He was having a little private war with that other Albatros the last I saw of him. Don't know what happened. All I do know is that he isn't back yet."

Just then Sergeant Fontana, who had been on the low patrol, joined us. Laguesse greeted him jovially. "Well, my ancient senatorial friend! You didn't——What is it, old man?" he added quietly.

"Marcantoni's gone. Oh, damn it to hell. What a beast of a war!" Then he sat down on a gasoline tin and began to cry like a child.

No one spoke for a moment. The other pilots of the low patrol were coming down the field. Lufbery walked over and shook hands silently with Captain Clermont. They stood in a little group, looking helplessly at Sergeant Fontana, as though all of them were wishing they could cry like that.

"The poor little devil! Little Napoleon! And we've been bunking together since——"

Captain Clermont nodded to us to come away.

"Let him have it out alone. Luf, I've just heard about your two-seater. Bully for you, old man!"

Laguesse, Golasse, and I were walking behind.

"How did it happen, Golasse?"

"It was north of Brabant, over the Meuse. We met a gang of Albatros. Little Napoleon got it right at the start. He was killed—no doubt of that. Crashed in a wood near Dannevoux where the river makes that loop to the west. They were a mordant lot, that crowd!"

"Just the same, honours were even," Masson added. "The captain knocked one down. That Boche didn't know what hit him."

"I saw him crash. It must have been about a quarter of a mile from where little Marc fell."

"My gun jammed, and I couldn't clear it. Had to fly the whole patrol without a gun!"

"That's some battery, north of Étain! Lord, but they were stickin' 'em close!"

Volokoff came in the next day. His Spad had been so badly shot up by the second Albatros that he had been compelled to land near Ste-Menehould.

Dinner that evening was a very noisy one. Everyone talked at once; Golasse cracked his funniest jokes, and the squadron phonograph was never allowed to stop for a moment. I have never seen a more gallant or a less successful attempt to drown the eloquence of one empty chair.

VIII

OVER THE RAID

AFTER dinner I put on my bearskin coat and strolled across the field to the "bar." Each Groupe de Combat had an institution of this kind, maintained by the flying personnel. An orderly was to be found there throughout the day and until bedtime at night, ready to dispense various sorts of drinks as well as tea, hot chocolate, and sandwiches; and a small truck was detailed to move the equipment of plates, glasses, wines and liqueurs, furniture, and the like, from field to field. Major Beaumont, in command of our Group, believed in making his pilots comfortable, and he did everything in his power to give the bar the atmosphere of a little club. Once or twice a week he found time to drop in for a chat with the squadron captains and to glance about in a fatherly way. In the bar all differences of rank were laid aside; the war was forgotten for the moment, and all men who wore wings played bridge, shook poker dice, or swapped yarns in an atmosphere of good comradeship.

Several bridge games were in full swing when I entered the bar. In a corner, sitting by the almost red-hot stove, I saw Forbes. He beckoned to me and pointed to an empty chair.

"Well, how did you make out?" he said.

"Don't ask! I'm the rottenest pilot in the Army! I'm ashamed to tell you!"

Nevertheless I described in detail the events of my first patrol. When I had finished, Gordon nodded.

"I know, I know," he remarked. "I was just the same at first, but you'll soon get the hang of it. And don't think you're the only one who can't see Germans. You know that Slater got an Albatros in flames to-day? Well, I was on the same patrol, and I didn't even know there had been a scrap! Neither did the other man, and he was the lieutenant leading us! We were easing along at five thousand right at the bend of the Salient. There was nothing in sight; but the lieutenant, who is a pretty wary old bird, was banking almost vertically back and forth, hoping for the glimpse of a Boche below. Then, all at once I saw that Slater was gone. A few minutes passed. The lieutenant kept on as though nothing had happened, and of course I had to follow him. I was wondering what to do and planning to run alongside and signal him, when I glanced up and saw that Slater was with us again. We finished our patrol and landed, and our captain was slapping the lieutenant's back before he could climb down from his machine. 'Splendid!' he was saying. 'Got him in flames, eh? The confirmation came in twenty minutes ago; he fell behind our balloons directly in front of Avocourt!' The lieutenant's mouth opened in astonishment. He thought there had been a mistake—told the captain we'd had no combat. Slater was on the ground by this time, and he came up to the captain with that cold-blooded little grin of his. You know how well he speaks French. He saluted. 'I was about to report to the lieutenant, sir,' he said quietly, 'that I took the liberty of leaving his patrol when I saw an Albatros directly below. I was afraid he might get away if I took time to speed up and signal the others, so I dove on him at once. I got him at the first burst, and saw the plane burning on the ground as I took altitude to rejoin the patrol.' The lieutenant and I were flabbergasted. When Slater was gone I heard the captain say, 'Mark my words; he will become famous. He's not the type that fights the Boches—he assassinates them!' "

Gordon stretched out luxuriously, feet to the stove. Five minutes passed before he spoke again. "Remember that letter from your uncle?" he asked. "I've thought of it many times. I wonder if he would let me in—if you and I get through the war. What do you think?"

"He'd be delighted, and so should I!"

"Why not write him, then, and put it up to him? Lordy! It sounds good to me. I've been wondering what on earth I could find to do when the war's over. I love the sea and everything to do with ships. I could put up any extra capital that was needed, and I think I could soon learn to run the schooner. Suppose I ran the schooner and you looked after the work on shore?"

The stars were all out and there was a sharp autumn chill in the air as I walked home to turn in. Laguesse was reading in bed by the light of a candle; he laid his book down on his knees at sight of me.

"A bit of excitement in the morning," he announced; "I suspect that the infantry's staging a raid in the vicinity of Avocourt. At any rate, four patrols from the Group are ordered to be on the job at daybreak. And you're elected—you and Golasse and I. Wish it would start to snow and keep on for forty days!"

I heard a rather unsteady step outside the door, then a husky tenor voice raised in the litany of the French Air Force:

"*Bidons d'essence!*

Carburateurs!

Sauvez, sauvez la France!

Et tous les avateurs!"

It was Sergeant Golasse, and, as usual at this hour, he was in a mellow mood. He burst open our door without knocking and stood there, swaying a little as he regarded us with mock solemnity. No more than five feet tall, hard as nails, physically and spiritually, humorous, full of courage, and incapable of respect for anything, Golasse was the incarnation of the spirit of Montmartre. It was impossible to imagine him as a baby or as a child; he made one fancy that he had sprung into the world full-grown, as Aphrodite did from the sea, though Golasse, of course, would have sprung from the asphalt of the Paris boulevards.

"Made your wills?" he asked. "I should if I had anything to leave, or anyone to leave it to! But maybe you haven't heard the news?"

"You mean the *coup de main* to-morrow morning?" asked Laguesse.

"No, no! That's nothing! Our new neighbours over the way. The captain just got it from the Intelligence. No more cold meat, boys! The Jasta Eleven has moved in! Richtofen's gang—Red-Noses, Checkerboards, Tangos! They've been sent down from Flanders for a rest! Rest! *Eh bien!* I hope they take it! I hope they're all too tired to fly! The Group they're replacing was bad enough!"

Laguesse greeted this bit of news with a groan. "And just as we were settling down to a nice quiet winter! Curse the Teutonic martial spirit—what'do they call it?—*Schrecklichkeit.* Summer's the time for fighting, when a man can get out of bed without being frozen stiff. In winter, soldiers should be encouraged to hibernate, like bears."

I fell asleep with the anticipation—half painful, half pleasurable—of a morning of keen excitement, and it seemed that I had scarcely slept an hour when I felt a hand on my shoulder and opened my eyes to see old Felix standing over me, like Father Christmas in the candlelight. "Corporal! Corporal!" he called deferentially. "Your patrol leaves in thirty minutes. The chocolate is on the table." He turned to rouse Laguesse, but though he shook him gently by the shoulder, calling "Sergeant! Sergeant!" the leader of our patrol gave no slightest sign of life. The old man straightened his back, gathered his enormous grey beard meditatively in one hand, gave a despairing shrug, and shuffled out of the room, candle in hand. At that moment, from the messroom, I heard the preliminary scratching and grating of the squadron phonograph—it must have been in the war since 1914—and then some female artist of the music halls gave tongue:

"Poor But—ter—fly . . . da—da—deedee—ah—da!"

Like the plague of influenza, this honey-sweet song flew around the world that year, as popular in France as in the country of its origin, and the needle grated no more unpleasantly on the record, already worn-out, than on my nerves. Laguesse sprang up in bed as though he had been stung by a scorpion.

"Golasse! Golasse! For the love of God, shut that damn thing off!"

The lover of early-morning music laughed heartlessly, with a sound like the twitter of a Parisian sparrow.

"Shut off nothing! It's my favourite song! I have a premonition I may never hear it again!"

I glanced at the luminous dial of my wrist watch twenty-five minutes before we were to take off. Time for another five minutes in bed. It was still pitch-dark—the hour when the tide of a man's vitality is at the lowest ebb. No Quaker ever disapproved of war more heartily than I at that moment. The phonograph rasped on. It seemed to me that if Golasse had had his pick of every disc recorded since Mr. Edison invented the "talking machine" he could not have made a worse choice. Poor Butterfly! I felt like one myself. And in thirty minutes I should be high in the stinging autumn air on the way to the lines. And in forty minutes . . . Tangos, Checkerboards—Germans so ferocious that they sent them to the Verdun sector for a rest!

Laguesse and I crawled gloomily out of our blankets and pulled on uniforms and boots without a word. I felt more cheerful after a bowl of Felix's chocolate and the brisk five-minute walk to the hangar. The sky was beginning to brighten, though the stars still sparkled frostily overhead; and I could hear the deep-throated exhausts of our three Spads warming up. Cartier was in the cockpit of my ship, opening and closing the throttle as he listened critically, his head a little on one side. And a new windshield was in place. He nodded. "Listen to her take hold!" he said. He pulled the throttle lever wide open and the engine burst into a deep, trampling roar. The plane trembled; the propeller sent an icy hurricane through the hangar; bits of rubbish rose and eddied high in the air.

Cartier shut down to idling speed, and climbed stiffly down. "She'll do!" he remarked dryly.

He helped me on with my combination and flying boots; then I thrust my hands into silk gloves, paper gloves and fur-lined leather gauntlets. I crawled into the cockpit, wincing at the blast of cold air behind the whirling stick. Cartier helped me with my belt; then I leaned forward to load my Vickers. Last of all I handed down my goggles to be polished, adjusted the elastic over my soft leather helmet, and pushed them up on my forehead.

Captain Clermont, whose patrol was to leave later, was standing by Laguesse's Spad. He reached down to stroke his little fox terrier, glanced at his watch, and nodded to Laguesse. "*En l'air!*" his voice rang out cheerfully.

I was the last to take off, while the others circled overhead. Cartier ran alongside with giant strides, holding to one wing as I taxied out to the middle of the field. At a signal from me he held back strongly while I gave her the guns for an instant, causing the Spad to whirl into the light westerly wind. I nodded and pulled my goggles down over my eyes. Still sleepy and heavy-headed in the grey dawn, I felt no desire to fly, and less to fight. Cartier stepped away from the wing and stood regarding me critically, hands on hips. I settled myself in the little seat and pulled the throttle open.

The motor roared out its full sweet music, up came the tail, and we swept down the field in a buoyant, bounding rush.

Next moment the Spad was in the air. I held her nose down to gather speed, gave her her head, and roared up swiftly over a line of tall trees. In an instant all the dismal hesitation had gone out of me; I was in the air now, with every faculty on the alert—happy and full of confidence.

Laguesse was circling at a thousand metres, with motor reduced. I saw Golasse fall in behind him on the left. My Spad was climbing like a rocket, and in a moment, it seemed to me, I took my place beside Golasse. I looked down at the field, where other patrols were taking off; then I saw Laguesse's head—a ball of black leather in the cockpit of his machine—turn swiftly to glance back at me. His plane seemed to float upward magically as he gave her full throttle and began to climb toward the lines.

We were heading for Avocourt, and far away over Germany, across the St.-Mihiel Salient, the sun was coming up. There was not a cloud in the sky, and no fog to veil the earth from us. We were at five thousand metres when we reached the lines, and the landscape below, over which the Battle of Verdun had raged so long, was indescribably, appallingly desolate: trees, houses, fields, villages—all the landmarks of a once rich countryside—had been blotted out by hurricanes of high explosive and steel. Nothing remained but the raw upturned earth, threaded by an inconceivable zigzag network of trenches, scarred by shell craters filled with stagnant water, so thickly set that they seemed to overlap. Along one section of front directly below us, a furious barrage fire was under way, the exploding shells winking like fireflies. Golasse, twenty yards away, glanced across at me and pointed down. I knew I was witnessing the start of the raid Laguesse had foretold the night before.

As I banked steeply and craned my neck over the side, I had a glimpse of the two French ships directing barrage fire—informing the gunners by wireless how to elevate and traverse their seventy-fives. These artillery planes were Caudrons, with two motors, and from our height they seemed to be crawling back and forth, barely above the surface of the ground, bracketed in bright flashes of fire. I didn't envy them their job. Our job was to stay above and drive off any German single-seaters that might appear.

Laguesse was throttled down, flying this way and that in great curves as he banked to scan the air below. I saw a patrol of Spads, and then another, hovering like gnats over the artillery machines, but for a long time there was not an enemy plane in sight. An hour passed; I was so cold that I wondered whether I should be able to pull the trigger of my gun. Then, as Laguesse turned west for the tenth or eleventh time, I saw his Spad rock violently, nose down like a rolling porpoise, and plunge out of sight. I followed, but he was diving so fast that when I next sighted him he was far below. I opened the throttle a little; the wind screamed about me furiously and tears came into my eyes.

I knew, of course, that Laguesse had sighted enemy planes, but it was not till that moment that I caught sight of them. The Caudron to the west, toward Avocourt, had been attacked by a strong Albatros patrol, but almost before the first exchange of shots two patrols of Spads had attacked the Germans in turn. Fifteen or twenty single-seaters were circling, diving, and banking in an indescribable mêlée. The other observation plane had edged off unnoticed toward the Meuse, and was being hotly attacked by a brace of grey, sharklike Albatros, detached from the patrol. Laguesse was diving to the rescue, and, glancing over my windshield as we rushed downward, I now perceived another Spad ahead of us. The Caudron—a slow, awkward ship—was having a bad time of it, though the pilot manœuvred skilfully and the observer plied his gun this way and that. We were still a thousand yards away when the lone Spad, approaching unobserved, took a hand in the game. What followed happened so fast that it is hard to describe coherently.

The Spad swept over the two Germans into the sun, banked vertically, nosed down for an instant to let fly a short burst, rose in a beautiful climbing turn, and dropped like a thunderbolt, spitting smoke and fire. The first Albatros seemed to stagger in the air, fell off in a wing slip, and went down slowly and aimlessly, like an autumn leaf. Flames enveloped the cockpit of the second German plane, and it fled earthward like a comet, trailing thick black smoke. As the victorious Spad turned and passed within twenty yards of me to speed back to the "dog fight" west of us, I saw the black-horse insignia of Spad 602, and Tommy Slater's tombstones on the upper wing. Laguesse turned sharply to the west.

With two short bursts, and in a breath of time, Slater had shot down two Albatros, and during that moment the dog fight must have broken off as abruptly as it began. The Caudron, its work over for the morning, was moving back into our lines at a leisurely pace, and, strain my eyes as I might, I could see neither Spad nor Albatros. Even Slater had disappeared, and save for our patrol of three the sky was empty. As we flew westward, at about two thousand metres, I made out two machines burning on the ground, but whether friends or enemies, I did not know. Then: *Rauf!* My Spad staggered violently, as if shying at the deep racking roar and at the same instant—ahead and a little to the right—a black mass appeared as if by magic: an inky sphere with scarlet flame at its heart. Next moment the sickening odour of high explosive was in my nostrils. *Rauf! Rauf! Rauf!* The deep growling voices of the hundred-and-fives spoke out on all sides of us, so close to me that twice I nearly lost control of my plane. Our propellers whirled through the dense smoke of their bursts, and at each explosion I hunched my shoulders instinctively and crouched lower in my frail seat. It was hard to realize that far below me a man—a kindly man, with human interests like my own—was directing the fire and ordering the lanyards to be pulled. The bursting shells gave one a sense of dull, monstrous hostility, impersonal as a volcano in eruption, and quite as impressive when first experienced. I felt deeply thankful when Laguesse banked, opened his throttle, and climbed back steeply to the east, to make one more turn toward the Meuse before heading for Sénard. The shelling continued, of course, as we took altitude, but the batteries to the east were wretched shots.

At three thousand metres, with motors reduced, we flew eastward for ten minutes before Laguesse gave the signal that the patrol was over. It was the "Russian Mountains," a short series of zooms and dives. Once this signal was given, the members of the patrol were at liberty to make their way homeward as they wished—together or singly. Laguesse turned south-west, and I was about to take a line of my own when I heard a faint short crackle of machine-gun fire. The flight commander's plane banked up sharply, wing-slipped, recovered itself, and nosed down easily for the distant aerodrome. Golasse swept past me to the rear in a climbing turn; I circled, craning my neck, saw Golasse pull up and let drive a long burst while his Spad hung vertically and almost stationary. Then, far above us and speeding back into the German lines, I made out a small plane with a red nose and a silvery livid body. Golasse fell off, dove into it, ranged alongside me, and signalled that pursuit was useless. Side by side we headed for Sénard.

Even to-day, after the passage of years, I can feel the emotion of those moments at the close of a patrol. The strain of two hours with every sense on the alert was over; one had done one's bit for that morning, and the time had come to relax, to throttle down for the long easy glide over friendly territory. Putting the war out of mind, the pilot could now lean back at his ease, and allow his senses to drink in the beauty, the romance, the poetry of the air, his element. The motor, at half speed, hummed soothingly, almost sleepily; the little plane seemed to drift back toward its aerodrome, impelled by a homing instinct to return to the men who groomed and fed it. And, securely perched on its back, the pilot was free to feast his eyes on the vast panorama of forests, and farms, and towns, stretching away to horizons such as only the airman knows.

We had lost Laguesse during the moment of circling, and Golasse and I coasted home happily, with no inkling of trouble to come. Presently, miles ahead of us, I made out the Sénard aerodrome, scaled down as though seen through the wrong end of a telescope. The field looked no more than a yard across, and the hangars, placed irregularly here and there, were like matchboxes dropped at random round about.

Approaching the field at about two thousand metres, I saw Laguesse's blue-striped Spad gliding down to land. It levelled off at decreasing speed, and came to a halt while pygmy figures sprinted out from a near-by hangar. I pulled up in a tight spiral, lost fifteen hundred metres, came out a little dizzily, glanced down at the landing-T to make sure the wind had not changed, and slid in over the hangars of 602. I stopped within twenty yards of Laguesse's Spad, still standing with its motor idling. His mechanic astride the fuselage, was fumbling at the pilot's safety belt, and other men stood about, talking excitedly.

Golasse landed close alongside, and, glancing that way, I saw Captain Clermont crossing the field at a trot, while his little dog frisked at his heels. "*Le toubib! Le toubib!*" I heard him shout over his shoulder to Flingot; and this slang Arabic word for doctor was my first intimation that something was wrong. Then I heard Cartier's voice, brusque with emotion: "Get down—I'll taxi her to the hangar for you."

"What the devil's wrong?" I inquired.

Cartier's pock-marked face looked paler than usual, and his black eyes gleamed with an expression almost ferocious. Usually laconic in his speech, his reply was a burst of picturesque profanity. Then, mastering his emotion: "They got Laguesse—he's dying—two bullets through the chest."

The captain arrived, followed by the Group medical officer, and when they had lowered Laguesse on to a stretcher the doctor pronounced life extinct. Laguesse's mechanic shrugged his shoulders despairingly; he and the others ceased their anxious whispering and grimy hands went up to remove their caps. Golasse and I followed the little procession across the field.

"How did it happen?" the captain asked.

"The patrol was over, *mon capitaine*," said Golasse. "He had given the signal and turned to come home. At that moment I heard a crackle of machine-gun fire and saw Laguesse back, wing-slip, and recover himself. I turned and saw a lone red-nosed Boche high overhead, making into his own lines at full speed. Gasoline was low, and there was no hope of catching him, so I signalled Selden that it was no use. Laguesse was heading home; we didn't dream, of course, that he had been hit."

The captain was deeply moved. Laguesse had been one of the pillars of the squadron, always eager to fly, and a comrade to rely on no matter how desperate the pinch.

"It was like him," he said, "dying in his cockpit, to bring his plane home and land it like a feather! Never fear! We shall revenge you, André!"

An hour later, in the bar, I met Forbes, Slater, and the C.O. of their squadron, a great friend of Captain Clermont's. The officer was in high spirits over Slater's two Boches and hopeful that both would be officially confirmed. Slater seemed as apathetic as usual. He didn't appear to care in the least whether he got credit for his victories or not. When he spoke, I had the impression that he did so only to please the captain. We were sitting round a table by the door. Slater turned to me.

"Was that you I saw just after I attacked those Albatros? I thought I recognized your palm tree."

"Yes. That was marvellous shooting, Tommy! I saw both planes strike the ground, not far in the German lines." The captain looked up eagerly.

"What! You saw them? I telephoned the balloons at once—with a little luck we shall hear from them soon." I could see that he was very keen to have Slater's victories confirmed.

The French Army granted confirmations of enemy planes destroyed only after searching investigation and on the strength of unimpeachable evidence from the ground. The balloon observers and the infantry were consulted, and unless they reported that at the time and place specified a plane had been seen to crash, the pilot was not credited with a victory. The moment one of his pilots reported that he had brought down a German, the captain of the squadron worked with might and main to have the victory confirmed, partly, of course, from the selfish motive of running up his squadron's score, but much more, it seemed to me, for the unselfish pleasure of seeing that a good man got credit for good work. The captain of Spad 602 was no exception to the rule.

An orderly opened the door, closed it carefully to keep out the cold air, and snapped his heels together with a salute. He grinned broadly as he handed the officer a slip of paper. "From the telephonist, sir," he explained. The captain glanced at the short typed message and sprang out of his chair, giving Slater a hearty slap on the back.

"Eh, Lagache!" he shouted to the little red-faced barman.

"Champagne for all hands! Two Boches *homologués!*" Slater hunched his thin shoulders with a grimace. He seemed the least excited, the least interested man in the room.

"You saw the big dog fight," Gordon was saying. "Yes, I was in it. There must have been twenty of us, French and German, all circling like mad. I was on a Boche's tail, and one of them was on mine. Every time I got my gun to bear, the fellow behind me started to shoot! The Roosters got an Albatros and lost one of their own men; I saw both planes burning on the ground afterward. Then the Caudron turned into our lines, and the whole flock of Albatros dove away toward the Argonne like a school of fish. I think we could have got some of them, but orders were to stay with the *réglage* machines."

Laguesse was to be buried next day, at a village not far off—Triacourt, I think it was. Captain Clermont had wired his mother in Paris, who would be allowed to enter the Zone des Armées to attend the funeral of her son. His body lay in state that night in the squadron bureau—the coffin, a rough pine box hastily knocked together by the mechanics, draped in the tricolour, on which the pilot's decorations were displayed. His two mechanics, in full uniform, and with fixed bayonets, stood guard, and during the course of the night every flying man on the field came to pay his respects to the dead. Most of them crossed themselves as they entered; some knelt down as simply as children by the coffin to pray for Laguesse's soul.

Fontana, the bluff hearty pilot from Aries, touched me with his display of emotion and simple faith. He went down on his knees to pray long and earnestly.

Mme. Laguesse arrived toward noon next day. She came into our barrack on Captain Clermont's arm, giving me just time to put on my tunic and brush my hair. Then I heard a knock at the door of the tiny room I had shared with her son. She was a slender woman in black, with grey hair, and a firm, sweet, courageous face. She held out her hand to me, smiling as the captain murmured my name.

"You are the American friend André wrote me about," she said. "I hope you will come to see me on your next leave. You live in California, *n'est-ce pas*? And your mother is living? Ah—it is easier for us mothers in France!"

She glanced down at Laguesse's cot, on which I had arranged the small belongings of a soldier's simple, nomadic life. She turned to us. "May I be alone for a moment," she asked, with magnificent self-control, "here in André's room?"

The captain bowed, without trusting himself to speak, and walked into the corridor. As I followed, closing the door, I saw Mme. Laguesse kneel beside her son's rough cot and hide her face in her hands.

Captain Clermont and I waited for her in the messroom. He was silent for a long time. Finally he cleared his throat and spoke. "And she is a widow," he told me, as if putting his own reflections into words, "who lost her other son at the retaking of Douaumont last year. War is a rotten thing for mothers!"

When Mme. Laguesse opened the door and rejoined us, her eyes were dry and she smiled as she held out her hands. "I want you to accept this, Captain," she said. "It's only a cigarette case his father gave him long ago, but André was devoted to you, and he would like you to have some little souvenir." She turned to me. "And you, M. Selden, will you accept this tiepin, and wear it sometimes, and think of the comrade who liked you so well?"

I could only bow, for I am not ashamed to say that I dared not speak. Mme. Laguesse's superb courage affected me as no display of emotion could have done.

Presently the motor cars that were to take us to the village a few miles away drew up outside. Two pilots from each of the four squadrons of the Group were sent to do the last honours to Laguesse. Golasse and I represented Spad 597. Flingot, with a serious face for once, and driving at a sober pace, led the procession in the little Fiat that contained the coffin, and Captain Clermont followed with Mme. Laguesse in his car. As usual at the innumerable funerals of those days, the sky was grey and a fine rain drizzling down. There was a short service in the church, and a long walk afterward in the rain to the soldiers' cemetery, a mile and a half away. I remember the feel of the rain on my bared head, and how we stood about the new grave while the guns along the Salient boomed and muttered fitfully. Facing the coffin, Captain Clermont bade farewell to his pilot in moving words.

"Farewell, Laguesse!" he concluded. "May you sleep in peace. You have earned your rest, for the example of your life will be an inspiration for your comrades who still have work to do. Our memories of you are imperishable and will ensure the lasting glory of your name. And now—*Vive la France!*"

The coffin was lowered and a bugler blew the *Extinction des feux*, putting into the beautiful old French "Taps" something I shall not attempt to describe. The village priest came forward with a vessel of holy water, and we filed slowly past our comrade's grave, each man sprinkling the coffin with a few drops. The funeral was over; we took our places in the waiting cars and drove back to Sénard, silent in the rain.

Passing our squadron bureau on my way back to our barrack, I heard my name shouted joyfully, and was surprised to see Harvey McKail rush out to seize my hand. At Avord both Gordon and I had grown very fond of the little fair-haired chap from Illinois; now he had been sent up from the G.D.E. to replace Marcantoni. Captain Clermont was speaking to another officer nearby, and as they separated I introduced McKail to his new C.O.

"Yes," remarked the captain with a friendly smile. "I thought you might like to have another American in the squadron. He can have Laguesse's Spad and his mechanics. Show him the ropes, will you, Selden? I suppose you two would like to room together?"

McKail took Laguesse's place at dinner that night. Fontana, Volokoff, and Golasse drank long and deep, and when the meal was over the Russian fetched his guitar and a bottle of brandy. The guitar was a fine one, with a sweet resonant tone, true as a bell, and when Volokoff had tossed off three or four glasses of brandy, he took up the instrument, leaned back with a far-away look in his eyes, and struck a series of minor chords that silenced the hilarious talk. He seemed to have forgotten our presence. Next moment his rich voice rang out in a strange song—some folk-song of the Steppes, I suppose. The last notes of the chorus died away to a minor diminuendo on the guitar. There was a moment of silence, followed by a knock at the door.

Lieutenant de Chalais, our second in command, limped into the room, a jolly ex-cavalry officer with a game leg, acquired on the Marne in 1914. We sprang up to make a place for him, but he only smiled, and held up a protesting hand. "I wish I could stop," he said. "Lucky beggars to have a comrade like Volokoff! I could sit here all night and listen to those Russian songs! But I must hurry off. I came to tell you that the infantry wants the Saint Juvin balloon shot down. I'm going to tackle it at daybreak, and I want another man. Who'll go?"

Every man in the room shouted at once, but Volokoff dominated the rest. "I'm your man, *mon lieutenant!* I'm the worst shot in the squadron, but I believe I could hit a balloon!"

Golasse burst into a twitter of laughter, and the officer grinned. "Very well," he assented. "Goodnight, all of you."

There was a finger bowl still on the table, and beside it one of the little dumb-bells of glass used as a rest for knives and forks while the plates were being changed. It had a certain resemblance to the holy-water sprinkler the priest had brought to Laguesse's grave a few hours before. "You're welcome to the job," Golasse was saying as the door closed behind de Chalais. "I tackled that balloon once, and once was enough! They've got a whole corps of machine gunners around it, every one of them a murderous shot! Have you made your will, Volokoff? What about giving me your guitar? "

The Russian was pouring himself another drink when Golasse's roving eye caught sight of the finger bowl and the knife rest. He took up the little dumb-bell of glass, dipped it into the water, and stood over Volokoff, making the sign of the cross and sprinkling him with a few drops. Then he chanted solemnly, in Gregorian tones:

> "*Bidons d'essence!*
> *Carburateurs!*
> *Sauvez, sauvez la France!*
> *Et tous les aviateurs!*"

Next morning Volokoff and the lieutenant ran the balloon to earth, but the Russian's bad luck persisted; his bullets missed their mark, and he had to make off without the satisfaction of having destroyed it.

IX

IN PYJAMAS

ONE morning early in November, Harvey McKail, Golasse and I were loafing around the messroom stove. The other members of Spad 597, with the exception of Captain Clermont, were out on an eight to ten o'clock patrol. A new motor was being installed in the captain's Spad, so he was doubtless having as luxurious a morning in his own barrack as we were in ours. The other three squadrons of Group 31 had gone off at eight-thirty to furnish protection to a lot of Bréguet bombing planes sent out to drop huge bombs on ammunition dumps near Metz. McKail, Golasse and I were to go up at ten-fifteen for a high patrol, so we had slept till nine, and now, a quarter of an hour later, still dressed in pyjamas, we were crunching buttered toast and drinking chocolate. McKail was reading Henry James's *Gabrielle de Bergerac*, and Golasse and I were exchanging boyhood reminiscences. Our lives up to the war had been as different as possible. His had been spent wholly in Paris; he had never been farther from the boulevards than to St.-Cloud, and it was hard for him to understand what ranch life in California could be like. Still less could he picture the South Seas.

"Do you mean to say you really enjoyed being there?" he asked incredulously.

"Enjoyed it! That's a mild way of stating it," I replied. "I'm going back after the war; Forbes and I are going together if we get through."

Golasse shook his head. "You Americans are a queer lot. Well, you can have your South Sea island. Give me Paris. Give me the Café Maxéville on a fine summer evening, with a glass of *porto* on the table beside me, plenty of money to buy more when that one's gone, and nothing to do till to-morrow. Give me——"

He didn't finish the sentence. Just then old Felix came in, and his beard fairly bristled with excitement. "Gentlemen! I don't like to disturb you, but there's a Boche coming this way! I thought you might like to see him."

We rushed outside, and heard at once the far-off brisk detonations of anti-aircraft fire. It was a windless, cloudless morning; eight or ten miles away to the south-east, the sky was dotted with the tiny white smoke blossoms of French seventy-fives. The smoke from the French anti-aircraft shells was always white, and that of the Germans black, so we knew at once that the plane was a Boche. He was still too far away to be seen, but we could follow his course by the shell bursts, and he was evidently coming our way.

"Another of those photographic buses," said Golasse.

"Selden, there's some cold meat for us. Let's go after it! What do you say, McKail?"

"I looked at my watch—a quarter to ten. "Haven't time," I said. "We're due for high patrol in half an hour."

Just then an orderly from Group Headquarters scorched across the field on a motor cycle. It was Flingot, the chauffeur who had met me at Châlons the night I joined the squadron.

"Now then! Now then!" he said. "Don't stand there looking at him. That won't win the war. Hop along, you two! Captain's orders."

He handed Golasse a pencilled note which read;

GOLASSE: You and Selden take off at once after that two-seater. Never mind the ten-fifteen patrol. McKail will wait for the scheduled formation. Good luck!

There was no time to dress, of course. We sprinted down the field, bearskin coats over our pyjamas. Orders had already been sent to the hangars: the mechanics had trundled out our Spads and were warming up the motors by the time we arrived. We jumped into our flying suits and were ready for the take-off within three minutes. At least I was, but Golasse's mechanics were having trouble with his motor. It spluttered and back-fired, and refused to turn up more than a thousand revolutions. Golasse was cursing and waving his arms. "Go on!" he yelled. "I'll be along in a minute." So I waved and started off alone.

My little ship had never climbed more beautifully. I took height over the aerodrome, watching it shrink and shrink until the great field with its row of barracks and hangars looked no larger than a playing card. The horizons rolled back; soon I could see for miles in every direction, and above me, but still off to the right, the sky sparkled every little while with points of intense light where the French anti-aircraft shells were bursting. The minute puffs of smoke were climbing the sky in my direction. It looked as though the German meant to make a long sweep across the Salient and re-enter his own territory somewhere to the north-west.

I turned north-east and climbed in a wide circle so that I could have the sun at my back when high enough to attack, at the same time keeping a sharp lookout for other Germans. There were none to be seen, however, but far to the eastward the sky, at about three thousand metres, was plentifully sprinkled with shell bursts, both black and white. There was no lack of aerial activity over the lines. Apparently the two-seater, taking altitude over his own territory, had sailed serenely across the front at a great height.

Presently I could make him out, a minute speck moving jauntily among the smoke blossoms. Every anti-aircraft battery along the sector seemed to be blazing away at him, and some of them were making good practice. They were putting them very close, in groups of three and four, but he moved on in a leisurely way, flying in wide detours and circles. As I watched him I was convinced that Golasse was right in thinking it a photographic plane, sent out to take long-range pictures with one of those marvellous high-altitude cameras the Germans had. The two men went about their business as calmly and methodically as though anti-aircraft fire was nothing to them and the possibility of pursuit by hostile planes had not crossed their minds.

I wondered whether they saw my Spad on their trail, climbing steadily up the sky. I could see them plainly enough now, not more than two miles away and about a thousand metres over me. "They must see me," I thought, "but it doesn't appear to worry them." Now and then they would make a wide turn, very slowly, as though they had throttled down for picture-taking, and then move leisurely on. I felt a little uneasy at their apparent disregard of me, and scrutinized the air below me, hoping to see Golasse. The sight of his Spad would have been a welcome one, but I was not to be granted it. No Golasse—no anybody save myself and the two Germans whose plane looked bigger and more sinister every moment.

While making a turn I was astonished to find that we were almost over the Sénard aerodrome, which now appeared to be about the size of a postage stamp. I had been looking overhead constantly and had paid little attention to direction except to follow the German. He had turned west without my knowing it, and was flying parallel to the front and about ten miles inside our lines. "Lord!" I thought. "Now's my time! What luck if I could bring down a German right over my own field!" He was almost directly above me now, but still a good five hundred metres higher. Useless to pull up and fire a burst at that distance, but I was rather surprised that the observer didn't spray a few bullets in my direction. He didn't, however; at least I saw no pencilled lines of smoke from tracers. They still flew in the most leisurely manner, as though they thought me not worth bothering about; and somehow their manner of flying told me that they were old pilots who knew their business thoroughly. Their ship, with its silvered undersurface and the huge black crosses on the wings, looked like a veteran too, long accustomed to making flights deep into enemy territory. By that time I had made it out to be a Rumpler.

I didn't like the way they ignored my little Spad, and felt a welcome flush of anger surging through me. "Just wait a moment you two!" I thought. "You may be old hands at this game, and you may know that I'm a young one. Just the same you'll have to notice me."

I crept up, crept up, turning off from their course as I gained my last three hundred metres of altitude, and taking care to keep the sun at my back. "Now, my boy," I said, "go to it!"

I made a half turn to the left, at the same time crooking my forefinger around the machine-gun trigger on the joy stick, and started toward what I considered my prey. I had made my calculations with the utmost care, so that I could attack directly from behind and a little below the two-seater, approaching him under cover of his blind spot. The only mistake I made was in forgetting, momentarily, that the two Germans might do some calculating as well. As I have said, I started toward my prey, and to my great astonishment he wasn't there.

Then I heard a sound as peculiar as it was uncomfortable—*flac! flac-flac! flac!* I knew what it meant; bullets were going through the fabric of my bus. I made a steep turn and found that the German pilot had dived suddenly about fifty metres and levelled off again so that his observer could have me in full view. And so he did have me, and was giving me a full dose with both guns. I thought certainly I was lost; the muzzles of his two guns were pointing straight at me and my Spad seemed to be hanging motionless. But he didn't have me in his sights for long. I made a diving turn and had him broadside on and a little above me again. I pulled the trigger. My gun popped once and jammed.

Of all the exasperating things that could happen in the air, a jammed gun was assuredly the worst, and it seemed always to occur at the most critical moment possible. It was by no means easy to clear a stoppage; and in order to do so it was necessary to withdraw from a fight for several moments, and a pilot was lucky if his opponent permitted him to withdraw. I was grateful to those Germans for allowing me to do so in this case. They flew steadily on, I following at a safe distance, all the while hammering on my crank handle with the little wooden mallet we carried for such emergencies. I knew from the position of my crank handle that I had a bulged cartridge to deal with, but I got rid of it at last and went on again, full motor.

The two-seater was about half a mile in front of me now, flying at the same altitude. I gained on him rapidly, and in my excitement opened fire when still one hundred and fifty metres distant. My tracers appeared to be going directly into the plane, and yet, to my astonishment and disgust, it showed no signs of being damaged. I must have fired between fifty and seventy-five rounds when of a sudden the Rumpler loomed up directly in front of me. I had not realized how much faster I was going, and as a result I nearly got him by running into him. He turned just as I zoomed over him, and I had a vivid glimpse of my opponents. The observer was sighting down through his camera, but looked up just as I passed and seized the handle of his guns with an air of annoyance and surprise, as much as to say, "Oh, damn! Here's that pest back again!" The pilot turned his head over his shoulder, and I had a fleeting view of the vacant stare of his goggles and a flowing blonde moustache. I did an Immelmann turn to come back at them, and unfortunately, in making it, passed directly above them, whereupon the observer gave me another burst. I heard a loud *whang-g-g*, and knew that something had been hit, but it was not till several minutes later that I saw that one of my bracing wires had been cut through.

One of the most surprising things to me, in an air battle,

was the rapidity with which two planes could separate. At one second you were close enough to see the colour of your opponent's moustache and the kind of flying clothes he wore; a few seconds later, as you turned to come back at him, you found that he was half or even three quarters of a mile away. Two planes flying at a combined speed of perhaps two hundred and fifty miles per hour are soon separated when going in opposite directions.

My Rumpler was still not mine. He was a long way off, and I had to do my creeping up all over again. This time I determined to keep cool and reserve my fire until within fifty yards of him. He let me approach as before, and I knew that the observer was busy with his long-range camera, for I could see the muzzles of his guns pointing idly into the air. The pilot flew straight on as though so thoroughly convinced of my poor marksmanship that he meant to let me blaze away to my heart's content; but he was not quite so indifferent as that. I was still about three hundred yards distant, and had my head steadily braced against my headrest, and my sights in beautiful alignment, when the Rumpler began to rise as though being drawn up by invisible wires. Despite my resolution to keep cool, I pulled up steeply and fired a burst of fifteen or twenty rounds which doubtless missed him by twice as many yards, slipped off on a wing, and had to dive into it to regain flying speed. In doing so I lost a good fifty metres of altitude, and when I turned once more in pursuit the Rumpler was a long way ahead and climbing as though there were no limit to his ceiling. There was nothing to do but climb after him.

All this while we had not, of course, been circling over the same area. Our general direction had been east and a little north, but I had been so busy that I failed to notice how far we had gone. Now, with nothing to do but to climb for a while, I took notice of landmarks. Far below to the left I saw a great stretch of wooded country, another to the right, and north of that one a city. "Now what in the world can that town be?" I thought. Châlons was the first name that occurred to me, but I knew there were no forests near Châlons. I made a more careful scrutiny and presently recognized the cathedral of Rheims. There was no doubt of it. I had never seen Rheims from the air—or from the ground, for that matter—but for more than three months I had been studying aeroplane maps and photographs of the western front from the Channel coast to Switzerland, and knew it better than my native California. I easily identified the Marne-Vesle canal which makes a great loop from Epernay to Rheims. We were a good thirty-five miles from Sénard, and evidently the Germans meant to go still farther. The Rumpler was headed for Rheims, and within a few minutes we were directly over the city at a height of fifty-five hundred metres.

At least that was my own altitude; the Rumpler was at six thousand or more, and my Spad was doing its best to lessen the advantage. The motor sounded tacky; not the full-bodied roar to which I was accustomed. Something was wrong, but I didn't know what. By the time we had left Rheims behind I had climbed another fifty metres, but that was the best I could do. And there were my Germans, not five hundred metres higher, paying no further attention to me, knowing, apparently, that the only harm I could now do would be to get into the line of vision of their camera. Then it occurred to me that they might even want me there, provided that my Spad was far enough away and cut off the view of nothing essential on the ground. It would add a bit of local colour to their photographs to have a tiny French *chasse* plane clearly outlined over the towns, railroad junctions, aerodromes, ammunition dumps, and so forth, they were snapping. I could imagine them, a day or two later bringing their developed films to their squadron or group commander, who would glance through them with interest.

"Splendid photographs, *Oberleutnant*. Just what we want."

"*Danke schön, Hauptmann*. We had excellent weather—a perfectly clear sky all the way from St.-Mihiel to Rheims. It would have been impossible not to have taken good pictures."

"And you weren't molested, all that way?"

"*Nein, Hauptmann*. We had very good luck. We were heavily shelled, of course, as usual."

"Hello! Here's a Spad showing—in the photograph taken over that aerodrome near St. Hilaire."

"Bitte schön?"

"A Spad—a French Spad. He must have been about five hundred metres under you at the time. Yes, here it is again in the picture taken over the Montagne de Rheims. He must have been following you. Didn't you know he was there?"

"Oh, *ja!* . . . *Ja, ja,* I remember now. There was a Spad that trailed us all the way from the foot of the Argonne Forest. The pilot was quite harmless. We could have bagged him easily if we'd had time."

I could all but hear this conversation taking place, and it made me so angry to think that in all probability it *would* take place that I pulled up and fired another burst at the Rumpler, although he was a quarter of a mile in front of me and as much above. And I believe that I may have been lucky enough to hit him with a stray bullet, for the pilot made a leisurely turn, banking to look at me, then levelled out on his course again. The manœuvre said, as plainly as though he had spoken, "What! *You* still here?" It was as though he had waved his hand at a fly—troublesome, perhaps, but not troublesome enough to waste time over.

So it went for another ten or fifteen minutes. After leaving Rheims the Rumpler made another wide sweep into French territory, all the way from five to eight or nine miles behind the trenches. I had a map of the Verdun Sector in my map case, but we had long since flown out of that, over country I had never before seen from the air. The German pilot showed me everything worth seeing, from the military standpoint, behind our lines: aerodromes, hospitals, ammunition and supply dumps, and the like, all quite unknown to me. I wondered why I was not joined by some other friendly plane until it occurred to me that other Spads below, seeing me, would refrain from joining up. Pilots would think: "That Rumpler is his victim. I'll not horn in on his victory. Hope he gets the blighter. Awful crust he's got, that Boche, coming all this way back." The anti-aircraft batteries too had ceased firing, doubtless from the fear of hitting the wrong ship; for all this while I was trailing along very close behind, vainly trying to coax my Spad up the last short slope of sky that would give me another chance to attack. It was damnable to think that A-A battery commanders were perhaps watching me through binoculars, counting on me to do something and wondering why the devil I didn't.

"I will!" I said. "I will! Don't worry. If he gives me half a chance." I had forgotten to be afraid, or even in the least uneasy about my own skin. I had forgotten my severed bracing wire and my coughing motor. I had forgotten what time it was, how long I had been flying, how much gas I had left—everything but my intense longing to knock down the cheeky Rumpler that had already flown with impunity across seventy-five miles of French territory.

And then my chance came, more quickly than I had bargained for. The Germans had just made a circle over a flying field I was later to know very well, deep in our territory, at the village of Fère-en-Tardenois. It was not an aerodrome, but a small Aviation-supply depot furnished with only two hangars. The Rumpler circled over it, so I circled too, as I had already done a score of times while they took their photographs. Then, their mission over apparently, they headed due north to cross to their own lines. But they held that course for no longer than a minute. Suddenly the pilot went down in a steep turn and I saw the observer seize his guns and swing them round to fire at me.

This time I was not caught napping, and I wasted no precious seconds trying to get under his tail. I turned left as the Rumpler did, and got in a beautiful burst of about thirty rounds, again broadside on, and from a distance of not more than fifty yards. The observer repaid me with a shorter burst, but a murderously accurate one. Again I heard the ominous *flac! flac-flac-flac! flac-flac!* but it was only for a second. My Spad flopped over in a half turn and came back in the opposite direction so prettily that the thought, "Did I do that?" flashed through my mind. So it was always in the air: the manœuvres one made instinctively were always better than those made with deliberation. It was from that moment that I began to learn how to take care of myself in the air. Every old war-time pilot must have had some such illuminating experience which taught him more in five seconds than his flying instructors could do in three months. Thereafter, when I met a German ship, I kept my eye on that and let my Spad do its own manœuvring.

Turning, I found the Rumpler coming for me from a distance of about two hundred yards—straight for me this time, the pilot firing the guns mounted on his motor hood. So I made for him, my guns crackling steadily. Our motors seemed to be eating each other's bullets; in fact they were, as I discovered later, but we flashed past each other, both seemingly still intact. I made a vertical turn to the right and then saw something that made me shout for joy. The Rumpler was going off, and his propeller was standing stock-still. He had "a dead stick," as we used to say. I thought for a second or two I had imagined this, for not infrequently pilots thought they saw what they hoped to see. It was true, however. The propeller was standing vertically, motionless. What a thrill it gave me to see it! "Now I've got them!" I thought. "I'll force them down in our lines!"

But the Germans had other plans about where they meant to land. They were planing very flatly, making a straight course for their own territory. I glanced at my altimeter. Forty-eight hundred metres. They had sufficient altitude to enable them to land behind their own lines if they were careful not to lose height unnecessarily. My motor was coughing and spitting as though at its last gasp, but I quickly overtook them. The rear gunner was waiting for me; I could see him turning his guns this way and that, trying to get a line on me; but his pilot was afraid to lose altitude which he could not regain, so I had little difficulty in keeping the observer guessing. He fired two or three bursts, but they went wide of the mark. "I'll have to shoot them," I thought. "These men are old hands. They can't be frightened into landing." So I went after them again, hoping that my marksmanship would be good enough to wing them both but not good enough to kill either. I had a wonderful chance now. They were planing all the while, of course, tail up at such an angle that I could see the surface of the underbody. I pressed the trigger. My gun fired twice and stopped. This time it wasn't a missfire or a bulged shell casing. I had run through my entire belt of cartridges.

I didn't know what to do then. I had never thought of such an emergency as this. I confess that what I felt like doing was crying with vexation and disappointment. I had tried hard for that Rumpler, and to have him escape me at the last moment, when victory was all but in my hand—it was too much for me. And all the while the wide belt of desolate country that marked the trench lines was drawing nearer. Soon they would be sailing over it to safety. I made a feint at an attack from the side so that both pilot and observer could see me, but that didn't frighten them in the least. The observer swung his guns round and gave me a dose of lead in the tail just as I passed under him. Had he been half a second quicker the chances are that I shouldn't be telling this story.

Help came in histrionic eleventh-hour fashion. Greased lightning decorated with tricolour *cocardes* streaked down the sky, turned left and fired, turned right and fired, flipped upside down, fired again, and vanished. I saw the German observer drop his guns and collapse in his seat as though he had been pushed down by strong, invisible hands. The little friendly plane flashed into view again; it was precisely as though it had the power of being everywhere at once, and visible or invisible as it chose. This time it came down from the side in plain view of the German pilot, but keeping well above him. The Frenchman, or whoever it was, did a barrel turn, at the same time cutting his motor to come down on the Rumpler, but the German didn't wait for him to fire again. He turned away from his own lines—slowly, and one could feel as well as see with what reluctance—and planed down into France.

We were right at his tail, the Frenchman on one side, I on the other. He was flying a Nieuport, type 27, and on the side of his fuselage was painted a black dragon, and another insignia which I made out to be a skull-and-cross-bones design against a black background. I waved and he waved back, then reached out and went through the motions of shaking hands. He pulled up till he was opposite the German pilot's cockpit and I followed to the same position on the other side. The Frenchman yelled something at the Boche and pointed down. The German looked over the side and waved his hand as much as to say, "All right." I looked too, and saw the hangars of an aerodrome off to our left front.

We were all three so close together that we could see each

other's faces. It gave me a curious feeling to be flying wing to wing with that Rumpler. The pilot's yellow moustache was even longer than it had seemed when I had my first fleeting view of it. The ends fluttered back in the wind around the sides of his flying helmet. The observer was crumpled down in his cockpit, his head hanging to one side. We weren't long in coming down. Two or three minutes later the German landed with his dead stick. The Rumpler rolled a little way and stopped, and I saw a crowd of mechanics rushing out to it. The Frenchman and I followed him down.

X

STILL IN PYJAMAS

IT was not until I taxied up to the hangars that I knew what field this was. The first thing I saw as I climbed out of my bus was a row of six Spads bearing the Indian-head insignia of the Escadrille Lafayette. Our arrival caused great excitement at the aerodrome. Pilots and mechanics ran out to the Rumpler from barracks and hangars all round the field. Others gathered about our two ships, and the first man to greet me was red-headed Bill O'Connor.

"Charlie Selden! You old son of a gun! What are you doing at Chaudun?"

"I didn't know till this minute that it *was* Chaudun," I replied.

"How's Gordon, and Tommy Slater? Are you still at Sénard? Where did you meet Nungesser? Who got the Rumpler?"

He fired questions at me faster than I could answer them, and when he mentioned the name of Nungesser, my eyes bulged.

"Nungesser? Is that who . . .?"

"Sure thing! Didn't you know? He belongs to our Group—

in Spad 65. But how did you two get together?"

Just then Lieutenant Bill Thaw, second in command of the Escadrille Lafayette, came up with Lufbery and Nungesser. Lufbery remembered me, which pleased me very much.

"Hello, Selden! Good work, old boy! Nungesser, this is your flying partner, Selden, from Spad 597, though what he's doing nearly a hundred miles from his own aerodrome is more than I know. Did you get lost again?" Then, turning to Lieutenant Thaw, "Bill, we'll have to have him transferred to Group 13. He seems to like flying with us better than with his own outfit."

Nungesser gave me a hearty handclasp. *"Félicitations!"* he said.

"Félicitations, mon lieutenant? For what?"

"For your Rumpler, of course!"

"But I didn't get him. *You* did."

Thaw grinned. "Now then, Selden! Don't tell your superiors what happened in the air, especially an old bird like Nungesser. But you might explain what you are doing up this way, hunting in our preserves. Mean to say the Verdun Sector's too quiet for you? It must have changed since we were down there."

I told them then of my long chase, of my jammed gun, of the Rumpler's high "ceiling" I couldn't reach, and how I had wasted my ammunition so foolishly that when the critical moment came I didn't have a cartridge left. "And he would have got away," I added, "if Lieutenant Nungesser hadn't appeared."

Nungesser shook his head vigorously. "Nonsense!" he said. "You'd have chivied him down all right. All I did was to persuade him to turn a little quicker." And to Thaw, "Bill, see that Selden gets credit for him, will you? I'll send over my report. Sorry I took a hand at all. Selden would have forced them down alive. As it is, I'm afraid that poor devil of an observer is dead."

I said nothing for a moment. I could think of nothing to say. I felt proud merely to have flown with Nungesser; such an honour was more than enough for me, and to have him show such kindness and generosity to a young pilot bowled me over.

He had had a remarkable experience in the war. In August 1914, he was a non-commissioned officer in the Hussars, and at the Battle of the Marne was given the Médaille Militaire for capturing single-handed a German staff car filled with officers. Later, when the cavalry was dismounted for trench warfare, he transferred to Aviation as a pilot in an *escadrille de bombardement* and took part in numberless bombing raids far into enemy territory. Then, transferring to an *escadrille de chasse*, he began his splendid career as a pursuit pilot, winning victory after victory until, at the time I met him, he had shot down thirty-eight enemy planes. Toward the close of 1915, while trying out a new machine, he had a fall in which he broke a leg and a shoulder and suffered internal injuries so serious that a man of less hardy spirit and constitution would have succumbed. But Nungesser refused a discharge and was soon at the front again, hobbling about his aerodrome with a stick, taking part in the battles for the mastery of the air during the great German attacks at Verdun. On May 19, 1916, his name appeared for the first time in the French *communiqué:* he had gained his fifth victory and was thereafter to be counted among the aces. On June 22 he won his eighth official victory, and on July 22 his tenth. It was then a race between Nungesser and Guynemer, who, on the same date, had won his eleventh victory. On September 26, Nungesser shot down two planes and one observation balloon, bringing his score up to seventeen, three of which had been balloons. Then another wound sent him back to hospital. During the war he was seventeen times wounded, and there was hardly a bone in his body that had not been broken at one time or another. In my opinion, had he not been compelled to spend so much time in hospital, he might easily have won the title of Ace of Aces of France. As it was, at the close of the war he had a total of forty-five enemy planes and balloons shot down and officially confirmed.

At one time—in the summer of 1916—he had been attached to the Lafayette Squadron, and thereafter to Spad 65, a squadron in the same Groupe de Combat with the Lafayette. Later, when all attempts of the military authorities to invalid him out of service had failed, they threw up their hands and gave him letters of marque to fly where and when he pleased—a Privateersman of the Air. There was no more picturesque or romantic figure in the entire French Army. He never liked the Spad. He always flew a type-27 Nieuport, and his famous ship, a gift from the manufacturers and especially built for him, was a welcome and familiar sight at aerodromes both French and British all along the western front, and his skull-and-cross-bones insignia anything but a welcome one to German pilots he met in the air.

I had long wanted to see his ship, and it was a great experience to inspect it in his company. He showed me his gun, his sights, and special little gadgets of various sorts he had had built into the plane, explaining everything carefully and with as much consideration as if I had been Maréchal Joffre, Then we went out to see the captured Rumpler. It was still standing in the middle of the field with a crowd of pilots and mechanics gathered round it. The body of the observer had been lifted out and laid on a stretcher. Two men carried it away as we were coming up. Nungesser was right—the German was dead with three bullets through the chest. He was a man of about twenty-five, with aristocratic features. His face looked as peaceful as though he were asleep. We removed our caps as the stretcher passed.

"Poor chap!" said Nungesser. "It's a pity his pilot wouldn't turn, Selden. But you've got to admire their pluck, trying to get their taxi home with a dead motor."

The pilot was an older man, with the physique and the imperious face of an old Viking. He might have stepped out of one of the Icelandic sagas. It was easy to imagine him in a horned helmet and chain armour, leaning on a great two-handed sword. He had removed his flying combination and I could see the breadth of his shoulders and the girth of his thighs and arms beneath his immaculate uniform. On his tunic was the Iron Cross of the First Class. He was talking with a French officer as Thaw, Nungesser, and I came up. Lieutenant Thaw saluted the officer, Commandant Féquant, chief of the Thirteenth Combat Group.

"*Mon commandant*, may I present Caporal Selden, of Spad 597? He's been chasing this Rumpler all the way from the Argonne."

The commandant shook my hand. "So it was you, Corporal? Well done!" He smiled as he added, "And it was thoughtful of you to bring him down on our field."

"But I didn't get him, *mon commandant*. I only shot up his motor. Lieutenant Nungesser forced him down."

"How is this, Nungesser? Did you have a hand in it too?"

And again Nungesser insisted on giving me all the credit. "I merely happened along at the last minute," he said, "when Selden had things his own way."

But I knew very well that I didn't have them my own way, and explained to the commandant how it had happened. The result was that we were both given credit for the Rumpler, And so it chanced that my first victory was a half victory, and as I think over those days there is nothing of which I am prouder than of the fact that somewhere in the military archives of France there is a record of a certain Rumpler forced to land in French territory at Chaudun, on November 10, 1917, driven down by Lieutenant Charles Nungesser and Caporal Charles Selden. While writing this very chapter of war-time reminiscences, on an island in the South Pacific, on the other side of the world from France, I have received from home papers three months old, containing the account of the death of Nungesser, lost with his friend, Coli, in the attempt to fly across the Atlantic. I hear again the tones of his voice, and see his jolly smile and the gleam of his gold teeth as he said, "NonsenseI You'd have chivied him down all right. Bill, see that Selden gets credit for him, will you?" That was my first meeting with Lieutenant Nungesser, and I shall never forget his courtesy and generosity to a young pilot at the end of his first real battle in the air.

Commandant Féquant introduced us to the German pilot, wha spoke French nearly as well as the commandant himself. He bowed stiffly and shook hands, first with Nungesser, then with me. As he shook mine he said, "Charmed to meet you again," with a faint ironic smile, and then, "Many thanks for the souvenir." He glanced down indifferently at his right leg, and I saw a small hole circled with blood through his laced boot at the calf of his leg. As he moved a few drops of blood trickled down his boot.

"But you're wounded, *Hauptmann!*" said Commandant Féquant. "Hard luck! We must attend to that at once."

"It's nothing, *mon commandant*. This young man," turning to me, "merely wished to show me how well he could shoot," Again he smiled his disdainful smile, and I felt ashamed and angry at the same moment. It was as though he had said, "Considering the number of bullets he sprayed at us, it would have been strange if one of them had not gone somewhere near his target." I said nothing, of course, but what I thought was "Well, old boy, I did get one in after all. And you and your observer fired a good few rounds at me. You were not what might be called saving of your ammunition, but here you see me, still intact."

But if I was intact my poor little Spad was not. The German pilot limped away with Commandant Féquant and I went with the Lafayette pilots to look at my bus. Several mechanics were examining it. Thaw spoke to one of them. "Have you given it the once-over, Valatron? What's the damage? Anything serious?"

"Serious! Sacred name of a sieve! This *coucou* will never fly again! How she got down without falling apart is more than I know. Have a look."

It is needless to give a catalogue of the wounds my Spad had received. Two cylinders were out of commission, one of the bracing wires severed, an aileron hinge cut through, and there were thirty-eight bullet holes through the fabric of wings and fuselage, most of them in the tail. Nearly every part of the plane had been hit, except the two most vital ones—the pilot's seat and the gasoline tank.

"*Vous voyez?*" said Valatron. "She'll have to be invalided out. She's done her bit. Corporal, luck's been with you to-day, that's sure!"

I loved my Spad and was just getting thoroughly used to her. "Can't she be overhauled?" I asked. "She's been a fine ship; I hate to lose her so soon."

The mechanic shook his head decisively. "Not a hope," he said.

"Damn the luck! What'll I do now? How am I to get to Sénard?"

"Don't worry about that," said Thaw. "We'll get you back. What we'd better do now is to go to Group Headquarters and phone your outfit. They're probably wondering what's become of you. By the way, you know Clermont, don't you, Luf? Suppose you call him up. Better go along, Selden, in case he wants to talk with you. Come over to the mess when you've finished. The ten-thirty patrol will be in soon; then we'll have lunch."

The bureau of the Thirteenth Combat Group was much like that of Group 31. On one wall was a complete picture of the sector made by fitting aeroplane photographs together so that one had a bird's-eye view of this part of the front, showing the first, second, and third lines of defence and the back-line areas on both sides of No Man's Land. On the opposite wall was a large-scale map showing the sector in great detail, with enemy anti-aircraft batteries, aerodromes, and observation balloons marked in red ink. Such maps were frequently changed as conditions altered, and I never tired of studying them. While the sergeant in charge of the bureau was calling Sénard, Lufbery showed me all the important features on the Aisne front. Presently the telephone rang. "Here you are, Lieutenant," said the man. "Captain Clermont of Spad 597 on the line." Lufbery took the receiver.

"Allo! Allo! Captain Clermont? *Bien!* René, this is Luf. Lufbery. . . . Yes. . . . Oh, rather quiet just now. . . . What? . . . No such luck. René, we've got one of your pilots here. Selden. . . . Yes, he's quite all right. And the Rumpler is down on our field. The observer was killed and the pilot slightly wounded. . . . What? . . . Of course he did! What happened was this: He'd chased him all the way from Sénard and was jockeying him down with a dead stick. Naturally the Boche didn't want to come and Selden was having a hard time trying to persuade him. The worst of it was that he'd fired away all his ammunition; the Boches still had any amount, so all Selden could do was make feints at them. Well, at that moment along came Nungesser. . . . What? . . . Yes, just back from hospital. Came in the day before yesterday. He was doing a high patrol on his own this morning when he met Selden and his two-seater. Nungesser joined in and had to kill the observer before the pilot would turn back. . . . Whose Boche? Well, Nungesser says it's Selden's and Selden says it's Nungesser's. They've been bowing and scraping to each other for the last hour, saying, 'After you, sir!' Ever hear of such delicacy? . . . Yes. . . . Yes, that's what Commandant Féquant has done: they're both to have credit for him. . . . What? . . . Oh, it's a wreck. His motor's a pile of junk. It will have to be scrapped. . . . Good! I'll tell him. . . . Right you are! . . . Yes. . . . Yes. . . . All right. So long."

He hung up the receiver. "A bit of good luck, Selden. You're to go in to Le Bpurget for a new Spad. Captain Clermont says to go this afternoon if possible; if not, then the first thing to-morrow morning. And you're to fly back to Sénard as soon as you can."

It was not till that moment that I remembered I was wearing pyjamas and had nothing but flying boots over my bare feet.

"Good Lord!" I said. "I don't see how I can go. I'm half naked."

"Ha, ha! Pyjamas, eh?"

It was by no means uncommon for pilots to make morning patrols in pyjamas. They would hop out of bed at the last possible moment, gulp their chocolate or coffee, slip on their bearskin coats, and exchange these at the hangars for their fur-lined combinations and flying boots.

Reluctantly I unbuttoned my combination and displayed

the frogs of a very loud pyjama suit. I had bought it in a hurry in Paris, the afternoon I left for the front, at one of those "One Hundred Thousand Shirts" stores every soldier visitor will remember; and it was not till I opened the parcel at Sénard that I realized how hideous these particular pyjamas were. In fact, I didn't remember whether they were plain or striped, white, pale blue, or Harvard crimson. Alas! the green and orange stripes would have been considered gaudy even in Birmingham, Alabama. Every pilot in the mess had ragged me, and Golasse had even made up a song about them, a rather indelicate song I must refrain from translating here. There after I had worn them for pure cussedness, but I had had no intention of making patrols in them, to say nothing of landing in them at strange aerodromes.

Lufbery took one glance, then put his hand over his eyes.

"Wow! Do you mean to say you can sleep in those!"

"They are pretty noisy," I admitted. "What'll I do? I can't go to lunch like this!"

"Of course you can! Come on and give the boys an eyeful! Bob Soubiran has some almost as bad. Maybe one of us can lend you a uniform to wear to Le Bourget." He looked at his watch, "Twelve-thirty. Time our low patrol was coming in. Look! There they are, right on the dot, All six of them, too."

Off to the north I saw the patrol coming in beautiful formation. There was none of the customary dallying— no exhibitions of fancy flying as they lost height over the aerodrome. They knew it was lunch time and dropped to land without the loss of a moment. A police dog raced across the field toward the first of the Spads taxiing to the hangars,

"That's Fram, Captain Thénault's dog," Lufbery explained. "If anything happened to Thénault I honestly think Fram would die of a broken heart."

We crossed over to join the little group making a bee line for the mess. I was introduced to Captain Thénault, the French officer commanding the Escadrille Lafayette, and the other pilots. They had had an uneventful two hours in the air, except that, as usual, they had been persistently and heavily shelled from the moment they reached the lines till the patrol was ended.

"That's a wicked battery the other side of the Chevregny reservoir," Ray Bridgeman, a pilot from Illinois, was saying. "The best shots on the sector."

"You've said a mouthful, Bridgie," another man replied. "I got a piece of iron as big as your hand through my tail. Not three inches from my seat, but oh, the difference to me!"

"I'd like to know how many shells they wasted on us in two hours. I started keeping count, but gave up after three hundred. We'd been out then a little over an hour."

"I've heard that those Boche Archie shells cost twenty-five dollars each. Let's see. Suppose they fire four hundred shells at us. That would be a conservative estimate. How much would that be in all?"

"There goes Pete, cost-accounting again! If he keeps on figuring he'll have the boys out of the trenches by Christmas, the way old Henry was going to."

"That's all right, Pete! Work it out. Four times five are twenty——"

"And four times two are eight and two are ten. One thousand bones!"

"Yea bo! And all Heinie got for his money was a hole through Dud Hill's tail!"

"Dud, you ought to frame that hole."

"Sure thing! You'll probably be married if you live long enough. And when your kids say, 'Daddy, what did *you* do in the Great War?' you can show them the picture and say 'See that hole? That cost the Kaiser a thousand dollars; and it's only one of the things papa did.' "

Food was being put on the table when we entered the barrack. All the members of the Lafayette Squadron, officers and non-coms alike, messed together, and they were all present that day. The weather was bitterly cold and the messroom stove had been stoked till it was red-hot. One of the pilots noticed that I still had on my flying clothes.

"Hell's bells, Selden! Why don't you take off your combination? I should think you'd be cooked. Do they mess in flying clothes at your outfit?"

I caught Lufbery's eye. He was sitting on a bench near the stove, rocking back and forth and hugging his knees in anticipation. I knew it was useless to delay, so I unbuttoned and unbuckled at once, and stood up, barefooted in my superb pyjamas. For a moment there was dead silence, but the uproar that followed must have been heard nearly as far as Sénard. Whiskey and Soda, the two lion mascots of the Lafayette Squadron, were lying in a corner. Whiskey at this time was almost full grown; Soda was about the size of Captain Thénault's dog, Fram. They got excited at the noise my pyjamas had caused and rose to their feet, wrinkling up their noses and giving voice to a series of rumbling growls. This added to the hilarity, although it didn't add to my comfort. I had not seen the lions till that moment, although I had, of course, long since heard of these strange mascots; they were known all along the western front.

Whiskey came toward me, still wrinkling his nose and snarling. Soda crouched in a corner, moving her tail swiftly back and forth as a cat does when excited or angry.

"That's all right, Selden. Whiskey won't hurt you. He's harmless as a lamb!"

"All he wants is those pyjamas! Better give 'em to him! He's not used to being trifled with!"

"Luf! I see it all now! Selden's been chased out of Sénard by his own outfit!"

"No wonder that Rumpler observer couldn't hit him! Selden must have opened up his combination and blinded him!"

"It'd be worse than having the sun in your eyes!"

"I've seen some passionate pyjamas in my time, but these get the aluminium medal!"

I had to go through with it, but at last the uproar died away; Whiskey and Soda calmed down, Fram stopped barking, and we all sat down to lunch, which was growing cold on the table.

I have the pleasantest memories of that meal. The pilots of Spad 124—as the Lafayette Squadron was officially called—were splendid hosts, and it was good to hear American talk once more. One of the records for the squadron phonograph in great demand just then was a male quartette, and the song was "I'm Going Way Back Home and Have a Wonderful Time." I felt that I was actually back home with all these Americans. The chief topic of conversation was the probable transfer of the squadron as a unit to the U.S. Air Service. The American military authorities had expressed a desire to have this done, and the Executive Committee of the Lafayette Corps, in Paris, had put the matter up to the men themselves. The decision was a hard one to make. Although the pilots were eager to fight under their own flag, they "were reluctant—as were we other Lafayette Corps men—to leave the service of France. They had formed lasting friendships in French Aviation, and had come to think of France as a second Mother Country, almost as dear to them as their own. But since the French authorities had expressed a willingness to release them for this purpose, it was the general opinion of the squadron personnel that the change should be made; and it was made, in February 1918. The *escadrille* then became the 103rd Pursuit Squadron, U.S.A.S., and was the first, and for two months thereafter the only, American squadron on duty at the front.

At the time I visited Chaudun, the squadron comprised Captain Georges Thénault, commanding; Lieutenant Verdier-Fauvety, a French ex-cavalry officer; Lieutenants Thaw and Lufbery; and the following non-commissioned pilots: Ray Bridgeman, Charles Dolan, William E. Dugan, Christopher Ford, James N. Hall, Dudley Hill, Henry S. Jones, Kenneth Marr, Edwin C. Parsons, David Peterson, Robert L. Rockwell, Robert Soubiran,—the chap I had met on the train the night I joined my squadron,—and my friend of the flying schools, Bill O'Connor, One reason why I remember their names so well is that, after lunch, a *prise d'armes* was held, when I was presented with the following citation, signed by all the pilots, including Captain Thénault:

The officers and non-commissioned officers of the Escadrille, Spad 124, cite to the entire Western Front the unique pyjamas of Caporal Charles Selden, of Spad 597, Groupe de Combat 31.

On November 10,1917, while attacking an enemy two-seater over Chaudun, these pyjamas, displayed in a single burst, brought down the Rumpler intact in our lines, killing the observer and slightly wounding the pilot. This citation carries with it the Grand Cross of the Order of the African Nightshirt, with Palm, Star, and Evinrude Motor attached.

I didn't leave Chaudun till the following morning, for Captain Thénault learned that a two-seater Spad was to fly to Le Bourget at that time, and he arranged that I should accompany it. One squadron, Spad 84, of the Thirteenth Group, had been equipped experimentally with two-seater Spads, but after a try-out at the front they were found to be unsuited for pursuit work; they were much slower and less adaptable for combat than the single-seaters, and so were being returned to the depot.

Not a member of that Lafayette crowd would lend me a uniform for the journey. They all professed to have no extra uniforms. They made a pretence of searching and were most apologetic.

"It's too bad, Selden," Bill Thaw explained. "You see what happened was this: we got into a big poker game with Spad 65 a few nights ago, and damned if that bunch of crooks didn't strip us of everything we owned, including our extra uniforms!"

"We'd certainly do something for you if we could," said Doc Rockwell. "We know just how you feel. Tough luck gadding all over France in pyjamas, but . . ." etc., etc.

They wouldn't weaken, and the result was that I left Chaudun still in pyjamas. The pilot from Spad 84 took off shortly after dawn at the time when an early patrol from the Lafayette Squadron was going out to the lines. Before I climbed into the rear seat of the two-seater Spad, they made me unbutton my combination and give them one last look at my gorgeous sleeping suit. Our two-seater left the ground just after their patrol. We took height over the aerodrome, and a moment later were over the forest of Villers-Cotterets, headed south-east in the direction of Paris.

I enjoyed that ride to Le Bourget. For the first time in my career as an aviator I had nothing to do in the air, was free from all responsibility, and I gave myself up to uninterrupted enjoyment of the countryside flowing beneath us. The French pilot followed the railroad line that runs from Soissons to Paris, and within fifteen minutes we could see the hangars and barracks at the G. D. E., Plessis-Belleville. We flew low over that familiar spot and passed not two hundred metres above the roof of the Hôtel de la Bonne Rencontre. I saw Mme. Rodel, wife of the *patron*, hanging out some washing in the backyard, but she didn't look up; the buzzing of aeroplanes over her roof was as familiar a sound to her as the buzzing of houseflies under it. We passed through flocks of machines. Some of them flew alongside for a little way to look at us. They could see our insignia and the machine guns mounted forward and in the rear cockpit, and knew, of course, that we were from the front. I felt proud and a little superior, and waved condescendingly to those school pilots awaiting orders.

For I was now a veteran whose plane had received scars in battle and with half a victory to my credit.

Le Bourget was an enormous Aviation Depot. It still is, in fact. The name of that village, just outside Paris, is now known all over the world, for it was there that Lindbergh landed at the end of his glorious flight across the Atlantic. I little thought, on that November day in 1917, that a young American was to bring such honour to himself and to his country by landing there ten years later. In fact, my thoughts were entirely concerned with getting a new Spad, and I was keen, of course, to have a good one. There were scores of hangars filled with hundreds of planes received from French aircraft factories, waiting for service at the front. In the Spad Division I enquired for Lieutenant Du Pont, the friend of my friend, Sergeant Laguesse. He was a test pilot whose business it was to try out new machines as they came from the factories. I had written to him at the time of Laguesse's death and had received a very kind letter in reply in which he asked that I look him up in case I ever came to Le Bourget for a new Spad.

He gave me a cordial welcome. "I've got just the ship for you!" he said. "I tried it out not half an hour ago."

"What is it?" I asked. "A one-eighty?"

"Yes. It's not another Hispano-Hispano, but just as good, or I'm no judge. Come on; you can see for yourself."

"You're making no mistake," he added, "in choosing

another hundred-and-eighty. The two-twenties have proved unsatisfactory so far. If you get fifteen hours of flight from one of them, you're lucky. As for this particular one-eighty"—he kissed the tips of his fingers—"she's a marvel! Look! There she is in front of that hangar."

She had no machine gun, of course, but was otherwise all ready for flight, and she seemed as eager to fly as I was to fly her.

"Try her out," said the test pilot. "Take a hop over Paris before you start for Sénard; and if you don't like her I'll give you another one."

I was not pressed for time, so I acted on this suggestion. I flew over Paris for nearly an hour. I couldn't have strolled up the Grand Boulevards in my noisy pyjamas, but there was nothing to prevent me flying over them, surveying them from a height of twelve thousand feet. My new Spad soared like a hawk without the least seeming effort, and when I throttled down the motor she skimmed through the fields of air singing softly to herself without a false note. I was reluetant to come down to earth again even for a moment, but I wanted to disburden myself of a little of the debt of gratitude I owed the *réceptionnaire* pilot for giving me such a splendid ship. So I landed again at Le Bourget, where I found him busy with another Spad.

"Well, how does she do? Are you satisfied?" he asked.

"Vastly more than that," I replied. "Thanks a thousand

times! You've done me a great service."

"Oh, don't speak of it. A flying partner of André Laguesse can have the best we've got in the shop. But you'd better fill your tank before starting off. You've been gone about an hour."

We chatted for another five minutes while the mechanics replenished the gasoline. I left Le Bourget at ten o'clock, followed the Marne as far as Châlons, then cut across country and landed at Sénard at eleven-thirty. I taxied over to the hangars; no one was about and the hangars themselves were empty. I taxied on down the field. The whole aerodrome was deserted, but a moment later I saw a small truck at the side of the road near the barracks of Spad 597. Someone came running toward me. It was Flingot, the chauffeur, or, as he preferred calling himself, "pursuit pilot flying a Fiat truck." He nodded in his off-hand manner.

"Breeze along, breeze along," he said. "You think you're at home, but you're not. You've still got a long way to go. We've moved."

"Moved? Where?"

"Down to the border of Switzerland. The whole Group's gone there on special mission. The pilots left three hours ago, and most of the camions at dawn. My truck's the last of the outfit. There's a new Group coming to Sénard—Group 28. Ought to be here now. Here's a note for you from the captain."

The note read as follows:

SELDEN: Group 31 has been ordered to the aerodrome at Chaux, near Belfort, for special duty. Come along as soon as you can. Flingot has a map for you. Follow the Moselle till you lose it in the mountains, then pick up the road that leads over the Ballon d'Alsace. Can't lose your way. Chaux aerodrome is about six miles due north of Belfort. Glad to hear about the Rumpler.

"Quite a sight-seeing trip you've had," Flingot was saying. "Well, you've got a good one hundred and thirty miles still to go. Bet you a dinner in Belfort that I get there within two hours after you do. Take me up? Right. Now we'll fill your tank and be on our way."

Ten minutes later I took off again. By that time Flingot's Fiat was travelling hell-bent-for-election down the road toward Bar-le-Duc. I whizzed over him not a hundred feet higher and saw him thumb his nose at me as I passed. In order to be on the safe side, I landed at an aerodrome near Toul for gasoline, and had a belated lunch with the pilots of a reconnaissance squadron stationed there. They had recently captured intact a German two-seater—a Roland—and were using it to good advantage in their work. The two men assigned to fly it were having all sorts of interesting adventures far in the rear of the enemy lines. Their chief danger had lain in crossing the French lines when they had been heavily shelled by our own anti-aircraft batteries, and once they had barely missed being shot down by a patrol of Spads. In order to lessen this danger, tricolour *cocardes* on strips of oiled silk had been made for the German machine, and these were attached to rollers operated from the pilot's seat by means of almost invisible wires, so that he could cover or uncover the German crosses at will. The rollers were marvellously concealed and could not be detected unless one made a minute examination of the plane. Several times they had landed spies and had brought them home again with much valuable information. The talk at the mess the day I visited them was of a flight to be made in this machine so far into Germany that it would necessitate landing at an enemy aerodrome for gasoline. They had German airman's papers, of course, and both the pilot and his observer were Alsatian Frenchmen who spoke German perfectly. I envied them that splendid and hazardous adventure, but at the same time I was glad I didn't have to tackle the job. I learned afterwards that they came home safely.

At one-thirty I was on my way again. My engine ran beautifully. I climbed to five thousand metres, far above a mass of cloud blowing up from the south-west, which at length cut off all view of the earth. So I then flew a compass course, allowing for wind drift, and hoping that I was well behind the front; for my new Spad was still without a gun and I had no desire to encounter any Germans.

When nearing the end of this lonely flight, I witnessed a

battle above the clouds which brought home to me anew the weirdness, the swift and terrible decisiveness, which often marked aerial combats. Far ahead and at least a mile below me I saw two planes, widely separated at first and considerably to the left of the course I was following. Whether hostile or friendly, or both, it was impossible to determine at that distance, so I descended cautiously for a better view. They rapidly approached one another, and I was still a thousand metres higher when one of them burst into flame—a conflagration that looked no larger than the flare of a match in that wide air. Both planes vanished at once into the sea of mist below them. Only a film of oily smoke, soiling the purity of the cloud bank, marked the scene of the encounter. I knew that I must be somewhere near my destination, so I too went on down through the clouds and, emerging within view of the earth, saw the conquered plane burning fiercely on the ground, the flames throwing a crude light in the gloom of a ravine where it had fallen. Hovering over it, I saw a welcome sight—the tricolour *cocardes* of a Spad, so I dove swiftly to join it, and soon recognized the red X of Lieutenant de Chalais, second in command of our squadron. We were close to the Hartmannsweilerkoft, north of Thann, and a few moments of flight brought us to Belfort and Chaux, where, thanks to good old Felix, I found my uniform, carefully brushed and pressed, laid out for me on my cot. The squadron gave me a welcome as boisterous as my pyjamas deserved and Golasse added two more stanzas to his song in their honour.

My machine gun was mounted the next morning, my coconut palm painted on the top wings, and for three days I took part in patrols over a sector that seemed as peaceful as a country churchyard after Verdun. In fact, the only air battle that took place was the one I had seen, in which Lieutenant de Chalais added another Albatros to his score. I have never enjoyed flying more than I did there, for we had the Alps in view to the south, and to the west the Valley of the Rhine, and no bothersome Germans to prevent our gazing to our hearts' content.

We were at lunch, the morning of our fourth day at Chaux, when Captain Clermont came in to read us the following extract from General Orders:

"The General commanding the Tenth Army wishes to thank the officers and non-commissioned officers of Groupe de Combat 31 for the aerial protection they have afforded His Majesty, the King of Italy, during his visit to the French lines of this sector."

"So that's what we have been doing!" said Sergeant Du Marmier. "Where are we off to next, I wonder?"

It was a purely rhetorical question and called for no reply. The events of to-morrow were glamorously veiled.

But in those days, whether veiled or not, adventures were

often glamorous enough. There was glamour in the air we breathed, fragrant with the never-to-be-forgotten odours of a flying field; in the noonday hush, when, from afar, ruffling the silence like cat's-paws, darkening the surface of quiet water, came the throb of motors of returning patrols and the mutter of gunfire—a world away, it seemed, from the quiet fields where we lived, and yet within ten minutes' flight of those very fields. Indeed, every day brought its glamorous possibilities; that is why I am glad that I preserved my noisy pyjamas, although I never wore them again. They and the citation they won are the only visible reminders I have now of the day when, setting out to pursue a German Rumpler, I had the honour to meet in the air that King of the Air, Lieutenant Nungesser, and to share with him a victory. They remind me too of a delightful visit with the pilots of the Escadrille Lafayette; of a journey to Le Bourget and Paris and back again to Sénard; and how from there I proceeded by route of the air to the extremity of a far-flung battle line, where I did what I could in a small way to protect the King of Italy.

XI

SILENT NIGHT

THEN we moved north again, to the Champagne Front, and were stationed at the Ferme de la Noblette, nine kilometres north of Châlons, on the main road—long cut by the battle lines—between Châlons and Charville. The aerodrome, an enormous one, was at this time the headquarters for our own Groupe de Combat and four squadrons flying Bréguet two-seaters, comprising the Thirty-fifth Day-Bombing Group. We patrolled the lines along forty mües of front, from Rheims to the west side of the Argonne forest.

Winter now set in in earnest, and those who were then in France will remember what a severe one it was. Winds swept unchecked down the North Sea, bringing icy rains, then sleet, then fine dry snow that whirled and eddied about the melancholy fields, drifting deeper and deeper against barracks and hangars.

We airmen didn't mind. As already explained, this was what we called superb weather, when we could lie comfortably in bed till all hours of the morning, loaf during the afternoons around the messroom stove, reading or chatting, visiting back and forth with the pilots of other squadrons, and swapping yarns at the Group bar. The war, both on the ground and in the air, was at a standstill, had ceased to exist, in fact, and the silence along the front was all but unbroken. Only at rare intervals did we hear the faint *br-r-rumble-rumble* of gunfire as though some monster in its cave had turned over in sleep and was growling and grumbling to itself. At night, as we looked out for a moment from the barrack-room door, we could see, far away to the north, the white glare of trench rockets suffused through the darkness filled with falling snow; then we would shut the door again, glad that we were airmen. But after nearly every storm there followed periods of clear weather, when patrols were at once resumed, and then, no matter how warmly we were dressed, we were nearly frozen stiff during our two hours in the air. The high patrols were the worst, of course. At fifteen or eighteen thousand feet the blood, it seemed, ceased to flow altogether. Hands and feet were lumps of ice, and one would have said that the current of air that swept around the windshield had come straight from the North Pole.

Cold though they were, I enjoyed those winter patrols—all but the getting out of bed in the grey dawn. We flew in small formations, two or three planes together and wandered up and down the sector, gazing down on a world wrapped in snow, which seemed as lifeless as the moon. Sometimes we did not meet, or even see, a hostile machine. Even the anti-aircraft batteries left us in peace; we would fly from Rheims to the Argonne and back again without attracting more than twenty or thirty shells. Snow had obliterated the trench lines, and it was only when coming down very low, flying over them at a few hundred metres, that we could see, occasionally, minute black figures—troglodytes standing in frozen clusters at the entrances to their caves.

One of our jobs during this uneventful winter weather, a job every airman loathed, was that of bombarding the helpless German infantry with paper ammunition—Allied propaganda. Hopeful and relentless officials—they must have been civilians—in some far-off Bureau of Propaganda kept this literature moving up to the front in never-ceasing streams. There was no damming it, except verbally, and the result was that it accumulated in enormous quantities at every French aerodrome—and doubtless at the British ones too—from the Channel coast to the Swiss border. When we moved from one flying field to another we left boxes, bales, cords of it behind, but upon arriving at a new aerodrome we would find that the airmen we were replacing there had considerately left us a legacy of this highly imaginative literature even more generous than that we had bequeathed to the incoming Group on our old field. It was of all sorts: speeches of French and English and American politicians, with portions underscored in red to attract the eye; broadsides informing German soldiers of the true military situation; neat cards prepared for the humblest kind of Teuton soldier unused to involved arguments, showing briefly, in parallel columns, the relative economic strength of the Central and Allied Powers; alleged letters from German prisoners in France and England—open letters to their comrades still in the trenches, giving such glowing accounts of their happy prison life that one almost envied them, and the like—all of it, of course, printed in German. Squadron cooks used it to start their morning fires, squadron rats to build their nests with, and the airmen themselves to paper the walls of their rooms in draughty barracks. But although much of it was consumed in these ways, fresh supplies came in in such quantity that at last, in despair, Group commanders would send us out to snow it down on the enemy, who, it was rumoured, used it for purposes still more practical.

The afternoon of the twenty-third of December was spent by Group 31 in clearing the squadron barracks of at least a ton of this paper. A light wind was blowing into Germany, and we worked like bees, from one o'clock till five, each pilot carrying out as many bundles of tracts as his Spad would hold, making several journeys out to the lines. The sector was apportioned off among the four squadrons. Spad 597 was given the smallest territory to cover—from the Butte de Mesnil to the Argonne—because it was farthest from the aerodrome. Each packet contained about a thousand leaflets, I should say, but we judged by weight. We would make a shallow turn into Germany, then slip off the rubber bands and toss the bundles over our heads, the wind from the propeller scattering the leaflets far and wide. They fluttered slowly down—it was as though millions of white birds were drifting idly here and there. We untidied the whole sector and gave forty miles of German soldiers reading matter and to spare for the rest of the winter, hoping they would receive with grateful spirits this largess snowed down upon them from the Allied heaven.

That evening Harvey McKail, Volokoff, and I went over to the Group bar. Gordon and Tommy Slater were there; in fact, a good half of the pilots of all four squadrons were present, some playing bridge, others reading or chatting or writing letters. We four Americans talked of home, Volokoff sitting near by with a bottle of brandy before him, listening in silence to our conversation. He had brought his guitar, but we knew it was useless asking him to play till the brandy had begun to take effect.

Tommy Slater sat hunched up in an easy-chair, his delicate hands clasped around his knees. He was in a talkative mood for the first time since I had known him. The nearness of Christmas may have been responsible for that. There was a happy, holiday feeling in the air; everyone seemed conscious of it except Volokoff, who gazed moodily through the open door of the stove.

"I hope we can have a really quiet Christmas," McKail was saying. "War seems all wrong at this time of year."

Gordon nodded. "You're right, Harvey. Well, you can have

your wish—we all can. I heard Commandant Beaumont telling our C.O. there would be no scheduled patrols on Christmas Day."

"That won't prevent our going out on our own?" Slater asked.

"No, I suppose not, but who'd want to?"

"Good as any other day for knocking down a Boche."

Volokoff brought his fist down on the table with a bang.

"That's the talk! Here's to you, Slater!" He tossed off his brandy and filled his glass again. "You're worth more to France than a million tons of propaganda! I wish I had your eye! Can't you teach me to shoot? Can't you? Or you, Forbes? I'll be the friend for life of the man who can teach me to knock down Germans!"

Slater shrugged his shoulders deprecatingly. "I doubt if there'll be any of 'em out Christmas Day. No harm, though, in looking for one."

"I'm sure there won't be," said McKail. "They love Christmas too much for that. Can't you hear them singing *Heilige Nacht*? Lord! I wish I could hear that song right now! It has more of the fine old spirit of Christmas in it than all of ours."

Tommy smiled his ghostly smile. "I'll sing it for you if you like, Harvey. Volokoff, play the accompaniment, will you?"

At first we thought he was joking. I remembered his telling me at Avord that he had been a choirboy in an Episcopal church in Philadelphia but none of us had ever heard him sing, or even so much as hum an air. But Volokoff took him at his word, reached for his guitar, and leaned back in his chair, striking a few chords that sent little shivers racing up and down my spine.

"What will you have—English, French, or German?" Slater asked.

"Sing it in German, if you don't mind," said McKail.

"All right. Ready, Volokoff? Wait! That's the key."

He began softly, in a voice of almost soprano quality, as clear and pure as any I have ever heard. The hard lines on Volokoff's face relaxed. He gave Slater a quick glance of amazement and delight, then leaned back with his eyes closed, playing as only a Russian can play the guitar. Conversation stopped at once—even the bridge players put down their cards to listen. At the end there was a silence so profound that one seemed to hear the melody echoing and re-echoing, farther and farther away. Then someone at the other end of the room said, "Sing it again, will you, Slater?" He sang it twice over and even then we were not satisfied.

That was the beginning of a concert I shall never forget. Those Frenchmen couldn't have enough of Tommy Slater; neither could we Americans, for that matter. He sang without the least effort; melody bubbled up in him as limpid as spring water. Afterward he and Volokoff, who had a magnificent baritone voice, sang together, French, German, and English folk-songs—they seemed to know them all. It was a privilege to be grateful for to hear them sing "*Au clair de la lune*," "*Ich weiss nicht was soll es bedeuten*," and an English song that began:

> Tom Pierce, Tom Pierce, lend me your grey mare,
> All along, out along, down along lea.

Later we all joined together in singing French army songs: "*Vive le pinard*": "*Bonsoir, les copains, bonsoir*," and the like; but the one I remember best was the "*Sambre et Meuse*," which Volokoff sang alone. It was an appeal that brushed reason aside and went straight to the heart. He made one think of war as the most glorious of all adventures.

Other men dropped in, and soon nearly the whole Group was present, including Commandant Beaumont. We all liked as well as respected the commandant. He had the faculty—a not uncommon one among French officers—of knowing how to unbend without the slightest loss of dignity, and he took a personal interest in every one of his pilots. He knew our names and remembered them, and made us feel, individually and collectively, that Group 31 was the *corps d'élite* of the entire French Air Service. That evening he gave us a little talk that is still fresh in my mind. I can recall it almost word for word.

"This has been a delightful evening," he began. "We owe Sergeant Slater and Sergeant Volokoff a debt of gratitude which I, for one, hope will increase as the winter goes on. Now, if you will permit me to talk shop at an unseasonable time, I should like to say something about the military situation as it affects us. I want to make clear to you, as briefly as possible, how we stand at present, and what the future probably has in store for us.

"Many of you will remember the struggle, in 1915, for the mastery of the air, and how, in spite of all the Allies were then able to do, Germany unquestionably gained it. They possessed the skies because they recognized early the possibilities for Aviation and the importance of the part pursuit planes would play in it before the war was far advanced. It is needless to tell you of the struggle for supremacy in aircraft and motor construction which then followed. You all know of it—of the rapid changes that took place in the types of planes and motors; of the appearance of our Nieuport; how it was superseded by the Spad; how the enemy has put in the field the Albatros D 2, followed by the D 3 and the D 5; and you are now beginning to meet in the air the Platz, Germany's latest attempt to contest the supremacy of the Spad.

"For France and her Allies now have supremacy in the air, and have had it since the beginning of the Battles of the Somme. This may be news to some of you. I observe that Sergeant Golasse is smiling; he is remembering that last patrol at Verdun when he and Fontana and Du Marmier were ambushed over Doncourt and considered themselves lucky to escape with whole skins. And so they were. Nevertheless, even Golasse will admit that, in order to be so ambushed, it was necessary to fly a considerable distance into German-held territory. And *I* will readily admit that you had no easy time at Verdun. The air over those scarred battlefields is probably more hotly contested than over any other sector of the front, except Flanders. We had grave losses there—irreparable ones—but the enemy suffered far more severely then than did we.

"And so it has been on the front as a whole. I do not mean to deprecate the fighting qualities of German pilots. Courage, initiative, intelligence, and skill are not the unique possession of Allied airmen. Our supremacy is due in part to the fact that we now have pursuit planes better than those of the enemy. How long this will be true is a matter only the future can decide. And this brings me to the chief purpose of these remarks.

"You have heard rumours of a great German offensive, to take place, it is said, in the spring. I have not the slightest doubt that it will take place, and that it will be on a scale exceeding anything yet attempted in the war. Command of the air is of first importance to the success of such an offensive, and we may be sure that the enemy will make every effort to gain it. There are rumours, as well, that Germany has in reserve, to put into the field at that time, pursuit planes far better than any you have met, and I am betraying no confidences when I say that we have reason to believe these to be something more than rumours. And I can promise you this, in case you like such promises: their numbers will be legion. The skies will be darkened by swarms of these hornets, which will try to drive us from the skies.

"Needless to say, we shall not be so driven, but I want you fully to realise the seriousness of the struggle before us. Russia has collapsed; Italy is defeated—though not destroyed, she has been so demoralized that England and France have been compelled, as you know, to send troops to her rescue. The Central Powers are now free to strike their last mighty blow in the West. It will be the last, and it will be mighty. It is now or never for Germany—it is now or never for us. But they shall not pass I Many of us, perhaps, will not live to see the day of victory, but it will come. Our lives, individually, count for nothing in this struggle. It is our part merely to fight with all our strength, all our will, with unconquerable tenacity of purpose, each man contributing his small share to the final result.

"Now I should like to read to you something that has pleased me. It is an extract from a speech, delivered in the House of Commons a few days ago, by Premier Lloyd George, of England. He spoke of the Air Service and the part it is playing in the war. He spoke of British airmen, but his remarks apply equally to all airmen of whatever nationality, not only those who fight for England, or France, or Belgium, but to those who are fighting against us. Listen—these are his words."

Commandant Beaumont then read us the following extract from Lloyd George's speech, beautifully translated into

French:

Far above the squalor and the mud, so high in the firmament as to be invisible from the earth, they fight out the eternal issues of right and wrong. Their daily and nightly struggles are like Miltonic conflicts between winged hosts. They fight high and low. They skim like armed swallows along the front, attacking men in their flights armed with rifle and machine gun. They scatter infantry on the march; they destroy convoys; they wreck trains. Every flight is a romance, every record an epic. They are the knighthood of this war, without fear and without reproach; and they recall the legendary days of chivalry, not merely by the daring of their exploits, but by the nobility of their spirit.

"Messieurs, if you will allow me to say so, that is true. You *do* comprise the knighthood of this war, not because you differ from the men in other branches of service, but merely because the peculiar conditions of Aviation have made it possible for you still to be individuals, dependent upon your own resources of skill and daring. For you war still has an element of romance. It is often a man-to-man adventure with fortune favouring the better pilot. I congratulate you. I take pride in your exploits. I am proud to be your chief. It is to you and to others like you that France owes her supremacy in the air——"

At that moment Commandant Beaumont was interrupted by an orderly, who made his way through the crowd, saluted apologetically, and presented him with a slip of paper. The commandant read it and looked up with an ironic grin.

"Messieurs, truth compels me to add to what I was just saying the words, 'by day.' This message, received by telephone from our front lines, informs me that a large formation of Gothas are headed this way. They probably mean to bomb Châlons, but it is likely that they will present their compliments to us on the way. Perhaps they are annoyed because we littered their front with paper this afternoon. However that may be, let us now scatter like rabbits to our holes!"

It was a frosty night, windless and clear. There was no moon, but the stars glittered with such brilliancy that they seemed to be doing their utmost to light the Germans on their way. We dispersed to our various barracks to wait there in comfort until it should be necessary to seek the cold but more adequate protection of a trench. There were four machine-gun pits scattered about the aerodrome, and these were always manned at times of an expected raid, in case enemy planes came low enough to be fired at from the ground. The one near our barrack was in charge of Sergeant Durand, our squadron armourer, and Cartier, my chief mechanic. Both men were already at their posts when Golasse and I walked down that way. Du Marmier, Fontana, Langlois, and several other pilots were standing about waiting for what might happen. The pit was a circular excavation five feet deep, with a boss of earth in the centre on which the gun was mounted. We walked up and down near by, stamping our feet and beating our arms against our bodies.

"I wonder why it is," said Du Marmier, "that there hasn't been more development in night pursuit. Here we are, all of us single-seater pilots, on the ground and waiting to be bombed! Personally, I'd a heap rather they sent us up to give the Boches a run for their money."

"A lot of good that would do," Langlois replied. Ever flown at night?"

"No."

"Well, if you had you'd know its a hopeless job looking for another plane in the dark. I was with a night-bombing squadron in 1916, before I transferred to *chasse.* We used to start off together, in formation, but many a time we'd lose each other and go on alone to our objective. It didn't matter, of course, so long as we got there and dropped our eggs where we were supposed to drop them. Hostile planes have a mighty slim chance of doing each other any damage by night."

"I've got a friend in Spad 476," said Fontana. "His Group is at St.-Pol. and he tells me they've been experimenting with night pursuit up there. It's been a fizzle so far."

"They'll develop it, very likely, if the war lasts long enough. Well, let 'em. As far as I'm concerned, I can find all the Boches I want in the daytime."

"Same here."

"Wish the blighters would come if they *are* coming. I want to go to bed."

"Listen! Hear anything?"

"No."

"What's wrong with your ears, man. They're coming all right!"

"Look! There go the German rockets up Sommepy way! That's to show them where the Châlons road crosses the lines."

"You're right! One on each side—a regular fiery gateway. They can't miss that."

"*Les salauds!* Listen to 'em now! There must be at least a dozen!"

The resonant chime of motors was becoming more and more distinct. The sound resembled the humming of telegraph wires on a cold winter night except that it was of much deeper quality. Durand and Cartier jumped down into their gun pit again. The rest of us edged toward our near-by trench and waited just outside to see what would happen. The sound of motors was almost directly overhead now. It seemed as though we must be able to see them against the starry sky, but they were very high up and we strained our eyes in vain. Soon they had passed, and a moment or two later we heard the Châlons anti-aircraft defences begin their bombardment, the bursting shells winking like swarms of fireflies. They made such a racket and we were so interested in watching the pyrotechnics that we failed to hear the engines of a second flock of Gothas closely following the first. We were informed of their nearness by the truly diabolical crescendo screech of a falling bomb. We fell into our trench without knowing how we got there, and at the same instant came a rending explosion followed by a concussion that seemed to burst my eardrums. Others followed it in quick succession. Then the stars seemed to withdraw and vanish; they were blotted out by a red glare that lighted up the whole field. One of the hangars of Spad 614 had been hit and was soon a mass of mounting flame.

The Gothas had their target beautifully lighted for them now, but luckily they had dropped most of their bombs. They loosed a few more without making a hit. Then they swept back and forth across the field, machine-gunning barracks and hangars. Their fire was hotly replied to from the machine-gun pits, fountains of tracer and incendiary bullets rising into the air. I don't know how long the battle lasted; five minutes, perhaps, or it may have been ten. I was too excited to think of time. Once we thought it was over and were rushing from all sides of the field toward the burning hangar when we heard the sound of motors once more and dove for our trenches again. The planes that now appeared were probably those returning from the raid on Châlons. Seeing our brightly lighted field, they turned aside to spray us with bullets on their way homeward. One of them circled so low over the field that we could see his black crosses and the great spread of his wings. He made three complete turns of the aerodrome, spraying everything in sight and receiving the concentrated fire from all four gun pits. He was making a fourth circuit and was directly over us when we saw a spurt of flame from his machine that threw it into lurid silhouette.

"By God, he's hit!" Golasse shouted. "Cartier's got him!"

The plane turned off, a jagged ribbon of flame flapping behind it, and disappeared behind a hangar. We scrambled out of our trench and ran in that direction. The Gotha was not more than five hundred feet up. Of a sudden we saw it nose down and crash to earth not half a mile away.

Golasse, McKail, and I were the first to reach the spot, an open field near a ruined farmhouse. By the time we arrived the Gotha was only a confused mass of metal parts lapped round with the fierce flames of burning gasoline and castor oil, a fitting funeral pyre for the three airmen. There was nothing we could do. It was impossible to approach that furnace, and I for one had no desire to approach it. Within ten minutes most of the pilots of both Groups were there, standing silently in a wide circle around the burning plane.

Golasse took my arm.

"Who wouldn't be an aviator!" he remarked dryly.

The weather on Christmas Day was just what it should have been. The sky was overcast at a great height, the ground covered with snow, and the silence was that of the sea on a grey windless day. I awoke early, dressed, and went for a walk down the Châlons road. The world was pure white except for the spot where one of the hangars of Spad 614 had stood. The hangar had been completely destroyed, with the six Spads housed there. Fifteen bombs were dropped by the Gothas, but the others had fallen in the fields, and, for all the hundreds of rounds of machine-gun bullets fired into the barracks, no one had been hit.

The Châlons road was all but empty. Only a few trucks passed, going down from the lines. I met a group of half a dozen infantrymen on foot, straggling boisterously along northward. They were carrying all their equipment and had parcels of various sorts hung all over them. They stopped to wish me an ironic Merry Christmas and to ask how long I thought the war would last. They had been on leave and were rejoining their battalion at Suippes, a wretched little village in ruins, three or four kilometres behind the front-line trenches.

"How's that for luck, Corporal?" one of them said. "Having to go back to that hell hole on Christmas Day?"

"They might have sent a truck down to fetch us from Châlons," another remarked.

"*Sacré nom de Papa Noël!* That's what I call rubbing it in with salt! Let's all have another drink."

They brought forth water bottles filled with cognac and

insisted on my having a nip with them. Then they proceeded on their way, a forlorn and lonely little group plodding through the slushy snow, but making the best of their hard luck as soldiers always do.

Felix was putting breakfast on the table when I returned to barracks—a breakfast of ham and eggs, freshly baked bread, plenty of butter, pancakes, and *café au lait*. We all tucked in with a will, even more heartily than usual, for there was to be nothing more till evening, when we were to have our Christmas dinner. While we were eating, Carnot, the orderly who posted patrols, stuck his head in at the door.

"Merry Christmas!" he said with a grin.

"What do *you* want, Kill-Joy?" asked Du Marmier. "What's the bad news now?"

"Big review this afternoon at two-thirty. All the heroes are going to be decorated by General Gouraud."

"That lets me out," said Masson, "unless I knock down a Boche within three hours."

"Who's Papa Gouraud going to kiss?"

"Oh, quite a lot of you. Here's the list; you can read it for yourselves. But this is no private show for airmen. There's a crowd of infantry to be decorated as well."

"Who's in it besides us?"

"Don't ask me. All I know is that before they pass out the medals General Gouraud's going to review a squadron of cavalry and the Forty-second Infantry Brigade."

"Good Lord! The whole Brigade? That *will* be a show!"

"Read the list, Fontana. Who draw the lucky numbers?"

Fontana glanced hastily over the paper. "Fifteen pilots from Group 31. That's not so bad! Here you are: Captain René Clermont, Spad 597; Lieutenant Jacques de Chalais, Spad 597; Sergeant Georges Daviot, Spad 614; Adjutant Henri Durmont, Spad 609; Maréchal de Logis Charles Fouquet, Spad 602 . . ." He read on down the list. Gordon's name was there, and Golasse's, and Tommy Slater's, of course. We were all particularly pleased to find that Sergeant Durand and Cartier were to be cited for the Gotha shot down the night of the bombardment. There had been some question as to which gun got him, although all of us Spad 597 pilots were sure that Cartier's had. When Fontana read out my name Du Marmier jumped up and slapped me on the back.

"*Épatant*, Selden! Good for you, old boy!"

"That's for your Rumpler."

"*Vive les cent mille chemises! Vive les pyjamas!*" shouted Golasse. "I'll have to add some more verses to that song of mine."

They jollied me again about my pyjama victory, but it warmed my heart to see how pleased they were. While we were talking over the list we heard the roar of a motor and rushed to the door to see who could be going up on Christmas morning. A lone Spad was taking off from the other side of the field. It zoomed over our roof and as it turned we saw

Tommy Slater's tombstone insignia.

"Well, I'll be damned!" said Masson. "Do you suppose he's going out to the lines?"

"I heard him say he might," I replied.

Golasse shook his head. "Catch me going out on Christmas Day, when I don't have to!" he said. "That boy's asking for it!"

"Anybody got any money they want to lose?" asked Fontana. "I'll give odds, three to two, that he doesn't even see a Eoche."

"Take you for a hundred francs," said Volokoff. "And I've got a thousand more that says he'll not only see one, but knock him down. Even money."

"I'll take a hundred of that!"

"I'll take fifty!"

"So will I!"

Every pilot in the mess who had any money was eager to bet against Volokoff, who met all comers to his last franc. I was appointed stakeholder and registered the bets, and the strange part of it was that I had no more than finished the job and settled down with a book by the stove when Flingot burst into the room.

"Somebody's got a Boche!" he announced. "The infantry's just phoned. Right over the lines! It's bound to be Slater; he's the only man up this morning."

Volokoff, Golasse, and I ploughed our way through the

snow to the hangars of 602. We had no more than crossed the field when we heard Slater coming in. We couldn't see him at first, for he was flying low down the road from Suippes; then he appeared over the barracks at the far end of the aerodrome, leveled off, and landed in a dust of powdery snow. Captain St. Cyr, the C.O. of Spad 602, Captain Clermont, and several pilots from Slater's squadron were awaiting him at the hangars.

"You've had a scrap, Slater?" his captain asked.

"Yes, sir."

"Over Navarin?"

"Yes, sir. I happened to meet one of those new Pfalzes just as I was crossing the lines. I went over to have a look at him and . . ."

The captain smiled, rather grimly I thought, and held up his hand. "I know that look of yours! Well, you got him. The infantry saw him crash. He's *homologué*."

"I supposed he would be. It was right over the lines."

As usual, Slater was neither excited nor elated. He jumped down from his Spad, removed his flying clothes, and carried them to his locker in the hangar. Captain St. Cyr looked after him with an expression half ironical, half puzzled. He turned to Captain Clermont.

"*Quel type!*" he said. "Did you hear him sing that old German song at the bar the other evening? An angelic-looking child! Peace on earth, good will toward men, eh?"

Captain Clermont nodded. "French Aviation could do with a few more angels like young Slater," he replied. "We'll be needing them in the spring."

At one-thirty everything was in readiness for the *prise d'armes*. The pilots had furbished up their best uniforms and polished boots and buttons. The mechanics had been at work all morning grooming Spads and Bréguets. The planes of the Thirty-fifth Day-Bombing Group were drawn up in a long line on one side of the field and those of our Group on the other. General Gouraud and his staff arrived in two limousines and were met by the commanding officers of the two Groups. Immediately afterward they reviewed the flying personnel. Each pilot stood at attention in front of his plane, and the mechanics of the various squadrons were arranged in platoons to the right and left. Events had been timed to the minute. As soon as the Aviation review was over the troops of the Forty-second Infantry Brigade began to arrive.

They came up the Châlons road, turned in at the aerodrome, formed columns of platoons, and marched in this order down the length of the field, going out at the eastern end. At their head came the squadron of cavalry, magnificent-looking men on magnificent horses. In advance were eight trumpeters who rode abreast. They carried long slender trumpets which they held with their right hands, resting them upright against their thighs. When they had reached the middle of the field opposite General Gouraud, they tossed their trumpets in the air with one movement, caught them, brandished them, and put them to their lips. I wish I knew the name of the call they played. It haunts me to this day, and I can feel my blood tingle at the thought of it.

The infantry followed with their tattered battle flags, the men marching in beautiful alignment. It was a splendid sight, and still more stirring to hear the music of their bands crashing out on the crisp winter air. *Sidi Ibrahim*, the *Marseillaise, Sambre et Meuse, Chant de départ*—they were all played that afternoon while we stood in the snow forgetting how cold we were, forgetting everything but the splendour and romance of war.

At the conclusion of the review the men to be decorated took places in a line six paces in advance of the others. We were arranged in alphabetical order for convenience in reading the citations. A staff captain with a sheaf of papers stood in front of us and read out the words of praise hurriedly, in a rather bored voice, as though he had performed this duty innumerable times. As General Gouraud had only one arm, the task of pinning the decorations to the pilots' tunics devolved upon another staff officer. The General then kissed the man on both cheeks. He had something to say to each of us, and, unlike his staff captain, there was nothing bored or perfunctory in his manner. He gave the appearance of being—and indeed, I think he was—genuinely interested in each man and what he had done to win his decoration, Tommy Slater stood next to me, looking very cold and pinched and miserable. He had piled up victories so fast that he received three citations at once, one of which conferred the Médaille Militaire. While they were being read, General Gouraud regarded him with an expression of interest. He turned to Commandant Beaumont.

"So this is the young man who fights Germans on Christmas Day? That's the kind we need! No holidays in this war—we can't afford them."

I can still feel the friendly pressure of his hand as he laid it on my shoulder.

"What! Another American? And you chased your German all that way? That's the spirit, my boy!"

He went quickly down the line, and a moment later we were dismissed. I went over to shake hands with Cartier and Sergeant Durand. They had each received a Croix de Guerre with palm for the Gotha they had shot down on the night of the bombardment.

"Good for you, Cartier!"

He smiled his dry little smile and glanced down his nose at the decoration on his tunic.

"It will please the old woman," he said.

That is as much of Cartier's family history as I ever learned.

XII

AT LUNÉVILLE

EARLY in January, Combat Group 31 received orders to move to Lunéville, in Lorraine. Down from a morning patrol with Fontana and Volokoff, I found an excited crowd of pilots in the bar, discussing the news and rejoicing at the prospect of a change. Lieutenant de Chalais beckoned to me.

"Good news!" he announced. "We're off for Lorraine this afternoon! Yes, Lunéville. Our field will be the parade ground right in town; we'll have cosy billets, and restaurants, and cafés to loaf in between patrols. I know that sector—you never see a Boche down there, and if you do run into one, he's not at all *méchant*."

"That sounds good," Fontana remarked; "so they're going to give us a rest, eh?"

"A rest!" muttered Golasse darkly at a near-by table, munching bread and drinking red wine. "Yes, the kind of a rest an ox gets when he's fattening for the butcher! Enjoy Lunéville while you can, boys! You won't be there when the spring attacks begin!"

Fontana seated himself at Golasse's table, fumbled in his

pockets, produced a clasp knife and a spud of garlic, and shouted to the barman to bring a glass. Then, without waiting for an invitation, he whittled off a chunk of bread, filled his glass, and proceeded with great gusto to eat and drink. He never flew over the lines without a pocketful of garlic, and it was well known that he had instructed his parents in Aries, in case he was taken prisoner, to start an unfailing supply of the odorous herb through the Red Cross in Switzerland.

Golasse wrinkled his nose and edged his chair away. "I dont mind your eating my bread and drinking my *pinard*," he said, "but to scoff up garlic as a cow eats grass—Whew! You go too far!"

"I say, Selden!" the lieutenant called. "Better go and pack up—we're all ready. The cars'll push off in less than an hour."

The mobility of the Combat Groups was marvellous. Our orders had only arrived an hour before, but many of the trucks were already packed and waiting for the word to start. AH hands were in high spirits at the prospect of life in a town. I found McKail stowing his belongings in his duffle bag, while old Felix lent a hand. He had a small bag of toilet things to carry in his Spad, and beside it, on his cot, I saw a volume of Captain Cook's *Voyages*. I carried nothing in my plane but a toothbrush, a cake of soap, and a roll of bills against emergencies.

Presently the trucks and cars of the Group rolled away in squadron convoys. Half a dozen mechanics, Cartier among them, stayed behind to start up the Spads, and a fast touring car waited to take them on when he had left. Lunch in the dismantled bar was like a big picnic of sixty men, all happy as schoolboys. Major Beaumont was in flying clothes. He was a pilot now, and he munched bread and sausage and drank red wine and cracked jokes like one of us, as at heart he was. At last he stepped out for a look at the sky, blue and almost cloudless.

"*En l'air mes enfants!*" he ordered. "Full throttle for the Promised Land! Like Moses, I shall lead you there!"

He was the first to take off, and, circling high over the field while squadron after squadron took the air, he put his old Spad through her paces of spins and loops. Then, tail up, he headed off to the south-east. We had no orders to fly in formation, but McKail and I had agreed to make the journey together.

We travelled for just an hour at five thousand feet, side by side with motors reduced—past our old field at Sénard, well to the north of us, past the foot of the St.-Mihiel Salient, over the walled town of Toul, over Nancy and the slag heaps of St.-Nicolas, and down the Meurthe to Lunéville. There was no mistaking the field, the parade ground of a garrison town. Spad after Spad was landing below us and taxiing to the hangars along the western side. We found Golasse waiting for us on the ground. He seized my arm, led me around the hangar, and pointed to the street, twenty yards away, where a crowd of women, children, and men in civilian clothes lined the fence watching the Spads land.

"Pinch me!" exclaimed Golasse. "Am I dreaming, or are those pretty girls real? Is there a war? Is this the Zone des Armées? Look at those kids with their fat pink cheeks!"

Captain Clermont smiled at Golasse's outburst.

"All real," he remarked. "As the major said, this is the Promised Land! And to prove it, here's the address of your billet. Volokoff, Golasse, Selden, McKail—27 Rue Jeanne d'Arc. Three rooms, it's marked."

Those days in Lorraine were the pleasantest I ever spent at the front. The sector, with the Vosges Mountains to the south, was one of great beauty from the air; the Germans, as de Chalais had said, were few and not *méchant*, and our occasional meetings with the enemy were just enough to give zest to life.

The war in Lorraine, as Golasse had remarked, was a *guerre de luxe*. Our billets, three rooms on the second story of a comfortable old-fashioned house, were almost indecently luxurious after barrack life. We had two bedrooms, each provided with a pair of great feather beds, much appreciated on those winter nights, and a big sunny living room, with a tiled stove and plenty of easy-chairs. Our host was a kindly, grey-bearded manufacturer, and he and Mme. Simonet spoiled us as if we had been so many prodigal sons. Old Felix came every day to make beds and polish boots, and the squadron messes were broken up, for we breakfasted in billets and lunched and dined in the restaurants of the town. From the Swiss frontier to Pont-à-Mousson, the war had settled down to a quiet state of siege, disturbed only by rumours of German attacks to come in the spring, and our squadron was required to furnish only two patrols a day—morning and afternoon. Two hours in the air out of each twenty-four was the most any pilot had to put in, and the weather was so bad that we were sometimes on the ground for three days at a stretch. Golasse revelled in the change and hoped the war would end before we left Lunéville. Volokoff and McKail, who had struck up an oddly matched friendship, had an orgy of reading and talk about books. The French pilots, after three years in the trenches and in the air, made no bones about taking it easy now. On this quiet front, with patrols a mere matter of routine, the old hands never flew unless ordered to; they were saving themselves for the hard fighting of the spring. But Slater, Forbes, McKail, and I were new to war and to the air, and the four of us made many a voluntary patrol.

Slater, whose nine official victories had brought him decorations and the rank of *adjutant*, was already something of a celebrity, and his Spad with its sinister insignia led our patrols. His name appeared often in the Paris newspapers of those days; items on the second page of *Le Temps: L'Adjudant Slater a abattu son huitième*, or *Slater, l'as américain, abat un biplace en flames.* Correspondents of the Press at home—

Americans in civilian clothes and horn-rimmed glasses—came to interview him at the front, and he answered their questions laconically. Not the least of Slater's oddities of character was his indifference to promotion and decorations and his increasing fame. But his exploits cost him the obscurity he seemed to crave.

A patrol with Slater was an education for me. If Germans were to be found in the sector he was sure to find them. He seemed to smell them out like a bloodhound; but once the enemy was in sight he was cool and wary, taking advantage of the sun, of altitude, and of the clouds. Then, with all the odds in his favour, he went in to kill, and his fire was so uncannily accurate that more often than not one short burst was enough. As Captain St. Cyr had remarked, Slater did not fight with Germans—he assassinated them. He was a killer, cool and skilful at his trade. But even Slater often failed to flush a German on that quiet Lorraine front, and when we did sight an enemy plane one afternoon I fancy that his bottled-up impatience was responsible for getting me into one of the most thrilling scrapes of my life.

It was a cloudless day for once, though bitter cold, and just after lunch Slater and McKail and Gordon and I took off for a turn over the lines, hoping that the good weather might have encouraged the enemy to do the same. As we climbed toward the front, over the Forest of Parroy, we saw, very high and remote against the blue, the white dots of French anti-aircraft fire springing out. A German plane had crossed the lines at nearly twenty thousand feet, and presently, as we turned, I caught a glimpse of it, weaving serenely in and out of the tracery of smoke.

Tommy turned north, then west, his Spad climbing with full throttle, so fast that I had difficulty in keeping my pace, above him and to the left. But the German's mission was done, or perhaps the pilot had sighted us; at any rate, still at an immense height, he turned back for his own lines. The French guns ceased firing. The German was so far above us and flying east so swiftly that Slater gave the signal to drop the pursuit. We were just under four thousand metres and not far behind our lines. I could see the trenches emerging on either side of the Forest of Parroy, and five or six miles farther, *chez Boche*, the fat succulent shapes of the German observation balloons. Three of them were in sight—one directly in front of us. It floated motionless on the still air at about four thousand feet, a corpulent yellow creature with a distended abdomen, and it had an irritating look of self-satisfaction and placid insolence.

I was thinking that if I had put some incendiaries in my machine-gun belt this would be a fine chance to puncture its fat belly and set it on fire, when I noticed that Slater's Spad had disappeared. Then I saw him, far below, diving away toward the Marine-Rhine Canal. We followed him down—a thousand, two thousand, three thousand metres. He pulled up not more than two thousand feet over the canal and crossed the lines with full throttle, heading straight for the Gisselfingen balloon. But we didn't take the Germans by surprise.

The soldiers had so little to do on that quiet front that I suppose they welcomed a diversion of any sort. As the four Spads roared over their trenches, in range of anything bigger than a pistol, it seemed to me that the whole German army began to take pot shots at us. The noise of machine guns was like that of riveting machines on Broadway, faintly heard. I pulled in my neck like a turtle and tried to sit in the smallest possible space; but the vitals of a Spad—the pilot's body, the engine, and the gasoline tank—make a tiny target moving at one hundred and thirty miles an hour. Glancing ahead, I saw that they were pulling down the balloon at an astonishing speed. It was at our level now, but we were very close. Little grey figures were running about on the ground, aimlessly, like disturbed ants. Slater, thirty yards ahead of me, let go a long burst and zoomed up in a climbing turn. I had no incendiaries, but I thought in my innocence that a tracer might set the fat thing on fire, so I let fly and banked, while Gordon and McKail swept past me to fire in turn. But the yellow air beast still fled toward its keepers below, seemingly unharmed. From the basket beneath the bulging abdomen one man and then another leaped off into space, to float down like a pair of beetles attached to toy parachutes. I was turning for another burst when Slater's Spad flashed past me in a steep dive, spurting fire and smoke. This time the incendiaries did their work.

It was over in an instant—a blinding flash of fire and a puff of thick smoke that hung in the air like the father of all shrapnel bursts. The explosion was so close that my Spad staggered at the blast. Slater had turned abruptly, diving off to one side after a parachute. I heard a faint stutter of his gun and knew that he had probably killed the observer, floating down helpless to shoot back. But I had other things to think of at that moment, for the machine guns were going like mad on the ground, and it seemed incredible that my Spad could escape their storm of fire. And, beside the guns, the Germans were treating us to a display of weird fireworks. Dazzling balls, like beads on a string—"flaming onions," I think the British called them, came whizzing up, and things that looked like what we used to call "flowerpots" on the Fourth of July. Under other circumstances I might have found them interesting, but I knew they were being sent up for something more than our entertainment, and they had a very evil look. Then I spied a group of Germans about a machine gun in a shallow pit, and nosed down for a long and satisfying burst at them.

I don't know whether my bullets hit any of them, for my finger was still on the trigger when I heard a gun going behind me in the air, and the *flac-flac-flac* of bullets going through the lower left wing of my Spad. I banked sharply, twisting my neck. There, sitting on my tail, was a small silvery German ship. It was just pulling out of a dive to keep above me. I had time to see a pair of superb black crosses on the upper plane, and Gordon's Spad flash past me, with another Pfalz on his tail. We had been attacked by a patrol of four Pfalz scouts, with every advantage of altitude and surprise.

My adversary was my master from the start, a pilot who seemed to know every trick of the trade and never gave me a chance to turn on him. I banked, twisted, and tried to climb, but he was always above me and just behind, and I had all I could do to keep out of his line of fire. Twice he lined his sights on me for bursts that came very close, and I was beginning to wonder if I should ever be able to shake him off. The Germans on the ground had ceased firing, of course, and we must have given them a rare show: eight single-seaters within a few hundred yards of the ground, milling in the closest kind of dog fight. Then, glancing back warily as I made a vertical bank to the left, I saw a Pfalz whiz past me, earthward, followed at a more leisurely pace by one of its own wings. Above, and upside down in an Immelmann, I had a glimpse of a Spad with tombstones on the wing, and the next moment my pursuer was nowhere to be seen. I pulled up instinctively to take altitude, and gazing this way and that, while the gunners opened up on me once more, I caught sight of two Spads flying east at full speed in hot pursuit of a single German plane. As I followed, nose down and motor wide open, three little groups of Germans were sprinting toward the wrecks of as many planes, all within a few hundred yards.

I soon caught up with the Spads, thanks to my advantage of altitude. I saw tombstones and a pair of big red F's. McKail was missing. Slater and Forbes had driven the Pfalz down till it was skimming the treetops, but as I ranged alongside and turned my head for a hasty glance at Slater, I saw him lean forward with a wooden mallet in his hand, hammering methodically at the crank handle of his jammed gun. At that moment Gordon gave the German a short burst, but the Pfalz was banking and the tracers went behind its tail. The Boche zoomed over a clump of trees, still turning to the north, and I got him in my sights for an instant. But I did not allow enough for the angle, and, instead of centering on the cockpit, I saw my tracers pouring into his wing. Working at his gun, Slater had given his Spad her head; he was now well above us and behind.

Fields, clumps of trees, and scattered houses streamed past beneath us at such a pace that the details of landscape were blurred. I was conscious of a stir of men running on the ground and of a faint fitful hammering of machine guns. One gunner, close to the Lake of Rohr-bach, sprayed me with bullets that came murderously close. Now the long narrow lake was just ahead, and at one side of it I saw a German aerodrome bordered with tiny hangars, camouflaged in green and brown, and barely large enough to house a pair of Pfalz scouts. Grey-clad figures sprinted for their gun pits and others drove into the hangars, and still others, working at top speed, began to push little silvery ships through the doorways and crank them up. My eyes took this scene in at a glance as I fired a burst at our quarry and missed, for the fifth or sixth time. I knew that the German plane must be riddled with bullets, but Gordon had no better luck than I, and now the Pfalz was roaring in over the trees to land on his own field. The pilot, extraordinarily cool and clever, though taken at a fatal disadvantage and pursued by ships faster than his own, had saved himself so far by a series of brusque manœuvres that offered us nothing but angling shots. But his doublings back and forth had given Slater time to clear his gun and to catch up.

As the Pfalz nosed down for the last time, to land, Tommy's Spad came plunging down like a man-o'-war hawk, full motor, and gun going in a long crackling burst. The range was a good two hundred yards, but the Pfalz seemed to wilt in the air—nosed up, slipped off on a wing, and crashed with a tremendous impact on the field. I let go at a group of men about a pilot who was climbing into the cockpit of his plane, and saw them scatter like young quail. Slater dove on one of the machine-gun pits and silenced its gun in two short bursts. Gordon was shooting up everything in sight—hangars, planes, and every man that showed himself. Then all three of us, as if at a prearranged signal, dove simultaneously on the remaining gun emplacement—a wide shallow pit with a pair of guns mounted on a central mound. Their hammering ceased, two of the men sank down, and the third began crawling toward a zigzag trench near by. Three little Pfalz planes stood before the hangars with propellers idling, and we gave them a parting spray of bullets as we turned for the lines.

We headed straight and fast for Lunéville. The wings of my Spad were riddled, but she was going strong. Gordon was on my right, and as we passed south of Gisselfingen his Spad lost speed and nosed down over a wide field. I saw him motion us to go on. I banked to watch him; we were too low for the anti-aircraft batteries, and at the moment only one machine gun was firing at us. Gordon sailed down, levelled over the grass, and landed perfectly, and I saw with mingled hope and despair that his propeller still turned. A dozen Germans rushed toward him from the edge of a little wood. Slater and I went into action together and the Germans lost their enthusiasm for capturing an Allied plane, but other guns were getting the range now, and infantrymen were potting at us with Mausers. The situation was getting too hot for comfort; I fancy that, in another minute or two, one or both of us would have been brought down.

But Gordon's Spad was under way now, moving with increasing swiftness over the grass. I found myself shouting like a madman as he took the air and zoomed over a line of trees at the far end of the field. Slater and I fell in behind him, crossed the lines so low that we got nothing but a few wild bursts of machine-gun fire, and sailed over the Forest of Parroy to land in Lunéville. Fontana still sat where I had left him, in the sunny lee of a hangar, reading an old copy of *Le Rire*.

"What!" he said. "Back already?"

We had been an hour and twenty minutes absent from the aerodrome.

The French Air Service had a slang phrase, *explication des coups*, translatable with the utmost precision by our own expression, "ground flying." Every squadron mess had a conspicuous sign on the wall, "*Défense d'expliquer les coups!*" but in the bar the pilots read, "Ground Flying Permitted here."

When we had taxied our Spads to the hangars that afternoon, there followed what I can only describe as an orgy of excited talk. A crowd of civilians, attracted by the mechanics and pilots clustered about our machines, lined the fence, welcoming any diversion in the monotony of their war-time lives. As I climbed stiffly down among the men crowded about my plane, Captain Clermont was the first one to speak.

"Where's McKail?" he asked. Slater, who was the first to land, was standing close by.

"Shot down," he answered for me, laconically.

"I saw him land," said Gordon, "close to the Gisselfingen balloon. I don't believe he was badly hurt, for he landed well and set fire to his plane."

"So you were the balloon-burners!" exclaimed the captain. "They telephoned half an hour ago that it had been shot down."

"Slater got it," I said.

"And three Albatros," added Gordon.

Tommy gave him a wan little smile. "What about *your* Albatros?" he said. "He splashed right by one of the gun pits."

Gordon's captain had arrived by now. "Four Albatros," he exclaimed, "and a balloon! Splendid work—but I'm afraid we can never get you official credit for the planes. They could see the balloon, of course, miles away."

"And we shot up an aerodrome," Gordon told him. "I had to land in Germany on the way back. They nicked the top of my tank; I couldn't keep the pressure up, and the valve of the auxiliary tank was stuck. I landed, managed to keep my motor turning, and got the valve open at last. Thought I was a goner for a minute or two; if Selden and Slater hadn't driven off the German infantry, I'd be a prisoner now."

I turned to Slater. "And if you hadn't knocked that Boche off my tail," I said, "I'd be something worse than a prisoner—dead, very likely. He was bad medicine!"

Oblivious of the conversation, Cartier had been making. a hasty examination of my Spad. He touched my arm. "You're in luck," he told me. "In theory our *coucou* is incapable of flight! It will have to be scrapped. How you got back is more than I know."

"What's that?" asked Captain Clermont. "Scrapped, you say?"

"*Oui, mon capitaine*"

"In that case, Selden," said the CO. briskly, "I'll send you off to Le Bourget for a new one. You can leave to-morrow, and how about forty-eight hours in Paris?"

I felt depressed that evening as we sat around the stove in our comfortable living room, and Volokoff seemed gloomier than usual. He missed McKail, and so did I, but Gordon had insisted that the little chap could not be seriously hurt. His motor had been put out of commission, he thought, for he had glided down and made a beautiful landing close to a group of Germans. What was more, he had set his plane on fire. Golasse looked on the bright side, for McKail, at least.

"He's a prisoner, and probably the luckiest one of the bunch. At any rate, he'll live to tell his children yarns about the war."

There was a knock at the door; Gordon and Tommy Slater entered.

"I hear you're going to Paris?" said Slater. "Will you do me a favour? Bring me a couple of pairs of Meyrowitz goggles—here's an old pair to give them the size."

"Sure! What about you, Gordon? Anything you want?"

"No, thanks. But give the Héraults my regards."

Slater was turning to leave. "Excuse me if I run along.

I'm sleepy, and I'm going to take a turn over the lines at daybreak."

Gordon stretched himself out in McKail's empty chair, and Volokoff poked the fire. Golasse was chuckling over some joke in the *Vie Parisienne.*

"I suppose you'll soon be transferring to the American Army," Gordon remarked to me. "Are you glad?"

"Yes, in a way. I'd rather fight in our uniform, and Doc Gros says I'll have a good chance of being sent back to the Squadron. Of course, there's always the risk of being sent to teach in a flying school."

"That's why I didn't accept; I'd hate to leave our outfit, and Captain St. Cyr's a fine chap. Did I tell you that he's going to make Tommy and me lieutenants as soon as the papers go through?"

"Good work! You fellows deserve it!"

"Of course, I'd rather be in the American Army, too. But St. Cyr's been so decent, and I'm' so afraid of being sent back to instruct that I'll stay where I am. When they send for you, do your damnedest to get back to the Group!"

"Trust me! Doc Gros promised to pull every wire he could."

Gordon fell silent; the prospect of separation depressed us both.

"Heard from your uncle lately?" he asked, after a time.

"Not for a month or so."

"I'm keen to see what he says. Think he'll let me in?"

"I'm sure of it!"

"Funny what a grip that idea has taken on me! Do you know, Charlie, if it weren't for that, I shouldn't care a hang whether I got through the war or not!"

He stood up to say good night; Golasse was turning in, and Volokoff was deep in the *Voyages* of Captain Cook—a legacy from Harvey McKail. I stifled a yawn as I opened the door of the bedroom of which I was now the sole occupant.

I was awakened by a steady knocking at a near-by door, and the voice of old Felix. He was calling Golasse and Volokoff.

"Gentlemen! Gentlemen! The captain wants you at once! There's a German plane headed directly for our field!"

I heard growling replies; a moment later the door opened and slammed, and there was a sound of slippered feet running down the stairs. My Spad was out of com^ mission, of course, but I sprang out of bed, pulled on uniform and boots, and sprinted for the field. German planes were rare on our side of the lines.

The sun was half an hour up and the morning was bitterly cold. The mechanics, taken by surprise, had trouble in getting the motors started. They were cranking and cursing and casting glances aloft, toward a pattern of white shell bursts in the sky. Golasse, in his cockpit, was trying to make his coughing motor take hold, swearing in his vehement picturesque way. The enemy plane, a tiny silver Pfalz, was now directly overhead at about three thousand metres. I heard Captain Clermont shout, "Look! He's dropping something! Wait! Don't take off! It's a message!"

A tiny object with a long fluttering streamer attached had been dropped from the Pfalz. The German turned, with the air of having finished his job, and headed back for his own lines.

The message from the enemy struck the field about two hundred yards away. A dozen mechanics raced for it, and the winner came puffing back with his prize to Major Beaumont, who stood with a group of officers. It was nothing but three or four yards of coarse white cloth, wrapped about a stone, and containing a brief typed note in French. We were sure that it came from the Pfalz Group opposite us.

"Corporal Harvey McKail," the major read aloud to his circle of eager listeners, "was forced to land in our lines while attacking the Gisselfingen balloon yesterday. He is slightly wounded by machine-gun fire."

The Great War was waged with a relentless savagery unprecedented in the history of the white race. Most of the amenities which distinguish the fighting of human beings from that of beasts were cast aside, but among airmen a spark of traditional chivalry toward a gallant foe was preserved. Notes such as the German pilot dropped that morning were freely exchanged, in a spirit of humanity which kept alive one's faith in mankind at a time when it was ebbing low. Not a man on the field would have taken off—unless ordered to—after the Pfalz, returning from its kindly mission; but, unfortunately for the German, Slater had gotten away before sunrise, and was now on his way back from a turn over the lines south of Baccarat. He had a habit of going out at dawn for a solitary patrol at very high altitudes. On that morning he was trying out a new Spad, the first 220 h.-p. to reach our Group. It was very fast, though a little awkward in manœuvre, and it mounted two guns.

The anti-aircraft gunners, of course, knew nothing except that an enemy plane was overhead, and they continued their shelling as the Pfalz made its way back toward the lines. Glancing up a moment later, I saw that the white bursts had ceased. The captain gave an exclamation of dismay. "There's a Spad I If it's Slater, that Boche pilot's out of luck!"

High above the Pfalz I saw a darker speck in the sky plunging down like a meteor. It seemed to overtake the German plane in a flash; for a minute, perhaps, the two single-seaters turned this way and that, with the Spad always above. Then, in plain view of the scores of spectators on the field, the German ship began to fall—a spin, a steep dive, a "falling leaf," and another spin. It disappeared over the trees in the direction of Jolivet. Forbes swore in disgust.

"What a damned shame! Tommy didn't know what he was doing here, of course. The poor devil!"

"Yes, but if he had," Golasse put in, "he'd have shot him

down just the same."

Slater came in to land, approaching the field nose down, at tremendous speed. He roared in over our heads before the wind, lower and lower until his wheels almost brushed the withered grass. Then, with the wind screaming through his struts at a hundred and fifty miles an hour, he cut his motor, zoomed up like a rocket, and did a beautiful Immelmann, turning with a dead stick. Down he came, turning again within a few yards of the ground; the wheels and tail skid touched at the same instant, and the Spad drew up in a little cloud of frosty dust, within ten yards of the hangar door. Slater climbed down stiffly, stood for a moment swinging his arms like a milkman on a winter morning, and made a sign to his mechanic to help him out of his combination. We gathered about his plane.

"*Eh bien*," said Captain St. Cyr, without a smile, "you got him. Of course you didn't know that he'd just dropped a message to tell us that McKail was not dead. Damn it all, Slater! Why did you have to happen along just then?' "

Tommy shrugged his shoulders.

"Another dead Boche, sir," he remarked indifferently; "they all look the same to me. May I have your car for a run out to look at him?"

Gordon, Golasse, and I went along. We travelled the rough country road at headlong speed and drew up with a screaming of brakes near a group of soldiers talking excitedly at the edge of a little wood.

The German plane, striking the treetops in its fall, had lost its wings, but the pilot's body lay in the cockpit, quite unscratched. He was dead, with blood on the breast of his flying suit and flecks of blood on his lips—a fair-haired boy of twenty. One of his arms hung over the side and there was a bracelet of heavy gold on his wrist. Slater forced his way through the gaping infantrymen and reached in to extract the papers from the blood-soaked tunic.

"Poor chap! Poor chap!" I heard Gordon mutter. Even hard little Golasse shrugged his shoulders pityingly.

"You know more German than I do, Forbes," Slater was saying. "What's all this?"

Gordon glanced through the sheaf of papers. "This one's a letter from his mother; and this—why, the poor devil had his leave in his pocket! Seven days' leave, to start this afternoon!"

"I never knew it to fail!" exclaimed Golasse. "It's suicide to fly when one's *permission* arrives! Worse than lighting three cigarettes with one match!"

We had asked the infantrymen to lay out the German's body on the ground, and when Gordon glanced up from his reading Slater was unbuttoning the dead man's tunic to examine his wounds. Gordon's eyes blazed.

"Lay off that, Slater!" he ordered. "I mean it—lay off!"

I saw the knuckles of his clenched fist turn white. Slater stood up, shrugging his thin shoulders. "All right, if you say so," he replied; "but there's nothing to get sore about. He's only a Boche, and how's a man going to shoot unless he can check up now and theft?"

XIII

SHOT DOWN

MY train for Paris left just before noon, and during the slow journey half-way across France I had time for some quiet reflections concerning my own small affairs. In the autumn, while I was at the G. D. E., Dr. Gros had driven out from Paris with Majors Glendinning and Hoffman of the Signal Corps, and Major Goldthwaite of the Medical Corps, to interview the Americans then at Plessis-Belleville. Those who expressed a desire to transfer to American Aviation were given a physical examination, and their records looked into with a view to commissioning them. Gordon and Slater had declined, but Dr. Gros—by that time a major in the Signal Corps-had assured me that my acceptance would not prevent my continuing at the front, and that, after my transfer, he could probably have me sent back to my French squadron, where I had been made a sergeant.

The trip from Lunéville to Paris was interminable in those days. We passed Vitry, Châlons, and Épernay; night fell before we got to Meaux. I was wondering when the French would release me, and how long it would be before my American commission came. Several men I knew had been released some time before, and were still waiting for their commissions, flying and fighting in their French uniforms. Things of this sort were inevitable in the confusion of those days, complicated by the red tape that seems inseparable from armies everywhere, but I hoped that I might have better luck. What I feared most was being sent to the rear as a flying instructor just now when I felt that I was beginning to be of some use at the front.

The train reached the Gare de l'Est at last; I made a run to engage the nearest taxicab and found the Héraults still up.

My first thought in the morning was to call on Dr. Gros. I had no business with him, but I wanted to shake his hand and hear his friendly voice. No pilot in the Lafayette Flying Corps was too insignificant to be accorded five minutes of a busy man's time—a smile and a handclasp and a word of inquiry that proved Dr. Gros's warm personal interest in the flying men. For they were his—bound to him by ties of affection and gratitude. I had the luck to find him at a moment of comparative leisure.

I told him briefly of what had happened since I had seen him at the G. D. E., and he made me feel unmistakably his pleasure in my small successes. He offered me a cigar, lit one himself, and snapped his fingers suddenly.

"By Jove! I'm glad you came in to-day! Forty-eight hours' leave you said? You've time to do the job and fly your new Spad back day after to-morrow! Yes, you're released from the

French Army, and your commission's come. Let's see." He ruffled hastily the pages of a railway time-table.

"Yes, you can make it; you've an hour to catch the Chaumont train. I'll have your papers ready in ten minutes. You're a first lieutenant, Signal Officers Reserve Corps, and when you've taken your oath of allegiance you'll receive orders to rejoin your French squadron. I've fixed that. You'll be sent for when the American squadrons are ready for the front, and if you keep on as you've been going you'll soon be a flight commander with captain's rank. The American Army will be needing pilots with experience at the front."

I left Dr. Gros's office walking on air. Commissioned an American officer! Ordered back to Spad 597! What splendid luck! I remember little of my rapid trip to Chaumont and return, except the kindness of Captain Frederick Zinn, who took me in hand at the G.H.Q., cut through miles of red tape as if by magic, had me sworn in, procured my travel orders and A.E.F. identification card, and saw me to the train for Paris that same evening. Zinn had fought through the war since August 1914, in the trenches with the Foreign Legion, and afterward as an observer and machine-gunner in the Lafayette Flying Corps. He waved at me from the platform as the train got under way. "Good luck!" he shouted. "Wish I were going back with you!"

My companions in the train were all Americans, but I was too happy to want to talk and took refuge in their supposition that I was French. Presently I took out my orders, to read them for the fourth or fifth time. I have them still—frayed and yellow with the years—a reminder of one of the happiest days of my life:

Pursuant to instructions contained in War Department Cable No. 686, First Lieutenant Charles Selden, Aviation Section, Signal Officers Reserve Corps, now at these headquarters, is assigned to active duty and will proceed to Paris, France, for temporary duty for a period of one day, and thence to the station of the French Escadrille Spad 597, reporting upon arrival to the commanding officer for duty. The travel directed is necessary in the military service.

By Command of General Pershing:

JAMES G. HARBORD, *Brigadier General, Chief of Staff.*

The next day was a busy one for me. As an officer, I should now live and mess with the officers of the squadron, and I wished, naturally, to be a credit to the American Service. So I resolved to order plenty of boots and uniforms, the smartest Paris could provide. And, with the memory of my adventure in pyjamas in mind, I allowed myself sufficient leisure to lay in a supply of those garments, in patterns I should not blush to display. Then there were the Meyrowitz goggles to buy for

Slater, and a visit to the dentist to repair a tooth broken in horseplay one evening at mess.

The dentist I visited that afternoon was—and still is, for all I know—an American long resident in Paris, with luxurious offices on the Champs-Élysées. A smart Swiss manservant bowed me into the waiting room, where I was the only patient at that hour. On a beautiful mahogany table, where the current numbers of French, English, and American weeklies reposed in perfect alignment, I saw a box of heavy chased gold, a foot long, and of a width to hold the fabulously expensive Abdullah cigarettes with which it was filled. Inside the open lid was a card lettered in handsome Gothic script: "Help Yourself." The atmosphere of the place made me pull out my pocket-book unconsciously, to reassure myself by counting the bills it contained.

At that moment the door opened and the servant—with a manner several degrees more impressive than that he had employed toward me—ushered a man into the room. The newcomer was dressed very plainly in horizon blue without a sign of gold braid on tunic or cap. But on his breast, so minute as to be almost unnoticeable, I saw the rosette of an officer of the Legion of Honour, and on his sleeve, equally small and inconspicuous/the stars of a general. I sprang out of my chair.

"Sit down, Sergeant," said the general. He spoke with the charming paternal familiarity that marks the attitude of

French general officers to enlisted men. I obeyed, and watched him as he strolled about the room, smiling behind his grizzled moustache as he examined its furnishings. He was a fighting general from the front—the finest type of Latin aristocrat, with a profile that made me think of a Roman coin. Finally he stopped before the box of cigarettes. He took one, lit it, and turned to me with a wink.

"I don't like the look of that gold box," he remarked; "and that invitation, 'Help Yourself,' and these cigarettes de luxe! Something tells me that you and I shall walk out of here decidedly poorer than we came in!"

Another door opened, and the dentist stood bowing before his torture chamber, a small dapper man all in white. "Come in, General," he said, as his quick eye caught the small gold stars.

"No, *chacun à son tour*. Go ahead, Sergeant."

I obeyed, as before, and lay for half an hour in the chair, while the dentist fixed my broken tooth and talked soothingly and ceaselessly about "the boys." I gathered that "the boys" were the Allied soldiers, and he seemed to be bursting with affection and admiration for them. He asked me if I knew Nungesser, and if I had noticed the Ace's gold teeth. "My work!" he said, proudly. "A nice job, eh? It's such a pleasure to work for you boys! As you see, I'm not a soldier, but I'm doing my bit." Presently the job was done, and he ushered me into the waiting room. Standing in the doorway while the dentist clasped my hand warmly, I ventured to interrupt his flow of talk to inquire how much I owed him.

"Oh, yes," he said, as though he would never have thought of it unless reminded. "Let me see." He glanced down at my sergeant's stripes. "I try to do everything I can for you boys. You're a sergeant . . . you fellows are very poorly paid. What is it? One franc fifty per day? Yes . . . something purely nominal. Let me see . . . shall we say one hundred francs?"

I paid him and he turned to the general. "Just a moment, sir, while I get ready for you." He gave me a final bow and disappeared, closing the door. "A hundred francs!" I was reflecting ruefully; "twenty dollars for thirty minutes isn't too bad! I wonder what he would charge if I didn't happen to be one of the boys!"

As I restored my purse thoughtfully to my pocket I found the general regarding me with an air of humorous solemnity.

"A hundred francs for a sergeant!" he said in a low voice. "And I'm a major general! *Bon Dieu!* No wonder he offers his clients cigarettes!"

I found Laguesse's friend, the test pilot, still at Le Bourget, and accepted gratefully his tip to take a beautiful little Peugeot-Blériot Spad he had tried out only the day before. She had an Éclair propeller that let her turn up to eighteen hundred revolutions, and she was rigged precisely to my taste, so that she climbed of her own accord when I gave her the guns. But she was destined for the shortest of lives—to die in infancy, if I may express it so. One hour in the life of a Spad corresponded roughly to a year in human life. After forty hours Spads were middle-aged, and at the end of eighty or ninety hours in the air we considered them senile veterans, unfit for further service. All pursuit ships were temperamental, short-lived creatures, very expensive to maintain. The statistics of the French Air Service show that it cost £36 to keep a Spad at the front one day.

I landed at Vertus, in the Champagne, lunched with some hospitable French airmen there, and hopped on to Lunéville. Everyone congratulated me on my commission, and Captain Clermont gave me leave to stop in my old quarters till my uniform came. I spent the next morning with Cartier and the armourer, mounting a gun on the new ship, and at noon, strolling across to my billet to wash and change after the grimy task, I felt thoroughly satisfied. Plane, engine, and gun, all brand new and in perfect condition, were rigged, tuned, and sighted to a hair. Cartier had given the ship the accolade of his measured approval. "She'll do," he had said, and then, with rare enthusiasm, "I couldn't have picked a better one myself!"

There was an unwritten law in French squadrons that every man commissioned from their ranks must *arroser ses galons*, "sprinkle his stripes," and my bars of an American lieutenant were to be sprinkled that night, I had ordered a barrel of good red Bordeaux for the men and asked Cartier to preside as master of ceremonies; and with Fontana's help in selecting food and wine I was giving a dinner at a restaurant in town for the pilots of Spad 597. But I missed the good time I was looking forward to with so much pleasure, for I was shot down the same afternoon.

Volokoff seemed even more melancholy than usual when I met him in our living-room. He had been reading a long letter from Russia, which he tore into bits and tossed idly into the stove. Then he stood up, towering over me and running a hand through his hair as if to brush away depressing thoughts.

"Want to take a turn over the lines at two o'clock?" he asked.

"I'm your man! I'm keen to try out my new bus."

"If we can find any Boches," he said quietly, "I'm going to knock one down to-day."

Though he had taken part in innumerable combats, and had had his plane riddled time after time, Volokoff had never succeeded in bringing down a German plane.

The sunlight filtered down through masses of light, scattered clouds that afternoon—an ideal day for ambushes in the air. Dodging in and out of the clouds, to throw off the gunners who shot at us at every chance, Volokoff and I flew north-west along the front, past Nancy, and on towards the bend of the Salient at Pont-à-Mousson. I was in the lead, and just east of Nomeny we sighted a lone German, high above us, dodging from one cloud to the next. We were at about three thousand metres.

Climbing with full throttle close alongside Volokoff, I saw that his gun had jammed while firing the short burst every pilot fired when going out to the lines to make sure that his gun was working smoothly. With his stick in his left hand he was leaning forward to tug at the crank handle of his Vickers, which resisted his efforts stubbornly. It must have been a bad jam, for he was still working to clear it when he dropped behind and out of sight.

I had such confidence in my new ship, and in the gun I had tested long and carefully, that I climbed on among the clouds, higher and higher, and always deeper into the enemy lines. I thought the German had not sighted us, and that, once at his altitude, I might be able to take him by surprise; but he must have been waiting all the time I was climbing up to him, and when he attacked he came in grimly to finish me.

I was in a space of open sunlight, with a wall of snowy cloud to the east; and my first inkling of the attack was a swift-dropping shadow on the screen of cloud. I turned sharply, but I was too late. I saw no smoky lines of tracers, heard no crackle of gunfire, but at that moment, turning to stare back, I felt a smashing blow in my left shoulder and a burning stab, as though it had been thrust through with a red-hot iron. As my Spad went into a spin, still with full motor, my side felt sticky and wet. I managed to reach over and reduce the throttle; then, pushing forward the stick, I straightened out of that frightful spin, marvelling dully that my ship had not lost her wings. I came out in a steep dive, turning toward the friendly lines; and that turn saved my life, I think, for the German, suspecting that my spin was a ruse to escape, had come down after me, full motor, and the moment I ceased spinning I heard his gun going behind. The bullets were whipping through the wind a yard to one side of me; then with a loud *ping!* one struck some part of the engine, and my propeller stopped dead. For all my sick faintness, I turned in a still steeper bank. The Pfalz pulled up just over me to get on my tail once more, and as I turned my head for a hasty glance I saw something that gave me a faint thrill of hope. Above me and a little ahead, Volokoff was diving on the German plane, roaring down almost vertically. I had just time to wonder dully why he didn't shoot, and to think, "My God! What if his gun's still jammed!" What followed was wonderful and terrible.

Still without firing a shot, the Russian flashed over me at tremendous speed, straight for the German. The Pfalz nosed down to pass under him, but Volokoff steepened his dive till he was almost on his back. The two ships, moving at a combined speed of three hundred miles an hour or more, met head-on, with a rending crash I heard distinctly. Their wings buckled, and they seemed to fly into bits as they disappeared. Volokoff had gotten his Boche at last.

Stunned by the shock of my wound and the horror of what

I had just seen, I straightened out and began a long glide for the lines, still far away. My altimeter read two thousand and eight hundred, and I wondered in a queer impersonal way whether I was high enough to fetch the French side. Weighing a ton, and supported by only twenty yards of wing surface, the Spad lost altitude at disquieting speed. I was growing dizzy and faint. Presently I saw trenches, and the roofless houses of the front; there was a rapid distant hammering of machine guns, and I knew that in another minute I should be on the ground. There was no place anywhere ahead of me where a plane could be landed without a smash—only trenches, shell holes filled with ice, the splintered stumps of trees, and a tangle of barbed wire everywhere. Down I came, the wind whistling through struts and bracing wires. I was struggling to keep a grip on my remnant of consciousness when I made out ahead of me a broad deep communication trench. It was straight at the point where I saw that my ship would strike, and wide enough to let the fuselage down, while the smashing wings might break the force of the fall. I was heading for it when I seemed to fall asleep.

Consciousness came back to me by slow degrees. I was stretched out comfortably and in little pain, though my arm and left side were numb. My eyes were tight shut, and the effort of opening them was more than I could face. Cautiously I moved my feet, my legs, my right arm. I thought no bones were broken, but my left arm seemed to be paralyzed. Then I heard a sound that has been described without success a thousand times—the noise of an approaching H. E. shell, ripping its way through the air. It exploded with a roar somewhere near by, and I heard the wasplike buzzing of splinters of steel. A husky voice remarked indifferently, "*Tiens! Les mouches!*"

A moment passed before I realized what this meant to me. "Thank the Lord!" I thought. "At least I'm not a prisoner!" Making an effort, I opened my eyes.

I lay on a stretcher in a bay of a deep communication trench. Two middle-aged infantrymen were muttering as they straightened weary legs to take up their burden once more. They wore helmets, their faces were almost obscured in grizzled hair, and their uniforms so faded and stained with mud that they suggested the field grey of Germany more than the blue of France. Another shell came—a big one, and very close this time—and the stretcher-bearers crouched for a moment as the splinters whizzed overhead in a shower of icy slush. I looked up at the sky, now clouded over in the grey light of a winter afternoon, and a paraphrase of a foolish song began to run through my mind. "I'd rather be up there looking down," I thought, "than down here looking up!" I must have been a little off my head, for I pronounced the words aloud, thinking them very witty and wise. The soldier in front of me turned at the sound of my weak voice. He had faded blue eyes surrounded by a pattern of fine wrinkles. "*Eh bien,*" he said, with a tone of professional, forced optimism;

"you feel better now?"

"Yes . . . Where's my plane? What happened?" The stretcher-bearer, standing up once more, put his hands on his hips and stared down at me dramatically.

"Your plane? It no longer exists! Tell me, do you carry a *porte-bonheur*—a little amulet of some sort to bring you luck?"

I grinned feebly and glanced toward my helpless left wrist, where, on the bracelet that carried my identification disc, I had fastened a small gold medallion of one of the saints, given me by Mme. de Thouars.

The soldier nodded. "I shall get one like it on my first leave," he said.

My odd brand of French had aroused the other man's curiosity. "You are English?" he asked. "Oh, American! We've heard that many of you are arriving nowadays. How long do you think the war will last?"

Another shell burst, and when the commotion was over they picked me up and carried me down the broad deep trench toward the first-aid dressing station. Our progress was slow; we were continually passing small parties of soldiers bringing up ammunition, rations, and water to the front line. I was very thirsty, and when I asked for water my carriers tapped their empty canteens regretfully. A dozen weary-looking men festooned with *bidons*, in which French soldiers carried their water and wine, came along the trench. The corporal stopped them.

"Give us a drink," he said. "This chap's shot through the shoulder; he's an aviator—an American." He turned to me. "What'll you have, water or *pinard?*"

"Make it half and half," I said.

The infantrymen gathered about me, glad of an excuse for a rest, and interested in the spectacle of an airman on the ground.

"I saw you come down," one of them said. "*Mon vieux!* If you hadn't struck in that trench just as you did!" He nodded solemnly, and then asked, "How long do you think the war will last?"

Those men of the trenches, with the pathetic eternal question in their minds and on their lips, brought home to me the realization of what war meant to the infantry. Mud, shellfire, wet, cold, the misery of perpetual discomfort, and the prospect of wounds, mutilation, or a lingering death . . . airman knew none of these things. Their life was one of comparative luxury—good food, warm beds, and long hours of leisure; and when death came it was swift, merciful, and glorious—such a death as any man might crave in the fullness of his years.

On we went, while the shells burst, and tired, silent men shuffled over the duckboards on the frozen ground. And another realization came to me: the immensity of this maze of trenches, which looked so insignificant from the air. Presently we came to the first-aid dressing station, a deep roomy dugout, lit by a glaring acetylene lamp, where a medical officer dressed my wound temporarily and gave me an injection of anti-lockjaw serum. There were other wounded men in the dugout, one of them with his face half torn away by a shell splinter, moaning faintly.

"You're in luck!" the young doctor told me, when I lay on his table in the full glare of the lamp. "The Boche drilled you, all right, but I don't believe he even nicked the bone!"

I lay on my stretcher in the dugout for a long time, light-headed, but suffering little pain. It was night when they carried me out at last. We went for a mile or more, it seemed to me, before we emerged from the trenches, and my stretcher was placed on a two-wheeled carrier which jolted atrociously as they trundled me for at least another mile along a cobbled road. Somewhere between Nomeny and Manoncourt the jolting ceased and I was carried to a Ford ambulance parked beside the road with all lights out. The driver was an American, but I was too tired and in too much pain by this time to want to talk with him. He drove skilfully during the long, pitch-dark journey to the Evacuation Hospital. I was thinking of my squadron far off in Lunéville. The pilots would have finished eating my dinner by now, and the mechanics would be enjoying their barrel of red wine. By this time, very likely, they would know what had happened to me—that I was not badly hurt.

The Evacuation Hospital was a group of barracks, whitewashed inside, and furnished with innumerable folding cots. We were unloaded close to the operating room and our stretchers set on little wagons that rolled smoothly over the floors on rubber tires. The chap with his face shot away was taken first, and I saw compassion in the eyes of the white-robed surgeons as he was wheeled in. He had never lost consciousness, but his moans and cries ceased suddenly as the anaesthetic took effect. At last the door opened and they wheeled him out, silent, motionless, and muffled in bandages.

"*L'aviateur!*" one of the surgeons called. My turn had come.

In my weakened state, I was prepared for a bad half hour, but I might have spared my fears, for they hurt me scarcely at all. While waiting I had been bathed and dressed in a suit of course pyjamas. They laid me on the operating table and washed my wound with the greatest care. Then one of the doctors broke the end of a little tube of glass and sprayed my shoulder with a liquid that felt like the touch of ice. He smiled down at me.

"A nice clean wound," he remarked approvingly; "the bullet didn't touch the bone. You must have been twisting your shoulder like a contortionist when the Boche let fly at you!" He took up a pair of scissors and snipped them suggestively. "I'm going to trim the edges here where the ball came out. Watch if you like—you'll feel nothing, I promise you."

I did watch, and felt no pain whatever, as he snipped and trimmed the living flesh. Ten minutes later, clean and bandaged and greatly relieved, I lay on a cot in one of the wards, and an old orderly, who made me think of Felix, was bringing me a pitcher of lemonade.

They kept me a week in the Evacuation Hospital, until a hospital train was made up for Paris. I saw sights there and heard sounds which I shall never forget, and on which I shall not dwell; and I began to ask myself for the first time what justification man could find for inflicting such horrors on his fellow men. Until then I had thought of war as the most glorious of sports—as, in a way, it was in the air; now I began to perceive the realities of war. I had leisure for a lot of thinking in those days. I saw clearly that this war would have to be fought to the end and won, but I hoped that its lessons might sink into all mankind as they were sinking into me, and that some day, in an uncertain future, the nations might convene to outlaw war for good.

Finally they entrained us for the long slow journey to Paris. The coaches were cattle cars, cleaned, painted, and rigged with three tiers of bunks, and every bunk had its occupant. Ambulances met us at the Gare de l'Est; I was placed in one, which sped smoothly over the wooden paving of the Champs-Elysées to the American Hospital in Neuilly. There, in a sunny upstairs ward, they put me to bed.

Next morning I had a visit from Dr. Gros.

"Well, Selden! So you stopped one, eh? You were lucky, my boy, to get down as you did. I heard of it nearly a week ago, and asked them to send you here as soon as you were fit to travel."

An orderly pulled up a chair and the doctor sat down for a chat with me.

He asked about the fight and I told him how Volokoff had saved my life. "Whew!" he exclaimed, when I had described the collision in the air. "Yes, I knew Volokoff—half Paris knew him by sight. Poor devil! He'd been reading a letter from Russia, you say. . . . Well, he hadn't much reason to be in love with life! There are dozens like him in the Legion—estates confiscated and families murdered by the Bolsheviki; I know one former Colonel who is a private in the Deuxième de Marche. Pretty tough to be a Russian nowadays."

"By the way," he went on a moment later, "they've booked you as a French sergeant—how is that?"

I explained that the tailor had not delivered my American uniforms when I was shot down, and that, being in French uniform, I had let matters take their course. While I was talking, Dr. Gros gave my wounded shoulder a critical professional glance. They had put thick wet dressings on the bullet hole, and a glass container hung overhead, arranged so that a turn of a valve allowed a supply of Dakin solution to drip over dressings and wound. The doctor nodded his approval.

"Great stuff," he remarked. "You'll be healed up before you know it!"

Dr. Gros was not my only visitor. M. Hérault and his daughter came the next afternoon, and Mme. de Thouars dropped in nearly every day thereafter. She spoiled me with cigarettes, cakes, and reading matter; and I accepted everything gratefully, for there were plenty of others to share the gifts. We were thirty in the ward, some of the men desperately wounded, others almost well. Every morning the doctor made his rounds, accompanied by two nurses, who pushed a little rubber-tired wagon, fitted with glass cases containing instruments, antiseptics, and gauze, and other tools of the trade. Some of my companions so dreaded the doctor's visit that they watched the clock long before he was due, gazing with terror-stricken eyes towards the door at the end of the ward. Poor devils! They suffered daily the tortures of the Inquisition. As for me, I got off easily until my wound began to heal, when it itched intolerably. Sometimes at night it took every ounce of will I could summon to keep from clawing the newly formed flesh. One day, just before they allowed me to sit up, I had a surprise.

I was reading the latest number of *La Guerre Aérienne*—the war-time illustrated weekly, read by every member of the Flying Corps. The leading article was intensely interesting to me, for M. Jacques Mortane, the editor, gave three pages to an account of Tommy Slater and his work at the front. Tommy had just knocked down his fifteenth official German plane. There was a picture of him, pale, slim, and childish-looking, in a short belted overcoat with flaring skirts, standing by the wreck of an Albatros he had shot down in our lines.

The editor [I read] had recently the pleasure of a visit to the Groupe de Combat 31, at the aerodrome of N——; and in the course of this visit to the front he was able to satisfy his curiosity concerning Adjutant Slater, the pilot of the Lafayette Flying Corps whose growing string of victories, won in so short a time, is a subject of conversation wherever pursuit pilots meet.

Picture to yourself a beardless boy of twenty or twenty-one—pale, slenderly-made, and with the gentle voice and manner of a girl. He cares nothing for decorations, rank, or fame, although he has won the Legion of Honour, the Médaille Militaire, and the Croix de Guerre with twelve palms. He talks little and asks nothing better than to be left in peace. He drinks nothing but water, and at mess I observed that he scarcely touched his food. Not the portrait of a fighting man, you will observe, but wait! When he takes off in his Spad, things are different! He flies with a delicacy and precision of manœuvre that made the writer think at once of Lufbery, the other American Ace. His shooting, they say, is so phenomenal that most of his Boches have been brought down with bursts of less than a dozen shots; and his comrades declare that he dives to the attack with a confidence profound and absolute in his power to overcome the enemy—a moral superiority which wins half the battle before a shot is fired. We hear a great deal about the mechanical efficiency of our allies, the Americans; well, here you have it embodied in a human machine for shooting down Boches! For Slater is a man without nerves, without temperament, and without imagination, so far as one can see. He brought down and had confirmed his fifteenth official enemy on the afternoon of the writer's visit to the aerodrome, and when he landed he stole quietly off to his quarters for the siesta he takes every day. But for all his hatred of publicity, his victories may be followed in the *communiqués* from day to day; and *La Guerre Aérienne* predicts for Adjutant Slater a future most glorious!

As I perused this well-deserved praise of the enigmatic Tommy, I was unaware that some visitors were approaching my bed, until I heard a soft murmur of interest run through the ward. I glanced up. An airman stood over me, gold teeth flashing, and a mass of decorations covering his left breast. It was Nungesser, and with him was Lufbery, almost equally resplendent with orders and crosses. There was a whispering throughout the ward, and I heard an old territorial mutter to a neighbour: "Whoever they are, it's not bananas they lack!" "Bananas" was the *poilu* word for decorations.

"Well, how's the Rumpler hound?" asked Lufbery.

"Just heard you were here," said Nungesser. "Hard luck, Selden! Better now? I know how it is—I'm always stopping 'em! If wounds were promotions, I'd be a Marshal of France!"

"Got everything you want?" Lufbery went on. "I'm in Paris for forty-eight hours, and I've plenty of time."

He wore the brand-new uniform of a major in the American Air Service, and he had an air of depressed discontent. An orderly bustled up with a couple of chairs for my visitors, and I was gratified when they sat down.

"Have you heard about Luf?" Nungesser asked, grinning at his companion. "They've made him a major, now that he's transferred to the American Service, and oh! such a useful one! They sent him to a flying school first—gave him an office, beautiful roll-top desk, a pencil, and a pad of paper. All he had to do was to whittle his pencil and draw pictures on his pad! He loved that—didn't you, Luf? Then they sent him to Villeneuve, in the Champagne, to be the boss of a couple of new pursuit squadrons. That's where he -is now. He's got pilots, mechanics, and planes—a first-class outfit. The only trouble is, they haven't any guns! What's the matter with you chaps, Selden? Isn't that six hundred million dollars the U.S.A. appropriated for Aviation enough to buy guns for a couple of dozen planes? They might at least buy one for Luf!"

Lufbery smiled gloomily. "I suppose they'll come some day, but we're getting mighty sick of waiting. Every day I take the boys up for a look at the lines with those damned dehorned

Nieuports of ours. We're the Ninety-fourth and Ninety-fifth Pursuit—the only American squadrons on the front, except the Lafayette. Pursuit hell! Pursuit backward! I've got the keenest crowd of pilots on the front! If they had anything to shoot with, those boys would be knocking down Boches right and left 1"

"Well, they'll be sending along your guns one of these days," said Nungesser, "and there'll be plenty of action this spring. One thing's sure: the Boches are going to pull off a tremendous show somewhere. Hurry up and get well, Selden! We'll need every pilot when the fun starts!" He stood up and took my uninjured hand. "Come along, Luf, we must push off. *Au revoir*."

I lay thinking of his words after they were gone. France was full of rumours in those days, for it was obvious that the time was at hand for Germany's great final effort to win the war. With American troops beginning to pour into France, it was now or never for the Central Powers. When and where they would strike were the questions in everyone's mind.

XIV

THE GREAT ATTACK

ON March 21, Germany struck the awaited blow—struck with sixty-two massed divisions, on a front extending from Croisilles to La Fère. The Allied lines gave back—gave back; the British Fifth Army was routed; the enemy was advancing at a pace unprecedented since 1914. The days dragged on. In the hospital on the outskirts of Paris, one was aware of the hushed, expectant city, tense with anxiety as each hour's news came in At last early in April, the attack came to a standstill; our lines had bulged, but now they were holding, and the attempt to separate the French and British had failed.

I was to be allowed to spend a few hours in town that day, with my arm in a sling and clad in the dark-blue hospital uniform of tunic and slacks. An orderly was helping me to dress when Forbes came in.

One of the nurses—a girl from San Francisco—ushered him into the ward. He looked thin and very tired; his face was pale and his eyes seemed unnaturally large and bright.

"Lordy," he exclaimed, clasping my hand with fingers that twitched, "it's good to see you out of bed!"

"And it's mighty good to see you, Gordon! This is my first day out; I was just pushing off for town. Couldn't we have lunch together?"

"Fine! I'm in for a new Spad, and the captain gave me forty-eight hours in Paris. A little rest, he said . . . well, I need it—we all do!"

An hour later we were sitting on the terrace at Fouquet's sipping *vermouth-cassis* and watching the traffic of the Champs-Élysées speed past. It was the first really pleasant day of the year. The sky was blue, with masses of light, gauzy cloud here and there, and the lime trees along the avenue were bursting into a mist of buds. The people about us were talking of the halted attack, with the air of sober rejoicing which pervaded the city. Gordon ordered lunch; we ate it upstairs, and descended to the terrace once more to loaf through the warm afternoon. Until that moment Gordon had dodged my efforts to get news of the front, and we had talked of everything but the war. He reached for his coffee cup and managed to convey it to his lips with a hand that trembled painfully.

"My nerves are shot to hell," he remarked, shrugging his shoulders with an attempt at a smile. "Two weeks of it. . . . My God! You were lucky to be in hospital! Four patrols a day—eight hours in the air; and the Boches thick as flies and mordant as the devil! Your crowd? Fontana's gone, and de Chalais, and Masson, and du Marmier. And it's just as bad in 602. Did you know they got Tommy Slater? He died of wounds night before last." He was silent for a time, and I waited while he drummed on the table with restless fingers. Then he went on.

"The Group got there a few hours after the attack started, and we've been in the thick of it ever since. . . . It seems to me I've lived a lifetime in the last two weeks. It's been a nightmare, too tremendous to comprehend, and filled with a kind of horrible beauty. When we arrived, there wasn't a balloon left on our side of the lines; the British were simply beating it for the rear, and the Boches had swept the air clean. They broke out hundreds of little triplanes—Fokkers—they'd been reserving for this show, and they flew in formations of a dozen and fifteen and twenty, attacking everything in sight, in the air and on the ground. They're slower than a Spad, but they can outclimb and outmanœuvre us, and they have a stunt of hanging on their props and shooting up. We've had to fight these birds, and shoot up troops on the ground, and do half the infantry liaison work. Eight hours a day of it—a lot of the time only a few hundred metres above the ground. That stuff gets on your nerves. None of us has had a real night's sleep from the start—you turn in, lie awake for a long time, doze off at last, wake up in a cold sweat, and do it all over again. Old Beaumont came into the bar one night and saw some of the fellows spilling the drinks they were trying to hoist, and when he'd looked around for a minute he held up his hand.

" 'I know I'm asking you to do more than flesh and blood

can endure,' he said; 'but it's got to be done, and remember—if we can hold them, you'll get the rest you deserve.' Well, the French held them all right!

"What do they say in Paris? What's wrong with the British, anyway? It hasn't been a retreat, but a rout—everything left behind. What a sight from the air! Cavalry galloping madly along the roads, ammunition dumps exploding, towns blazing—Lassigny, Ham, Noyon, Roye, Montdidier! And all the time the German infantry creeping forward as though it never would stop! All the Allied aerodromes were abandoned, of course, many of them so quickly that half the material was left behind. Remember that night when Beaumont made us the little speech about the supremacy of the air? Well, let me tell you, the Boches have had it for the last two weeks!"

Gordon stopped to wave at a group of American officers passing on the sidewalk. He had aged astonishingly since I had seen him last; he seemed to have crossed the divide between youth and manhood in a few short weeks.

"Tell me about Tommy Slater," I said.

"It was just north of Montdidier. They sent us out to try to locate the lines. There were four of us with Tommy in the lead, and it did my heart good to see the continuous flash of the guns as we flew along the front. Our lines were beginning to hold. Montdidier looked like a slag heap, and the whole country to the north was smoking and blazing, and strewn with dead horses and dead men. We found the German infantry dug in on a line of new shallow trenches, with French shrapnel bursting overhead; there had been no advance since the day before. The clouds were low, with patches of sunlight here and there, and the ceiling at above five hundred metres. Tommy took us over the clouds into thfe Boche lines, dove through a hole, and found a long line of cavalry on a national road. Lordy! We played the devil with them! The horses went wild! But right in the middle of the fun a flock of Fokkers came down out of the clouds.

"There were more than a dozen of them, and they had us cold. Do you remember Rousseau, that young lieutenant of ours we used to shake dice with in the bar? I saw him go past with three of them on his tail and fold up in the air. They simply shot his Spad to bits! Believe me, I had my hands full, but I had a glimpse or two of Tommy out of the corner of my eye. Four or five Fokkers were turning with him, taking pot shots from above and below and behind, but they couldn't get him in their sights and I saw him knock down two of them not thirty seconds apart. He could have ducked into a cloud, but that wasn't Tommy's style. He was glorious! I swear, if his guns hadn't jammed, I believe he'd have ruined the lot of them! Once, when I was in a vertical bank with a stream of bullets going through my fuselage, I thought he was a goner. Three of them were shooting at him at once, but he did one of those marvellous turns of his, so abrupt that he came right up under their tails and almost bagged one of them. Then both his guns jammed, and while he still turned with them, pounding at a crank handle, a little green Fokker came up underneath and behind him, hung on its prop, and gave him a point-blank burst. Tommy zoomed up and ducked into a cloud, and that's the last I saw of him till later on. . . .

"Me? Oh, I nearly got mine! It was a miracle the old ship hung together, but she did. The wings and fuselage looked like Swiss cheese. It was no place for a minister's son, so I called it a day and made for a handy cloud, climbed up to sunlight, and gave her the guns for home. Talk about *réformé!* You ought to have seen that old Spad of mine! She was a museum piece! They were making out my papers to go to Le Bourget for a new ship when the captain sent for me to say that Tommy had come down near Royaucourt. He was badly wounded, the skipper said, and, as the hospital service was disorganized, he told me to take his car and run up to fetch Tommy. Everyone else was off for another patrol, but I had no plane, of course.

"I wish you could have been with me on that ride! It would have sobered down some of our jingoes at home. The roads were full of troops, so dead tired out that they seemed to be marching in their sleep. And the wounded! I tell you, they sobered me! But the refugees were the worst of all. Old men, and women, and girls, and little kids, trudging along not knowing where to go, carrying pathetic little bundles of odds and ends—hungry, cold, homeless, and absolutely out of luck. Think of them—this is the second time they've been through all this. I saw one old white-haired woman, all alone, struggling to push a broken-down baby carriage along the road. She had a rooster and two hens in it—all she had left in the world, I suppose. At last I got to Royaucourt.

"The Germans were shelling the place, and I found Tommy in a wrecked farmhouse, on a dirty bed under the only bit of roof that was left. A doctor—a very decent young two-striper—met me at the door. He told me Tommy hadn't more than an hour to live—three bullets through the stomach. He'd brought his Spad down in a wretched little field without breaking a wire.

"Tommy's head was quite clear when I went into the room; if he was suffering he gave no sign of it. He greeted me with that ghostly little smile of his. 'Well, I got mine,' he said. I sat down by the bed while he told me briefly and calmly, about the fight.

"I can't say that I liked him—I don't suppose many people did—but I tell you, his courage, his calmness, the thought of what I'd seen him do—it brought a lump to my throat. We're taught to think of men as good or bad, but human nature's not so simple as all that. By God! That boy had guts! While I was sitting there a *padre* came in—a fine old ruddy, white-haired priest, with the eyes of a saint. The doctor must have told him the situation, for he walked straight to the bed and went down on his knees. 'Is there anything I can do for you, my son?' he asked. 'Yes, Father,' said Tommy, with another faint smile; 'you can give me a cigarette.' Without a word the old priest fumbled in his cassock, produced a cigarette, and struck a match when it was between Tommy's lips. Then I saw his own lips moving in prayer. When we looked up, the cigarette was burning a hole in the blanket, and Slater was dead."

Gordon's hand went up to his forehead, as if to brush away harassing thoughts. "Let's talk about something else," he said abruptly; "I've had enough war to hold me for a while. Heard from home lately?"

"Yes—I've had quite a batch of letters since I've been in hospital. And a long one from my uncle—he's keen on the idea of your coming down after the war."

"*Après la guerre fini*, eh? It's fun to think about what we'd like to do down there, but a fat chance you and I have of going to the South Seas! I reckon it's west we'll go, not south!"

We paid our bill and strolled off down the Champs-Élysées; I had another hour before it would be time to take a tram back to Neuilly. Gordon was gloomy and preoccupied. No doubt his thoughts, like mine, were dwelling on the war. I wondered whether America had come in too late; whether the Germans, heartened by their enormous gains, would not soon strike again. Could the Allied troops, worn out in Picardy, hold their fresh divisions, flushed with success? By the autumn, thousands upon thousands of Americans would be facing the enemy, but autumn was a long way off. Gordon put a halt to these reflections by seizing my arm.

He had stopped before one of the magnificent French war posters, on a courtyard wall: France, in the form of a noble-looking woman, standing on a shell-swept parapet. The tattered remnant of the tricolour she held aloft streamed in a great wind, and she was gazing back over her shoulder as if to cry, *"Hauts les cœurs! En avant!"* But the poster bore no legend, and none was needed. The splendid high-headed figure, the torn flag whipping in the wind, were more eloquent than any words.

"By God!" Forbes exclaimed softly. "That's France for you! The Boches'll never down her!"

That spring, after the severe winter, was warm and beautiful and I enjoyed it as much as one could in those anxious days. April passed, and the first half of May, while I convalesced, leaving the hospital in the morning and returning at night after a long day in places of quiet beauty like the Luxembourg Gardens or the Bois. It was at this time that I learned of Raoul Lufbery's death—how he had been shot down in flames in Lorraine. His loss was a blow to the entire French Air Service, and particularly saddening to the pilots of the Lafayette Flying Corps. On May 20, the day after Lufbery's death, I rejoined my squadron, at Villeneuve in the Champagne. I was now in the uniform of an American officer.

Villeneuve is south-east of Épernay—in a gently rolling country of vineyards and patches of pine forest and broad fields of wheat. Vertus, a village famous for its delicious pink wine, is close at hand. The aerodrome where I found Groupai installed was one of the largest in France.

Flingot met me at Épernay with the captain's car. It gave me a sense of home-coming to see his grin and feel the hearty clasp of his hand. We travelled at his usual breakneck pace, and he talked nearly as fast as he drove.

"We've been through it, Selden! By the way, I suppose I'll have to call you *mon lieutenant* now—you'll have to excuse me if I forget now and then. A lot of changes in the Group—new faces, and the old ones gone. Fontana's a prisoner—ha, ha!—that's the only laugh I've had for two months! A Boche came over—pretty decent of him at a time like that—and dropped a note to say that old Fontana came down without a scratch. Underneath the typed note they'd let Fontana scribble a message. What do you suppose it was? 'Send my garlic'! Your mess sent him a twenty-five pound package of it. When he gets it, the Heinies will probably let him escape—they'll be glad to get rid of him. You remember Masson and du Marmier? Both dead, and de Chalais was shot down in flames over our field in Picardy. They were a mordant lot up there! Bombed the devil out of us every clear night, and their pursuit came right over the field in patrols of fifteen or twenty and shot us up. They go too far, damn 'em! I didn't transfer from the Infantry to be machine-gunned twelve miles back of the lines! Golasse is the only one of your pals left among the pilots. They'll never get that bird—he's too tough. The captain's still with us—you'll be messing with him now—and Lieutenant Weiler, the Alsatian. How does it seem to be an officer? Remember that barrel of wine you gave us to sprinkle your stripes? We thought you were dead at first, so we changed the celebration into a wake till the telephone message came. We'd gotten through half the barrel by that time. When we heard you were alive we decided to keep up the good work. That was A-I *pinard!* I had a head like a pumpkin the next day, and old Cartier was a sick man! He doesn't often take a drink. Lord! That seems ten years ago!"

We flew down the white, dusty road, past Cramant and Avize, and at last I saw the hangars of the aerodrome. Flingot—the pursuit pilot on wheels—passed a line of barracks at a speed that brought heads to windows, and came to a sensational stop before the bar. "I thought so," he said. "There's the captain playing bridge."

There had been a lull in the summer's heavy fighting, and the bar was full of tired men. Thé warmth of the captain's welcome touched me.

"*Eh bien*, Selden! I'm delighted to have you back!" His face, full and ruddy when I had seen him last, looked grey, and there were dark circles beneath his eyes. His little fox terrier, a good friend of mine, frisked about my legs.

Forbes, Golasse, and other friends were there to welcome me, but, as Flingot said, there were many new faces. And the old faces that remained were changed, for flying over the attacks of 1918 was no bath in the fountain of youth.

The captain told me I might have Cartier and Vigneau back, so after I had been introduced to a bewildering crowd of new pilots, I set out with Forbes to greet my mechanics. As we passed the barracks of Spad 597, I saw old Felix standing in a doorway, loafing in the sun with a towel over his arm. His beard, if anything, had grown longer and more luxuriant during the attack; it was superb, and I thought that at this rate it would soon reach his knees. He came forward eagerly, dropping his towel.

"*Mon lieutenant!* It's good to see you—I had no idea . . ."

He seized both my hands, and was as glad to see me, I think, as I was to see him. "You and Golasse," he was murmuring; "the only ones of the old crowd left. . . . The old ones go . . . the new ones come . . ."

Cartier was working before a hangar, covering bullet holes in the wings of a Spad with little round patches, each one decorated with a miniature Iron Cross. He looked up from his work, took my outstretched hand, and smiled faintly, without a sign of emotion on his pockmarked face. "Hello, Selden. Glad to get back? This is your new taxi—not much good, but we have to take what they give us these days." Vigneau came out of the hangar with a can of oil, and shook hands shyly.

The Spad was one of the new 220 h.p. type, with two machine guns and a geared engine that made the propeller rotate left instead of right. They were very fast and had a high ceiling, but they were less manœuvrable and far less reliable than the one-eighties I was accustomed to. Many of their engines lasted only twelve or fifteen hours at the front.

Forbes got his lieutenancy during the third week in May. He had shot down and had confirmed six German planes, and several others too far in their lines for confirmation. I knew that he was now considered one of the best men in the Group. I have had little to say of his exploits because he seldom spoke of them himself, not so much owing to modesty as to the fact that he had a deep hatred of killing. But he believed, with so many others in those days, that this was indeed a war to end war, and, resolute in his belief, he carried on. As for talking about what he had done, he drew the line. Even if he had been an indifferent pilot, Gordon would probably have been made an officer, for Captain St. Cyr liked him and wanted him in the officers' mess.

For a week after my arrival at Villeneuve we led an easy life. We did routine patrols on both sides of Rheims, but the enemy seemed to have deserted the air. Those were long, warm, drowsy days of loafing and sleep. Nesting quail called in the wheat; the pale green of the vineyards was deepening; the peace and beauty of the French countryside made the war seem far away. But uppermost in every man's mind was the thought, "Where will the Germans strike next?" Some said at Belfort, on the Swiss frontier; others believed the attack would come in Lorraine; but most of us thought Ludendorff would attempt to drive through Amiens to the sea, cutting off the British in the Pas-de-Calais. The tired pilots of Group 31 congratulated themselves on being in the quiet Champagne. No man dreamed that our stretch of front would be the theatre of an attack, and the État-Major shared our belief, for the lines were held by only six more or less worn-out French divisions and two divisions of the British Fifth Army, which had been so roughly handled less than two months before.

My new Spad was a formidable little monster, squat and broad-winged, armed to the teeth, and with the power of two hundred and twenty wild horses bellowing out through its exhausts. I felt decided inward trepidations when I took it up for the first time, for the ship was unfamiliar to me, and a long time had passed since I had flown at all. It hurtled its way through the air, roaring and snorting and trembling with excess of power, and its speed in a dive took my breath away. But I managed to land without smashing up, and after the first hour or two I got the hang of it, though I never felt for the geared Spad the same affection I had had for the one-eighty—my first love.

Then came the twenty-seventh of May. This is not the place to describe in detail that great attack, nor am I capable of describing it. All I know is what we saw from the air. The whole country, to the west and south of Rheims, blazed and smoked and flashed with bursting shells as the enemy swept forward to the Marne. They reached the river on the night of the fourth day, but the French infantry, now numbering forty divisions, and stiffened by American troops whose conduct made me more than ever proud of the uniform I wore, held them there.

The attack came as a complete surprise. I remember that morning well. I was up before sunrise, for I had had a sound night's sleep. Captain Clermont and I strolled to the officers' mess to drink our chocolate. Weiler, the Alsatian lieutenant, rose, wiping his moustache, as we came in. He was a peaceable, blue-eyed little man, who had been revelling in the tranquillity of Villeneuve. He stretched his arms, yawned, and remarked: "This is almost as good as Lunéville. I've half a mind to go back to bed."

At that moment the captain's little dog began to bark. The door burst open and I was amazed to see Major Beaumont, flushed and breathing fast. He spoke without ceremony.

"I want every pilot in the Group in the air at once," he told the captain. "The Boches have attacked—they're breaking through all along the Chemin des Dames, and their aviation is reported to be very strong. Tell your mechanics to have everything ready to fill up quickly when the patrols return." Next moment he was off.

Captain Clermont wasted no time. He rang for Carnot, and dictated to him, crisply and clearly, the orders for the formation of patrols. The orderly set out for the pilots' quarters, and

Clermont and I crossed the field at a trot. Something in the major's manner had impressed us even more than his words—both of us, I think, realized the gravity of the situation. The mechanics had already been notified; they were wheeling out our Spads and beginning to warm them up. Major Beaumont kept his ship in the same hangar with mine, and, knowing him, I was not surprised to see that it was outside, with the motor idling. He had served his apprenticeship with Dorme, and Herteaux, and Guynemer, in the Cigognes—and the fuselage of his Spad bore the famous stork, the proudest insignia in France.

"We'll make two patrols," the captain was saying. "I'll lead one and Weiler the other. You can come with me." These are the last words René Clermont ever spoke to me.

Two Spads, both of the unreliable two-twenty type, were out of commission for the day, and three of our pilots were already over the lines. We were able to make up two patrols of five each—about the average number for the three other squadrons of the Group. The field buzzed like a beehive newly disturbed. One patrol took off—and another, and another. Weiler led his formation off toward the Montagne de Rheims—our turn had come. The clouds were low that morning, and under their grey ceiling we swept once around the field, bunching like a flock of teal. Clermont glanced back, then opened his throttle and headed low and straight for the lines. We crossed the Marne a little east of Épernay, and swept over the Montagne de Rheims—a rugged plateau with cliffs along the western side, and thickly wooded on top. Then, with the city and its ruined cathedral on our right, we passed over the Vesle.

The houses ceased to have roofs, bursting shells flashed and winked below, smoke rose from the villages, and the air was rocked and torn by the projectiles passing us. Patches of black sprang out on all sides, with the deep coughs of the one-hundred-and-fives, but we were too low and our speed too great for them. It was my first sight of a great battle, and I watched, fascinated, though I saw nothing I can describe coherently. A Spad ranged alongside me, and I saw Commandant Beaumont's stork. He was not a man to stay on the ground that day. The clouds were breaking up a little, and not an enemy plane was in sight.

The Fokker patrol must have come down out of the clouds; at any rate the air, empty a moment before, was suddenly filled with strange awkward-looking little ships, with N-shaped struts and black crosses on their wings. They were Fokker D 7's—by long odds the finest pursuit ships produced during the war, and the first any of us had seen, quite as fast as Spads, and far more manœuvrable; and they were piloted by the cream of the German Air Service, selected for this attack—the most formidable band of assassins I ever had the misfortune to meet. There must have been eighteen or twenty of them in this one patrol, and they flew together with the easy elasticity of migrating wild fowl.

One moment, as I said, the air was empty of enemies. An instant later, the Fokkers began to stream over as if driven before a hurricane—flashed past, banked up vertically, and came at us like a pack of wolves. The odds were three to one, and they had the advantage of altitude. I thought: "You'll be damned lucky to get out of this alive," But I fancy that their very numbers, under the low ceiling of clouds, may have saved some of our lives in the fantastic fight that followed. Thirty seconds after my first sight of the enemy, the air was criss-crossed with thin lines of smoke, and guns were stuttering faintly on every side.

Two Fokkers—murderously persistent ones—got on my tail at once, but I threw off their aim with a sharp climbing turn and managed to get in a burst at one of three that were attacking the captain. But the next moment flames began to stream from Clermont's Spad; he nosed down and sped earthward, leaving a train of dense black smoke.

I had resolved not to lose a metre of altitude, knowing that I should be lost if driven down; but, strive as I would to shake off my pursuers, or one of them, I found myself thwarted at every turn. The air was so thick with planes, banking, shooting, nosing down, zooming up, that I was as busy as a one-armed juggler. Several times I got a Fokker in my sights long enough to give him a burst, and as often barely missed being shot down; and the mere matter of avoiding collisions with friend or foe was an occupation in itself. Major Beaumont was in the thick of the fight; he handled his Spad like a true stork, and once, as he flashed past with three Fokkers on his tail, I saw him get in a burst at a fourth that sent the Boche coasting for the ground. At that moment my motor began to miss, and I realized that if I was ever to get home, this was the time to go. But the Germans—still three of them—were not willing to let me retire gracefully.

Climbing as well as I could while the engine skipped alarmingly, I made a sharp turn with tracers streaming past my tail, and ducked into a conveniently low cloud. I had my bearings well in mind as the grey mist enveloped me, and another turn headed my Spad for Rheims. Then, tail up, I fled. The exhausts of the big motor roared in syncopated time, very different from the song of a healthy Spad. I sped across a strip of sunlight, glancing to the rear, and ducked into a second cloud. When I came out of it. I was over the Vesle and there were no more clouds between me and the Montagne de Rheims. Half a mile behind me to the west, I saw three Fokkers, easily recognized by their short lower wings and single bays. They had spotted me again and were hot on my trail.

Now and then, for a few seconds, all eight cylinders of my motor would take hold, and though the Germans were gaining they were still too far behind for shooting when I reached the west side of the wooded plateau. Two of them banked and gave up the chase, but the third came on with an air of determination I didn't like. Close to the Marne, between St.-Imoge and Haut villers, he began to peck at me with short tentative bursts, though he was still too far for accurate shooting. We were approaching Épernay, and I realized with deep chagrin that thousands of eyes below might be watching my inglorious flight. Yet I knew that if I attempted to turn on the Fokker I should wing-slip and be driven down at the first brusque turn. "God damn this motor!" I thought bitterly. "If it would only run for two minutes I'd show that Fritz where to head in!" Strangely enough, at that instant my Spad ceased her jerking and the engine burst into its full deep-throated roar.

I made a steep climbing turn which took the German by complete surprise. A second later I had him full in my sights and gave him a long soul-satisfying burst from two Vickers that worked smoothly as a pair of sewing machines. The Fokker seemed to wince as the hurricane of lead took it fair amidships; up went its nose and off went one of the lower wings. The German pilot, riddled with bullets, had no time to close his throttle, and the Fokker went spinning down at ghastly speed, to splash in a field on the outskirts of Épernay. Dozens of tiny figures ran toward the wreck, and after the Fokker had struck the earth I saw its detached lower wing still eddying down like an autumn leaf.

I felt a glorious elation, untinged by the slightest regret at having killed a man, and there over the town I looped and did barrel turns till my engine began to miss once more, this time so badly that I headed straight and low for the aerodrome, eighteen miles away. The missing grew worse and I began to watch anxiously for landing places ahead. When I reached Villeneuve I was barely high enough to slide over the trees at the south end of the field.

XV

VILLENEUVE

CARTIER had everything ready to send me back to the lines at once—oil, gasoline, clean spark plugs, and patches for bullet holes. Vigneau set to work to patch the dozen or more holes in my Spad's wings, while I told Cartier how my motor had missed. He chocked the wheels, climbed into the cockpit, and opened the throttle. After listening for a moment to the stuttering exhaust, he shook his head.

"No good," he remarked dryly, and he snapped the switch and climbed down. "I can't fix it—no one can. But we've a spare motor—a good one, I think—and I'll have you in the air by morning if Vigneau and I have to work all night!"

My emotions as I turned away toward the bar were mixed. I felt deeply the loss of Captain Clermont, and eager to avenge him, and I knew that every available pilot was needed over the lines. But I was not available, and not entirely regretful of the fact. That morning patrol had left me very thoughtful; I realized for the first time, fully and no longer academically, that my chances of surviving the war were slim indeed. Youth shrinks, not from death, but from the realization of the fact of death; and now that realization came home to me, bringing a train of unpleasant reflections of the usual futile kind.

Spad after Spad was landing as I walked around the field, the pilots hastening to the bar for a sandwich or a drink, while their mechanics tuned up motors, loaded guns, and filled gasoline tanks. Half an hour later new patrols were taking off. I found Major Beaumont in the centre of a group of excited pilots in the bar. "Who got the Fokker over Épernay?" he was asking, and I arrived just in time to reply, "I did, sir." I told him of my motor trouble and that I should be *indisponsible* for the rest of the day. He gave an exclamation of disgust.

"Damn these two-twenty Spads! What with them and the losses we've had, a third of the Group is out of commission. And poor old Clermont's gone! Weiler! You'll take command of 597, of course. Who else have you lost? Charcot and Langlois and de la Tour? Tough luck! Well, we gave the Boches worse than we got, anyhow. By the way, Golasse has just phoned that he's down north of Fismes; he didn't crack up and he thinks a mechanic might be able to start his motor. Let Selden go up after him; he can take Golasse's mechanic and Flingot with your car." The major turned to me. "The main thing's to get Golasse. Start his bus if you can and let him fly back, but look out for the Boches! The road out from Rheims runs just south of the Vesle, and at the rate they're advancing they'll reach the river by night."

We pushed off fifteen minutes later, Flingot and the

mechanic, delighted at what they considered a lark, on the front seat, and I in the rear. Flingot settled himself at the wheel as if the outcome of the war depended on his driving, and if speed could have won the war it would have ended that day. We roared up the dusty road to Épernay, flashed through the town and across the Marne, and whizzed north on the long straight road to Rheims. The inconceivable traffic of soldiers and refugees, which I saw many times later from the air, had not yet got under way. As we sped bounding and rushing down the northern slope of the plateau, I had a view of the city and of the battle raging to the west. I knew how weakly our lines were held, and that it would take time to bring up our reserves, and I remember thinking, "Rheims is gone! We'll never be able to hold it!" But the French, as history records, held the city where their ancient kings were crowned, and the story of that defence is one of the epics of the war. Outflanked, shelled day and night, beating back wave after wave of attack, the defenders of Rheims earned grimly the glory that is theirs.

When we turned west to follow the Vesle to Fismes, the road was being shelled. The high explosive was not too bad, but the shrapnel, bursting overhead with flat reports, and spraying out balls that moved the tall wheat like hail, was a new and far from pleasant experience. Flingot drove on, faster than ever, if that were possible, shouting now and then to the French reserves lying in the wheat. The men looked old and tired and dishearteningly few, but I envied them their air of unconcern. Golasse's mechanic, who had been talking steadily with Flingot, grew silent and white. We reached Fismes, crossed the river on a bridge I feared might be demolished any moment by a shell, and found Golasse in a ruined farmhouse a mile to the north. His Spad stood unharmed in a field close by. The little pilot, who had been watching for us impatiently, gave me a curt nod and seized his mechanic's arm.

"You've got the wind up," he told the man; "but forget it! If you work like hell I think we can save the taxi. The Boches are just over that hill!"

We set out for the machine at a run, but just as we reached it Golasse gave a shout. We followed him in a dive for a ditch a few yards off, as a big H.E. shell shrieked down and burst with a roar and a shower of dirt and splinters. We stood up uninjured, but a glance showed that the Spad would never fly again. Golasse wasted no time. He opened the gasoline valve, touched a match to the fuel, and led the way back to the car, sprinting across the field while the wrecked Spad blazed fiercely. I could hear machine guns now, and as we tumbled into our car I had a glimpse of grey-green German uniforms where an advance party was crossing a wheat field disquietingly close. Golasse's mechanic was half paralysed by fear, but Flingot cranked his engine with a coolness that displayed a new side of his character. When the engine was running, he thumbed his nose deliberately at the Kaiser's troops before he sprang into his seat and released the clutch.

The Germans, advancing rapidly, were close behind us, and actually nearer the river to the west. We must have offered a tempting target as we covered that mile to the bridge; at any rate we got our share of fire. Twice I heard the spat of bullets striking the car. Flingot, never a conservative driver, fairly surpassed himself that day. The big Panhard seemed to leave the ground and fly. We flashed across the bridge, bouncing so high that I nearly went over the back of the seat; turned east in a cloud of dust, and broke all records from Fismes to Rheims.

It was late afternoon when we reached Villeneuve. Flingot was the hero of the Group chauffeurs, and five minutes after our arrival I saw him recounting our adventures with enormous gusto to a dozen of his peers, who stood about while he covered the bullet holes in his car with Iron Cross Spad patches. Cartier, Vigneau, and Captain Clermont's men had been working like demons on my bus; she would be ready to take off in an hour, they said. "And this motor's not too bad," Cartier added, wiping the sweat from his eyes. "Peugeot built it, and it won't let you down."

Another Combat Group had arrived at Villeneuve during our absence, and two more were to come that evening. The falcons of France were gathering. Patrols were landing and others taking off, for we flew till after nine o'clock on those long summer days. I found the bar filled with tired men, gulping drinks, eating sandwiches, and attempting to talk casually, though the air was vibrant with nerves. I saw Weiler, our temporary C.O., talking with Commandant Beaumont. Golasse and I went to report at once.

"Sorry about your Spad, Golasse," said the major; "but we'll have a batch of new ones out from Le Bourget tonight. Ought to be here now. Get your guns mounted and lined up the minute you pick out your taxi; you must be ready to fly at the crack of dawn. We'll have a dozen young pilots out from the G. D. E. to-morrow . . . a rotten time to be broken in at the front!" He chuckled grimly. "Fokker-fodder, eh?"

"I'll be ready to fly in an hour, sir," I put in.

"Good—you-can join Weiler's patrol."

I took a chair where I could be alone while I drank my cup of chocolate. The scraps of talk I overheard showed what was in every man's mind.

"They'll take Rheims to-morrow—we can never hold the place."

"I wonder if it's true they've crossed the Vesle?"

"We've no reserves anywhere near. . . ."

"They say the Boches are marching south in close order, by battalions, with everything but their bands!"

"Where's our Intelligence been—asleep?"

"Intelligence? Is that what you call it?"

"By God! Those new Fokkers are bad eggs. I didn't join the

chasse to fight helicopters!"

"Poor Clermont—the best man in the outfit . . ."

As I sat in a corner listening to this talk, I saw the captain's little fox terrier running anxiously here and there, looking for her master.

Presently the bar emptied and I heard the roar of Spads taking off. They were lining up my guns when I joined the group about my bus at the target, and the armourer had just pronounced the job O.K. I tried a burst or two to make sure, and taxied the Spad back to the hangar, where men were getting into flying-clothes.

"All right?" asked Lieutenant Weiler. I nodded, pulling on my combination.

"Take the left rear position, then. Well be twelve, with four men from the 602." He looked white and badly shaken by his day's work.

Major Beaumont came up, watch in hand. "*En voiture!*" he ordered sharply. "And I want every man to remember what I said: the object of this patrol is to locate the front. I shall call on each of you for a report."

Weiler opened his throttle to taxi out for the take-off, but the motor, which had run beautifully a moment before, now snorted and skipped, refusing to take hold. A minute passed and I saw the major raise his hand impatiently.

"*Assez! Assez!*" he exclaimed. "You're out of it—who's to take your place?"

In spite of his helmet and goggled eyes, I could see the relief on little Weiler's face, and I pitied him. He caught my eye.

"Let Selden lead, *mon commandant*," he said. "He's a good man, and the only officer we have left."

"Very well. *Allez*, Selden—*en l'air!*"

I had led patrols before, but never one so strong, and as I headed for Épernay, glancing back to make sure that my ten men were in place, I felt keenly my responsibility. To a certain extent the lives of the others depended on my individual judgment and skill. I had studied our orders, typed and posted at the bureau, and I knew them by heart. Briefly, we were to find the new front and find it unmistakably.

It was a cloudless evening—still and warm. As we flew north, low over the road I had travelled with Flingot in the morning, I saw that it was packed with refugees moving slowly southward—on foot, in wagons, and driving cattle and small flocks of sheep. Their homes, laboriously patched or rebuilt after the Battle of the Marne, were going up in dust and smoke a second time. I glanced aloft, and there, silhouetted against the sky, I saw the two strong Spad patrols sent out to protect us—one at two thousand metres, the other at three. They would bear the brunt of the battle if all went well, for our task was not to fight, but to observe. The fourteen ships of the lower group were directly overhead, moving in beautiful formation, like migrating geese, and well above them and behind I counted eleven in the high patrol. "Let the Fokkers come!" I thought with quickened pulse. "Those birds'll poison them!" The lower patrol, led by one of the greatest airmen in France, was an entire squadron, newly arrived in Villeneuve, and numbering among its pilots half a dozen grim old gunmen of the air.

When I turned east from Rheims, coasting down to a thousand feet, I began to devote all my attention to the ground. Presently the machine guns began to hammer at us, and time after time my Spad rocked in the wake of shells. But they were not destined for us, for we were far too low. The countryside north of the Vesle, all the way to the Aisne and beyond, smoked and blazed as far as the eye could reach—guns flashed incessantly, and all the villages seemed to be afire. South of the Vesle the fields and vineyards looked deserted, though shells were bursting everywhere, and now and then I had a glimpse of scattered men in horizon blue. But north of the river the fields were alive with advancing infantry. We swung down, weaving back and forth over them in storms of fire, and I saw clearly the great bucket helmets and the field grey of German troops. They had crossed the river at Magneux, and I could see their cyclists, rifles slung on their backs, pedalling down the Courville road. As I led my men over the river, I saw that only nine Spads were behind me now.

At that moment I had a dramatic reminder of the war in the air. A Fokker passed me, headed for the earth at a steep angle with throttle wide open. It rushed past, not twenty yards off; flames were streaming from its gasoline tank, and the pilot lay dead or dying in his cockpit, one arm hanging over the fuselage. Next moment another ship passed in a *vrille*—a Spad this time—and splashed terribly in the wheat below; and two minutes later a disabled Fokker sailed down across the Vesle and turned over in a vineyard. We were over Courcelles; I saw German soldiers running to the overturned plane, and I was sure they had not yet crossed the river south of there.

My instructions were to establish the lines from Rheims to where the railway turned south, about twenty miles west, and the mission was now accomplished. I was turning back toward Rheims, when one of the rear men, whose duty was to keep a special lookout for enemy planes, ranged alongside me, rocking his Spad. Our protection patrols above had been attacked by two strong gangs of Fokkers, and now a third, taking immediate advantage of the opportunity, had come down on us. They dove headlong, fired, pulled up, and dove again, manœuvring with the easy precision of frigate birds. And I must admit that during the six or eight minutes that followed I felt not unlike one of the boobies that are the frigate bird's favourite mark. We were at an altitude of five hundred feet when they attacked, and in the first few turns, low over the treetops of a little wood, I lost my patrol. I had a pair of assassins on my tail whose tracers were stabbing the air in streams, and another overhead who tipped up now and then, in a cool deliberate way, for a burst at me. I was alone, and, manœuvre as I would, I seemed to be at the mercy of these three skilled pilots, as implacable as any I ever met. Working to the south as well as I could, on a serpentine course that saved me from being riddled a dozen times, I found myself rushing over the open plains that surround Fère-en-Tardenois. I was not a hundred yards up by this time and had almost abandoned hope. Then my motor stopped dead. I whizzed down and landed beautifully in short grass. A blow on the buckle of my belt released me—I tumbled out of the cockpit and began to run, scarcely knowing why or where. The three Fokkers were droning and circling low overhead. There was a crackle of a short burst; bullets rustled the grass near by and one went whining off in a ricochet. Without reason or reflection I threw myself on my face and lay as if dead. Bullets clipped the grass and "pinged" off into space. Those wretches gave me the scare of my life—made me, lying there face down on the ground, *serrer les fesses*, as the French used to say.

The roar of motors grew fainter. I glanced up cautiously and saw the Germans a long way off, taking altitude again. Rising slowly to my feet to brush the inglorious dust from my clothes, I saw what I had not noticed before—the two small hangars of the Fère-en-Tardenois aerodrome. A group of men were running toward me, and in advance of them, bounding over the prairie and popping like a machine gun, I saw a motor cycle ridden by a man who brandished an immense automatic pistol. He drew up with a flourish, stopped his engine, and began to shout and wave his pistol and curse, all at once.

"*Les saligauds!* Are you wounded? What a dirty trick!"

"Easy with that pistol! No—I'm not wounded—my engine stopped."

He was a sergeant mechanician, I learned, and now, still puffing with indignation, he gave my Spad a quick professional scrutiny.

"It's nothing," he announced. "Your tank has been nicked, letting the pressure go down. *Mon vieux! Tu as de la chance!* If it had been an incendiary . . .!"

I was roasting in my combination and now I pulled it off. "*Officier!*" the man exclaimed. "*Officier Américain!*"

"Yes," I said; "and do you think I could get my bus fixed? It's important—I have information that must be turned in at once."

"Right! In half an hour she'll be soldered and ready to fly. You have information? You couldn't have come to a better place with it. Divisional Headquarters just moved in here—the General's in the village now." The sergeant, a thoroughly good fellow, turned to a couple of men who arrived, panting, at that moment, and ordered them to guard my Spad. To the next arrival he said, "Go back and get Lenoir—tell him to bring a soldering outfit, oil, and gasoline. I want this taxi repaired and filled at once. And wait—don't forget patches for the wings."

With that he took up his motor cycle and started the engine

with a kick of his foot. He patted the back seat.

"Hop on, *mon lieutenant!*" The sergeant was another Flingot, and he kept me busy holding on. But during the fast rough ride to the village he found time to tell me that orders had come to evacuate the field. The pilots were gone with their planes, and the mechanics were packing up to go. Half an hour later there would have been no one to repair my Spad.

A limousine with tricolour flag and stars, parked before the best house in the village, showed where the General was quartered. A staff captain received me inside and ushered me into the General's office without loss of time. The handsome grizzled man, bending earnestly over his work, looked up brusquely.

"Yes?" he snapped. "What is it?"

I explained briefly our mission, how I had come to grief, and why I was bothering him. "Go on! Go on!" he exclaimed impatiently.

"Their advance parties," I continued, "now occupy the line, Magneux, Fismes, Paars, Courcelles. At Magneux they are well across the Vesle, and I saw their cyclists moving south in advance of the infantry."

The General took up a pen and made four small red crosses on a map. "Thank you, Lieutenant." Then he glanced up once more, the stern lines of his face softened, and his eyes twinkled. "It seems to me we've met before. You were a sergeant then, I believe." He held out his cigarette case. "They're not Abdullahs, unfortunately; nevertheless I can say 'Help yourself'!" I had not recognized him till that moment. He kept me for a glass of wine and a sandwich before he would let me go.

When I landed at Villeneuve, the last of the patrol was in and it was almost dark. Men ran out of the hangars at the sound of the lone Spad overhead, and a crowd gathered round me as I taxied in. Cartier and Vigneau had given me up for dead, and my arrival at the bar caused a small sensation, tinged with mild regret. Someone had seen me head south with three Fokkers on my tail, and, as Golasse said, all hands had been trying to unearth a few decent things to say of me.

"Damn it all!" he went on with a disappointed air. "All this eulogy for nothing! You're supposed to be dead. The least you can do is to order champagne for the crowd."

So I ordered champagne, and the tired, nervous men drank it like water and called for more. Most of them had flown eight hours that day, facing enemies who attacked in great strength and with unparalleled bitterness. There was little talk of our losses, but they had been heavy, I learned. Our Group was asking for confirmation on seven Fokkers and one German two-seater reported shot down.

I felt worn-out and blessedly sleepy after this strenuous day, and soon headed for the barrack which I shared with Weiler. I kicked off my boots, hung my tunic on a chair, and stretched out on my cot all dirty and sweaty as I was. I was too tired to take a bath, and furthermore I was afraid that the touch of cold water might cost me my night's sleep. It was half-past ten.

A bedlam of machine-gun fire wakened me, twenty minutes later, and above the long crackling bursts from the gun pits I could hear the *Raum-m-m—raum-m-m—raum-m-m* of Gothas. Weiler, in pyjamas, rushed into my room. "Selden!" he shouted. "Wake up! They're . . ." The eerie scream of a bomb—most uncanny of all war-time sounds—drowned his voice, and it was followed by an appalling explosion close at hand. Another came, and another, and another. The uproar on the field was hellish—no other word can describe it. The sharp, nervous staccato of six or seven guns going at once, the unearthly screeching of bombs, the hateful chiming of Gothas overhead, and the accompaniment of racking explosions, roaring as if the world had come to an end—it made an infernal symphony.

Dimly in the moonlight, and sharply outlined in flashes of fire now and then, I could see little Weiler standing in the doorway—hesitating to run for our trench, and hating to stay. I pitied him, but I was so worn-out, so thoroughly disgusted at the awakening, that I felt more irritation than fear. In a brief lull, Weiler turned to me again. "Come on!" he shouted nervously. "Let's make a run for it!" He dove through the door as another bomb fell with a ghastly screech and a tremendous, earth-shaking roar. A hangar began to blaze fiercely, and I heard the monotonous cries of a wounded man.

It was over at last. I tried to sleep again, but found it impossible now. The wounded man was carried into an adjoining barrack, and moaned as though he would never stop. "Good God!" I thought. "What a life! Out of twenty-four hours only seven when it's too dark to fly, and a fellow can't sleep even then!" I was on the point of dozing off when a second lot of Gothas arrived.

There was no sleep for any of us that night. The Germans must have known all about Villeneuve; at any rate they sent us three generous assortments of eggs, at intervals of about an hour. In the grey light of dawn—horribly early on those long summer days—a haggard crowd of pilots gathered in the bar to drink coffee laced with cognac, and discuss, with heroic efforts at humour, the happenings of the night. Four men of Forbes's squadron, whose Spads had been destroyed when the hangar went up, were *indisponsibles*, and they rubbed it in, stretching their arms and giving exaggerated luxurious yawns as they took leave of us, to sleep through the day.

But there was no rest for me. Four times that day I led patrols over the rapidly changing front, and at nightfall, returning from the last sortie, I brought down a Rumpler in flames. The Germans did not bomb us that night, but my nerves were ragged, and in spite of my exhaustion I had great difficulty in getting to sleep. The next day was worse, if anything, and though the attack lost momentum, and came to a halt at last along the Marne, there was no slackening in the fighting in the air.

My clearest memory of those days is of an evening in early June. Forbes and I were down from a strong patrol led by Captain St. Cyr—all the available ships of Spad 597 and 602. It was only six o'clock and our work was over for the day. Forbes proposed that we have dinner together in Vertus.

We walked down the dusty road to the village, where there was a clean, cosy little inn. In the dining-room, almost deserted at this hour, we took a table by the window, and ordered omelets and a decanter of the rosy wine of Vertus, light and delicately perfumed. The window gave on a tiny garden, where hollyhocks and roses bloomed, and bees were still humming busily in the evening sunlight, The guns before Dormans and Châtillon muttered with a far-off sleepy sound.

"Curse those cannon!" remarked Forbes gloomily. "If it weren't for them a fellow could almost forget the war." He looked thin and ill; his face had a greyish pallor, and his eyes were hollow from lack of sleep.

"When do you get your leave?" I asked, feeling a sudden wave of concern for him. "It's long overdue, and you're looking like hell."

"What do you think *you* look like?" he inquired with a crooked smile. "A June bride? About leave, St. Cyr told me I could go last week, but the green pilots they send us from the G. D. E. get themselves knocked down like flies, and I hate to beat it just now. But I don't know how much longer I can carry on . . ."

A blowsy, red-handed girl interrupted him by bringing our food and wine. He filled his glass and held it shakily up to the light. "My father and I used to come here when I was a kid to drink this *vin rose*—it seems a lifetime ago. I remember how he loved it. It won't stand bottling or shipping, you know."

He set down his glass and tasted the omelet, hot from the pan. It was superbly cooked, an omelet of the kind only France can produce, but he laid aside his fork.

"I can't eat," he said. "It's the same every day—I feel hungry, but the moment they bring on the food, away goes my appetite." He drank another glass of wine. I nodded. I was suffering from the same malady.

It was dark when we started back for the field; the sky had clouded over, and a light rain soon began to fall. I turned in at once, but sleep eluded me, and as I tossed on my cot, hour after hour, I could hear Weiler in the next room, pacing up and down—five nervous steps, a turn, and five steps back. At last, in the small hours of the morning, the rain began to come down in earnest. The sound soothed me and I fell asleep.

I slept till ten the next morning, and the warm rain still fell. Forbes was tiptoeing out of the room, but he turned as I stirred in bed. He looked much fresher and more cheerful.

"I'm sorry," he said; "I thought you'd be awake by now."

I walked to the window for a look outside. The weather

could not have been more perfect from my point of view. Weiler's door was closed and I could hear him breathing irregularly in his sleep. I had reason to suspect that insomnia had driven him in desperation to the use of drugs. Gordon sat with me, smoking lazily while I had my chocolate; then we strolled over to see Golasse. We found him propped up in bed, perusing the *marraine* column of the *Vie Parisienne*. He held up his hand for silence as Forbes started to speak, while the rain drummed steadily on the tar-paper roof.

"Listen!" he said impressively. "They say the Fourth Zouaves has the finest band in France, but they never made music as sweet as that!"

XVI

JULY FIFTEENTH

ON July 15, Germany made her last great attack of the war. It is long since a matter of history how that attack was frustrated; how, through German carelessness, the excellence of the French Intelligence, and the development of night observation, the enemy plans for the attack with his Seventh Army east of Château-Thierry, between the Marne and Rheims, and with his First and Third Armies from Rheims to the Argonne, became known to General Foch early in July, giving him time to make adequate preparations for his defence. That battle marked the turning point of the war. It was Germany's final blow. Thereafter, the German Supreme Army Command was subject to the strategical law of the Allied Powers.

We airmen knew nothing of this, of course, at that time. Indeed, it seemed to us, overwrought and nervous as we were from many days of gruelling work in the air, that the enemy plans were carrying through. From Arras to Rheims their lines were miles—in one place, forty miles—in advance of any point they had held since 1914. Their Aviation was immensely strong. As Commandant Beaumont had foretold, the skies were all but darkened with swarms of enemy planes flying in formations of unprecedented strength. Our own Aviation, too, was now powerfully grouped south of the Marne from Châlons to Château-Thierry. Our most hotly contended battles, in 1917, were mere skirmishes compared to those we were now fighting on every patrol.

The night of the fourteenth of July was a memorable one. Orders had come early in the evening that every squadron in the Group, with every available plane, was to be in the air at dawn on the sector, Rheims–Château-Thierry. We were not told why we were to go out—it was not necessary that we should be told. Every man knew that the enemy was again expected to attack in force.

I went to bed early, but it was impossible to sleep. My nerves were on edge. I was fighting battles over in imagination, seeing ships falling in flames, hearing the incessant horrible staccato of machine-gun fire, smelling the nauseating fumes of high explosive. I lit a candle, sat up in bed and braced my book against my knees. Reading was no go, either; I couldn't keep my mind on my book for ten seconds; so I got up, dressed, and went over to the barracks of the non-coms, to see Golasse. Lieutenant Weiler, Golasse, and I were the only survivors of the squadron as it had been when I joined it in October, and we were among the dozen veterans of the entire Group. I found Golasse sleepless, too, lying in his pyjamas on his cot, staring at the ceiling as he smoked cigarette after cigarette.

The man he was rooming with had been killed that afternoon; I sat down on his cot.

Golasse hadn't shaved for three days, and looked as though he had not washed in an even longer period. The room smelled of stale sweat, like a gymnasium locker, and I told him so.

"Get out of here, then, if you don't like it!" he said savagely. "Who asked you to come, anyway?"

"Why don't you take a bath once in a while, so your friends can visit you? Water isn't as scarce as all that."

He sprang up.

"Are you going to get out, or do you want me to kick you out, you . . ."

He called me a name, but was sorry the second the wore was out of his mouth.

"Forgive me, Selden! I didn't mean that!"

I gripped his hand. "Done," I said, "if you'll forgive me first. Are you sleepy?"

"Yes, horribly, but I can't sleep."

"Neither can I. Let's go for a walk."

We crossed the fields and turned into the road toward Vertus. It was one of those heartbreaking beautiful midsummer nights that made one think of Shelley's lines in "The Indian Serenade":

> When the winds are breathing low
> And the stars are shining bright,

and I *was* thinking of them as we walked in silence down the road; thinking, too, of the incredible folly of war; of the German airmen on the other side of the lines, sleepless like ourselves, very likely—men who loved life as much as we did, looking forward with misgivings to the events of to-morrow, and drinking in all the beauty they could while there was yet time. Golasse broke a long silence.

"Selden, I have a feeling that this is the last time we'll ever be together."

"Rot! You and I will . . ."

"No, I mean it. We've had more than our share of luck so far. It can't go on—luck never does."

"Well, supposing it doesn't. *Tant pis pour nous.*"

I had never seen Golasse in a really serious mood before. Usually he was the gayest of companions, cracked jokes under his breath at funerals, and seemed to have an unconquerable belief in the luckiness of his own star. He was a remarkably fine pilot, and although Captain Clermont had thought him too reckless for a patrol leader, he was worth three ordinary men in a dog fight. Since the attack of May 27 he had shot down four German ships, and now had eleven official victories to his credit. That evening of the fourteenth of July was the first time he had given any indication that the pace was telling on him.

We walked on to Vertus. The little town was asleep, and we wandered aimlessly about the streets for a while, before turning back to the aerodrome. We met other pilots on the road, singly and in groups of two or three—men restless like ourselves. There was great activity at the hangars. The mechanics had been at work since the last patrol had come in, and they were still busy by lamp-light. Cartier was hovering about my Spad like a protecting angel, with the air of a man not willing to admit that his work was done. To Cartier, at a time like this, perfection was not enough.

"*Alors*, Cartier, *ça gaze?*" I asked.

"*Ça gaze la tonnerre!* You've never had a better motor, Selden. What's coming off to-morrow? Something big, eh?"

"You know as much as I do."

While we were talking we heard a sound that set our blood to tingling. At an aerodrome not far from us, the British and French had brigaded several night-bombing groups; Handley Pages, Voisins and Capronis. They were coming out from their lair in force—a great swarm of them passed high overhead. We could not see them, but the throbbing of their motors made the air quiver for miles. It was a formidable sound.

"Eh bien!" said Cartier, shaking his head solemnly. "Fritz is going to catch something to-night!"

"Hope it's aerodromes they're bombing," said Golasse.

A hand was laid on my arm, and I turned to find Commandant Beaumont beside me.

"Good evening, Selden. You ought to be in bed, my boy."

"I'm not sleepy, sir."

"I know. These are exciting times, but we mustn't let them interfere with our rest. We'll need all we can get from now on. But I'm glad I found you up. I've something to say to you."

We walked out into the field, beyond hearing of the others. The commandant paced up and down for a moment before speaking. Then he said, "Selden, Weiler's done for. . . . Yes, lost his nerve. Poor devil! He's in a really pitiable condition. He's doing his best to conceal it, of course, but it's plain that he can't go on. It would be criminal to send him over the lines."

I could think of nothing to say, so I remained silent.

"What I have in mind is this," the commandant went on." I want you to lead your squadron to-morrow, and I want you to understand thoroughly the situation, and what you have to do."

"Yes, sir."

"There is no longer any need for secrecy, and I can tell you now what you have doubtless guessed for yourself, that the Germans are attacking again at dawn, on a front extending from Château-Thierry to Rheims to the Argonne. This time we are not being taken by surprise as we were seven weeks ago on the Chemin des Dames. We know not only where the enemy will attack, but precisely when, and with what troops. The battle from Rheims to the Argonne doesn't concern our Group. We are to fly the sector, Château-Thierry–Rheims, opposite the German Seventh Army. They will attempt to force a crossing on the Marne between Jaulgonne and Verneuil. If they succeed, they will then advance on Épernay along both banks of the river. Our aircraft will be in great force there, as well as that of the enemy, for this is the critical point of the Seventh Army attack. Your patrol and one from Spad 602 are to have the posts of honour. You know what that means: you will do the dirty work, flying very low, machine-gunning infantry. Spad 602 is to disorganize their attempts to throw bridges across the river. Spad 597 will flyback of their attacking lines, shooting up transport and reserves coming into action. You are to go as far back as ten miles, even farther, if necessary. You will be underneath everything that flies and must look out for yourselves. Is all this quite clear?"

"Yes, sir."

"How are *your* nerves—all right?"

"I think so, sir."

"Good!" He looked at his watch. "Half-past ten. At this moment the German infantry is massed along the north bank of the Marne from Château-Thierry to Verneuil. As I said, they expect to surprise us again, but this time the shoe is on the other foot. In thirty minutes our artillery will open up along that entire front. There'll be little chance for sleep when that begins; nevertheless if I were you I'd try to catch a few winks."

I didn't, however. I was far too wide-awake. Golasse and I walked up and down in front of the hangars for a quarter of an hour; then we went to the bar for sandwiches and coffee. The room was filled with men, smoking and talking of the events of to-morrow. They were a hilarious crowd, but there was a forced note in their laughter and one could feel the tension in the air. Everyone now knew what was coming and that the enemy plans were to be forestalled. A moment or two before eleven Golasse, who was his old hard-boiled self again, mounted the zinc-covered bar and rapped with a spoon, for silence, on the hanging lamp.

"Gentlemen," he said, "by special appointment of General Foch I am to lead the grand chorus of kettledrums which is to furnish music for the Boches on *this* side of the Marne. My orchestra is ready. I will now demonstrate to you how well trained the musicians are."

He looked at his watch and waited for a moment. Then he again tapped the lamp, three times, with his bâton, shook back his hair, stretched out his arms like a conductor, and said: "One—two—one—play!"

Two or three seconds of profound silence followed, and Golasse looked about him with an air of comical dismay. But before he could speak, his orchestra crashed into an awe-inspiring overture. We were about twelve miles distant—far enough away to get the full effect of that incessant thunder. It was, in fact, as though a hundred thousand giants were beating kettledrums the size of brewery vats.

"*Bon Dieu de mille bons Dieux!*" shouted Golasse, beating

time with an expression of rapt virtuosity on his face. "That's music for you!"

We were off in the first faint light of dawn. Commandant Beaumont timed the departure of patrols; he himself was to fly with the high patrol of Spad 614. The formations from Group 31 were as follows: my patrol, Spad 597 and Spad 602, twelve planes each to machine-gun infantry; Spad 609, fourteen planes to fly up and down the river, at 2,000 metres; Spad 614, ten planes to fly at 4,500 metres. Spad 609 took off first. As soon as they were in the air Commandant Beaumont walked briskly over to my ship.

"Ready, Selden? Off you go! Remember, give the infantry hell wherever you see them coming up. Pay no attention to the river crossings—that's 602's lookout. Keep an eye out overhead. Good luck!"

We had no altitude to take, and the moment I saw that my patrol was behind me I headed north-west. We passed at two hundred metres over the Forest of Épernay and saw before us the Marne gleaming palely in a haze of smoke and dust. Soon our little ships were rocking crazily in the wake of shells coming from both sides of the river. There was no flying sensation more unpleasant. I often wondered why planes were not smashed to bits when flying low, by shells destined for the infantry, but strangely enough I never heard of such an accident. As we approached the river I glanced hastily overhead and saw flocks of planes at all altitudes. We passed over the ruins of Verneuil, and immediately I forgot everything but the work in hand.

Enemy troops were coming up in great force through the fields and along the roads. We did precisely as we had been ordered: gave them hell wherever we found them in the open. We attacked infantry, artillery, and transport, ranging farther and farther into their lines. But the giving was not all on our side, and the worst of it was that the men on the ground were not forced like us, to be sparing of their ammunition.

Twenty minutes passed; we had lost one man, and were about eight miles north of the river, and flying eastward to pick up the main road that runs from Rheims to Château-Thierry, when we were attacked from above. A patrol of eight or ten Fokkers came down on us. We had the advantage of numbers and they of altitude. They started shooting at three hundred metres, which convinced me that we had green pilots to deal with, men just out, very likely, from the German equivalent of the G. D. E. Their manner of manœuvring, too, was amateurish. This was the first time on the Marne that I had met clumsy Germans in the air, and I felt a mounting wave of confidence. One man singled me out, and was following above and behind me as I climbed, firing tentative bursts, but I had no difficulty in keeping out of his sights. I knew that I "possessed" this pilot, as the French say, as I had been possessed by more than one German during my apprenticeship at the front.

My motor ran splendidly, and I climbed up the sky like a beetle up a wall. The German hung on at first, making timid dives, but when he saw how I was gaining on him he left me to take height more rapidly himself. I followed him, and at three thousand metres caught up with him. He turned to meet me, and for some reason—inexperience, I imagine—dove to pass under me. I had him then, although he needn't have let me have him if he had known his business. He went down more in a glide than a dive, looking back over his shoulder, and allowing me to hold him in my sights. I had a feeling of compassion and annoyance at the same instant, and the thought flashed through my mind, "Why the devil doesn't he turn!" Then I opened fire.

I came away from that "combat" feeling like a murderer. Whenever I think of it now I have a feeling of shame such as a sportsman would feel who, by some fluke, had shot a sitting bird. The rest of my patrol had vanished. I was far in Germany with not more than twenty-five rounds of ammunition left. It was high time to be going home.

I was then at fifteen hundred metres, not far from Ville-en-Tardenois. Enemy anti-aircraft opened up on me, and the growl of the Archies was truly ominous. They had an enormous number of batteries thereabout. For all my twisting and turning, they bracketed me time and time again. I came down two hundred metres and levelled out, but one battery seemed to have divined that I was about to make this movement and had their shells already on the way to meet me on the new level. Suddenly I felt my Spad give a violent lurch. The motor spilled forward, wrenched partially loose from its bed, and down we went, plane and pilot, in a descent that still makes me shudder. I didn't know what had happened. All I felt convinced of was that here was an end of the war, and of everything else, for me. The suspense was not long drawn out. Aerial troubles often bring intense anxiety, but they have the merit of passing swiftly. I saw fields and clumps of woodland writhing up to meet me. "I'm finished," I thought, and then I thought no more.

When I opened my eyes I could see nothing at first but a reddish, greenish haze. Two or three minutes must have passed before I had any clear realization of who I was or where I was. Then memory returned and a panicky thought flashed through my brain: "I'm still in the air! I haven't yet crashed!" That was partly true: I *was* still in the air, but I had crashed right enough! My Spad with its wings torn out of all semblance of wings, was draped on a tree like a boy's kite and about fifteen feet from the ground. I tried to move my right arm, but a shock of pain told me that something was wrong there. My left arm was all right. I wiped my face with my sleeve and found that I was bleeding profusely. Then I noticed that my windshield of triplex glass was shattered—evidently I had bashed my head into it. My little clock on the instrument board was still ticking briskly away. I couldn't hear it, but it seemed to be saying, "Time-to-go-home, Time-to-go-home, Time-to-go-home, Time-to-go-home." I thought so too.

My ship, or what was left of it, was hanging tail down; it had crashed through the branches into the fork of three mighty limbs, and then, apparently, slipped backward till the stumps of the wings caught and held it, so that I was looking up through the foliage to the blue sky. My right arm was caught and I couldn't budge. I felt sick, and blood was running down my nose and cheeks into my mouth. I kept spitting it out over my windshield.

Guns, were making a tremendous racket somewhere close by, but in a momentary lull I heard voices—German voices, speaking the German language, with an authentic German accent. I didn't know what they were saying, and didn't care. I let my head fall back on the edge of my cockpit, and in that position I was staring straight up at a patch of blue sky. I saw a flight of Spads cross it, not a thousand metres up, but they were gone in a second, homeward bound, perhaps. I thought it likely that it was my own patrol; in that case they would soon be landing at the old aerodrome at Villeneuve. My own distance from that green, secluded, sunlit field I made no effort to compute.

A voice called out in French: "Hello, up there! Are you alive?"

"I think so," I replied.

A salvo of gunfire followed, then the voice called again: "Well, you've no right to be!"

The thought came to me: "That man's a good sort, whoever he is. I'm glad he's down there."

"Look down, can't you?"

"No. My right arm's caught."

"Are you badly hurt?"

"I don't think so, but I can't be certain."

"Right-o! Sit tight. We'll have you out in a jiffy."

I waited, listening to the continuous thunder of guns alone the Marne. It was a fearful sound, and heavier, if anything, than it had been an hour ago. There was a battery of enemy artillery within a stone's throw of my tree. I knew that I was behind them because of the peculiar, hollow, twanging sound the guns made. It was a four-gun battery, and they were firing rapidly: *Paoung! Paoung! Paoung! Paoung!* with not more than five-second intervals between the salvos. "Archies," I thought. "Seventy-sevens, very likely. Somebody's catching hell." Presently the battery ceased firing. A moment later I saw another flock of planes cross my patch of sky; this time they were Fokkers, very high up, and in steps-of-stairs formation. There must have been twenty of them. I was glad I hadn't met them with my patrol of twelve.

"Hello! Still all right?"

"Yes."

"We're coming after you now."

"Good!"

Turning my head slightly to the left, I saw a ladder being hoisted among the branches. A moment later a bearded man with deeply tanned cheek bones and blue eyes appeared, pushing his way through twigs and branches. His back was toward me till he had reached the top of the ladder; then he climbed out on a limb and turned to look at me.

"So!" he said, in a compassionate voice.

It sounded genuinely compassionate. I don't know why it was, but for the first and last time in my war experience I came very near to crying. I was overwrought, perhaps, and in the grip of half a dozen conflicting emotions—joy that I was alive, regret that I was a prisoner, and so forth. However that may be, tears certainly sprang into my eyes, and a few of them may have run down my cheeks. I smeared them away at once with my soppy left sleeve.

Another soldier came up with a saw, and the two of them set to work, carefully and methodically, to release me. My arm was wedged between a splintered limb that had pierced the fuselage and another that was bolstering up, a little farther along, the remains of my engine. They had a ticklish job to perform, cutting away limbs and branches in such a manner that I could be lifted out without letting my Spad slip on down to the ground. Naturally I took a profound interest in the operation, and when I saw how skilfully they went about it I felt easier. One would have thought that they had been doing nothing since 1914 but taking aviators out of trees.

A second ladder was put up, and there emerged at the top of it an officer of twenty-five or thereabouts. I knew at once that he was the man who had hailed me from below. He regarded me for a moment in silence.

"A nice mess you've got yourself into!" he said, in French. He didn't speak as I supposed all German officers spoke, with an air of stiff formality, but as one human being to another.

"Isn't it!" I replied.

"What brought you down. Were you wounded in the air?"

"No. Something happened to my motor, and here I am, most unwillingly."

He nodded. "I can understand that. You're not French, are you? You don't speak like a Frenchman."

"No. An American."

"An American!" He gave me a quick keen glance, then turned to examine my motor, spread out over a heavy limb as though it were hanging there to dry. Only a few bolts still held it to the rest of the plane. The officer turned to me with an exclamation of astonishment.

"No wonder you came down!" he said. "Do you know what you've got here? One of my small shells, unex-ploded, and stuck fast in your motor! My thirty-seven millimetre gun did that! Excuse me—I'll be back in a moment."

He went down the ladder like a fireman, and before he returned the soldiers had sawed away the limb that was pinning me. They lowered it carefully by means of a rope thrown over a higher limb; then I was lifted out and carried down the ladder. My arm pained like the devil, but I considered myself lucky to have got out as well as I did. In fact the only other injuries I received were a broken nose and various bruises and gashes about the head and face. I asked them to set me on my feet and was immensely relieved to find that my legs were all right. Nevertheless I sat down at once, for I felt shaky and weak, and leaned against my staunch old tree. It stood in the midst of a small wood, not more than an acre in extent. Beyond were open fields and other clumps of woodland. To the right I saw a road filled with motor lorries, each lorry crowded with troops moving up to the lines.

Half a dozen soldiers stood about, looking at me as though I were a museum specimen. Soon my officer came back with a man wearing a Red Cross *broncard*. They removed my flying combination, tunic, and shirt. That was a bad moment, but they made it easier for me by giving me a most refreshing drink of water with brandy in it. My right arm had been twisted and broken at the same time, and a big splinter of bone was sticking out through the skin. The Red Cross man bandaged it as well as he could and made a sling for me.

Meanwhile the officer went up the tree again for a second examination of my motor. He had his men cut away the branches so that a close-up photograph could be taken of the engine showing the shell rightly wedged in it.

"You know, I'll get my Iron Cross for this!" he said. "It's a red-letter day for me. You understand—I'm not trying to rub it in. Tough luck for you, but in my place I'm sure you would feel as I do."

"Of course I would! I don't blame you in the least."

"And you got one of our airmen. I saw the fight, of course. That's why I'm particularly glad to have got you."

We heard the far-off hum of Hispano-Suiza motors and the officer rushed back to his battery. A patrol of Spads went over, very high up. I went out to where the guns were stationed along one side of the wood with nothing but canvas camouflage for cover, and almost forgot my broken arm and the fact that I was a prisoner in my interest in watching a German A.A. battery in action. They had four seventy-sevens and one thirty-seven for shooting at planes at low altitudes. This latter was the gun that had ruined my Spad.

The battery got to work with amazing speed. One man at a range-finding instrument was calling out in a monotonous voice: "Five thousand—five thousand—four thousand nine—five thousand," as the planes changed altitude. Another man plotted direction, still others on the gun carriages spun the wheels which raised or depressed the muzzles, they were as busy as a nest of disturbed ants, and I felt a thrill of something like pride to think how many times formations from good old Spad 597 had kept gangs of men working like this. The four seventy-sevens would fire in quick succession, and after an interval I would see four tiny flashes, four tiny puffs of smoke—apparently right in the midst of the moving formation—and hear, eventually, four faint explosions: *plop—plop—plop—plop*, like seed pods bursting in the sun. It was hard to realize that each of these sounds, so seemingly innocuous, was in truth the terrific rending roar I had heard so often in the air.

The Spads flew on in a wide circle and were lost to view far down the sky. The battery ceased firing, and the officer rejoined me for a moment.

"No luck," he said with a faint smile. "There rarely is in this game. You chaps are too fast for us, and you have the exasperating habit of changing direction so often. Now if you would only fly in a straight line and give us a real chance now and then, we'd be very grateful."

"Well, you got *me*," I said.

"So we did, but that was pure luck; it doesn't happen once in ten thousand times. I've been commanding this battery since 1915, and I've never before made a direct hit on a plane. And you don't know how lucky *you* were when that shell failed to explode! If it had . . ."

While we were talking, a motor cyclist came put-putting down the road at top speed. He turned into the field where we were, threw down his bike rest, snapped his heels together, saluted and presented the officer with a paper which he read hastily. His face brightened.

"Our troops are across the Marne!" he said. "I've orders to

move four miles farther up."

He hurried over to his battery. The horses, which were tethered under the trees were immediately brought out; the camouflage screens were taken down, and within ten minutes the battery was on the move. The officer came back to me.

"I'll have to leave you here," he said. "It won't be for long, though. One of our Combat Groups is stationed at an aerodrome not far off. I'm sending word by this orderly for someone to come and get you. See here—will you give me your name and address? Your American address, I mean. If you will, after the war is over I'll send you a photograph of your plane and your motor with the shell sticking in it. You might like it as a souvenir of your last flight."

"Thanks ever so much," I said. "I'd love to have it. You won't forget?"

"Of course not. You shall have it if I live through."

(And he didn't forget. In 1920 I received the photographs and a letter from my friend—for I can truthfully call him that—who lives in Munich. We have kept in touch by letter ever since.)

Meanwhile I sat under a tree, with a soldier standing by to guard me, watching another long line of motor lorries, filled with troops, thundering past. The men were singing; I caught fragments of their songs as they passed:

> *Lieb Vaterland, magst ruhig sein . . .*
> *Lieb Vaterland magst ruhig sein.*

I wondered how long they would be singing with such confidence.

XVII

PRISONERS OF WAR

WE waited for an hour, perhaps, I sitting under a tree, my guard standing by the side of the road watching the traffic: staff cars, motor cyclists, trucks, ambulances, moving both ways in clouds of dust. At last he stopped a car, which turned into the field. Two young officers got out and came over to where I was sitting. I rose to greet them. One of them, who introduced himself as Lieutenant Müller, spoke English like an American.

"Hard luck," he said. "Fortunes of war, eh? Good Lord! What a superb smash! How did it happen?"

I told him briefly how I had been persuaded to come down. He listened with interest and translated what I had said to his companion. Then they examined the wreck and took some snapshots of it with a pocket camera. Both were airmen, and I noticed that Lieutenant Müller had the Iron Cross and two decorations I was not familiar with.

"We'll have to be getting along," he said. "Busy times, aren't they? By the way, how did you sleep last night?"

"To be quite frank, I didn't sleep at all," I replied.

"Neither did I. This pace is altogether too fast to suit any of us, I imagine. We've just come in from the lines and have to go out again immediately after lunch. Is your arm hurting much?"

"A good deal."

"Sorry. I'll tell the chauffeur to drive carefully. But it's a wretched road the first part of the way."

It was all of that. We jolted in and out of ruts and holes, turning out every other moment to make way for faster traffic. At last we came to smoother going on the Rheims–Soissons road a little to the east of Fismes, the same road I had travelled with Flingot on our memorable journey to fetch Golasse. I felt depressed at the thought that all this territory was now far behind the enemy lines. The Germans too were silent and preoccupied. Lieutenant Müller broke a long silence to tell me that four pilots of his Combat Group had been shot down that morning. He went on to say that he had been flying since 1916 and was the only man left of his original squadron. He asked whether I came from New York.

"I spent five years there just before the war," he added. "My father is a manufacturer of chemical apparatus. We had an office in New York. I little thought then that Germany and the United States would ever be at war."

"How do you feel about the outcome?" I asked.

He looked at me in a surprised manner, as though he thought that a strange question.

"Oh, we shall win, of course. It's only a matter of a few months now. America has come in too late."

He spoke with the utmost conviction. And indeed, up to that memorable fifteenth of July, the Germans had reason to be confident. They had made colossal gains at every point of attack, with the exception of Rheims, which was now all but surrounded. I kept my thoughts to myself, but I could not help wondering whether the United States had not, in truth, joined the Allies too late. As for our Aviation, even now, in the middle of July, but few American squadrons were actually on the front. We had been told that scores of them were ready to take the field, but they had not yet appeared.

The German aerodrome was on the outskirts of a village not far north of Fismes. The field was evidently a temporary one recently occupied. There must have been two Combat Groups there, judging by the number of tent barracks; and the hangars themselves, scattered around the borders of the field, were small portable ones, belonging to a mobile outfit. The planes were the new Fokkers we had been meeting continually in the air. Patrols were coming in and going out as we arrived. It gave me a strange thrill to see an enemy aerodrome from the ground so close at hand, and those single-seater pursuit ships with their provocative black crosses, skimming past just over my head. I was conscious too of a feeling of profound homesickness, sitting there, impotently watching them, knowing that for me the war was over, a least for a long time to come.

I was taken to a squadron mess in one of the houses in the village. The pilots were all talking excitedly as we came in, but they fell silent at once and turned to look at me with politely veiled curiosity. Lieutenant Müller introduced me all round, the men coming forward one by one, each of them making the same stiff little bow from the hips. They were fine-looking chaps, and it was plain from the decorations they wore, as well as from the trophies hung about the messroom, that they were a first-rate outfit, certainly not the one my patrol had met that morning. Among other trophies I saw two from Group 31: a red rooster and a spitting-cat insignia, cut from planes they had brought down on their side of the lines. Under the spitting cat was tacked a pilot's personal insignia—two red bars on a white field. I recognized it at once as that of Marcantoni, the little Corsican shot down on the afternoon of my first day with Spad 597. The walls were almost concealed with such trophies, and among them were two storks from Captain Guynemer's Group.

I caught a glimpse of myself in a mirror and was ashamed to see what a messy-looking object I was. My nose was swollen to three times its normal size, and my face and hands covered with scratches, cuts, and bruises, and smeared with dried blood. A very kind old orderly—another Felix in everything but beard—took me to a washroom, bathed my hands and face, and tidied me up generally, as gently as though I were a little boy and he my father. He drew up an easy chair for me in the messroom and placed before it a small table on which I had my food. They lived well, those German pilots. First we had an entrée, then an excellent roast, salad, dessert, and coffee to wind up with. And each man had a pint of delicious Rhine wine and a liqueur with the coffee. This latter was *Ersatz* coffee—a poor imitation—but not wholly bad; in fact, the meal was the most satisfying I had in Germany until the arrival of American Red Cross parcels from Switzerland. The old orderly cut up my meat for me and offered to feed me, but I told him that I could manage that part of the meal myself.

The pilots ate hurriedly, and although I understood little German I could gather something of their conversation. They talked of the morning patrols, of the fights they had had, all the while doing their best to ignore two empty chairs at the table. They spoke in the same nervous excited way we did on our side of the lines, and several of them were so shaky that they had difficulty in lifting their cups and glasses to their lips. It was curious to think, as I listened, that a few moments later they would be far away over the Marne, fighting with patrols from Group 31. Had it not been for my accident, I myself should have been hastily gobbling lunch at that hour before flying out on another patrol. More than likely I should have met some of these very men in the air. And here I was, sitting in their messroom, partaking of their hospitality! They treated me with genuine courtesy, and although half of them, I should say, spoke English, no one asked an embarrassing question. Several of them talked quite freely to me of narrow escapes they'd had that morning, but they were careful to avoid even a suspicion of trying to pump me for information. I was even informed by Lieutenant Müller that an Intelligence Officer would come to see me before I was sent to hospital, so I was ready for him when he did appear.

He arrived while we were having coffee—a middle-aged, soldierly looking man with a pleasant face and twinkling blue eyes, not at all the Prussian type of officer I had expected to see. He spoke English, of course, and the others gathered round to listen while we chatted for a moment about my accident and the various incredible sorts of adventures that happen to airmen. Finally he said: "Well, Lieutenant, tell us all about it. What are you people doing over there?" I decided that I could meet his friendly manner with one equally friendly without damaging the Allied cause greatly; so I said: "All right, Major. Ask whatever you want to know. I can't promise, of course, to give you any very remarkable information."

He began by telling me what he knew, or said he knew, of the movements of our troops, the organization of the American Air Forces, what squadrons were opposite that sector of the front, what others were soon to be there, and so forth. Evidently he thought that I belonged to an American Combat Group, and I let him think so. He showed me splendid photographs of Allied aerodromes all the way from

Château-Thierry to Verdun, watching me keenly all the while, but when, among others, I saw a beautiful one of Villeneuve, I believe that I successfully registered only polite interest. This cost some effort, I had seen that view of our field many times when going out or returning from the lines, and the thought that I might never see it so again was a bitter one. The piece of information he seemed to want particularly was where my Group was stationed. Finally I said: "I'll tell you what I'll do, Major. I will leave the matter to these officers. Suppose one of them to be in my position—a prisoner being questioned by one of our Intelligence officers. If any one of them will honestly say that under those circumstances he would be willing to give the location of his squadron headquarters, I'll tell you where mine is."

It would have been awkward not to have fulfilled this promise had there been occasion for doing so. But those pilots were gentleinen. They all said that in my place they would do precisely as I was doing.

The major was a very decent old fellow and didn't question me any further. On the contrary he gave me some very welcome information about prison-camp conditions. I was rather worried about this matter, for I had heard the usual tales circulated on our side of German cruelty to prisoners of war. I didn't believe the half of them, of course, but even so I imagined that my lot would be a hard one.

"Rubbish!" said the major. "We're just as humane as you

people are, if not more so. I know the stories you've heard; discount them 500 per cent and you'll arrive at something like truth. Of course, prison camps differ. In some you have liberties denied you in others; everything depends upon the officer in charge, but I can assure you that fair treatment is the rule, not the exception."

He went on to say that my name and the address of the hospital to which I was to be sent would be forwarded at once to the American Red Cross Committee in Switzerland. "As soon as the Red Cross receives this information, they send you a parcel containing a complete outfit of new clothing, with toilet articles, soap—everything you need, in fact. Every week thereafter you will be sent a parcel containing food: all sorts of tinned meats and vegetables, tea, coffee, sugar, tinned milk, tobacco, soap, et cetera. You prisoners with your Red Cross parcels live better than we Germans do. We lack any amount of things, such as tea and coffee and tobacco and soap, that you will have in abundance. And I can tell you this: 90 per cent of the prisoners' Red Cross parcels reach the men they're destined for. Of course, some are pilfered on the way—that's bound to happen; but 90 per cent is a fair showing, don't you think, when you remember that we are desperately in need of the very things your parcels contain? Well, so much for that. I must be going. Is there anything more I can do for you before starting you on your travels?"

I asked whether a note might be dropped on our side of the

lines, with the information that I was a prisoner.

"Of course," he replied. "We'll be glad to do it. Where shall we drop it?"

"It doesn't matter. Anywhere you please between Verdun and the Channel coast."

He laughed. "All right, my boy. I'll have it done for you."

And he did. After the Armistice I learned that the note had been dropped and the message phoned to my squadron that same afternoon.

We had talked for ten or fifteen minutes. Immediately afterward the pilots prepared to go out again. Lieutenant Müller came over to bid me good-bye. "We're flying at twelve-fifteen," he said. "Sorry you've had to be kept waiting this way, but you understand how it is to-day: with the attack going on, everything is a bit disorganized. But they'll be taking you straight to hospital now. Good luck!" He gave me what was meant to be a cheery nod, but I could see that he felt anything but cheerful. Each of the others bowed again as he hastened out the door, and one of them paused long enough to say, "I vish I vas you!"

I watched them take off, twelve planes in one formation. Their field discipline was a good deal like our own, the ships taxiing out in single file, taking off one after the other and meeting at a thousand metres over the field. They flew in steps-of-stairs formation, one man low, five planes about six hundred metres above and well to the rear, four more still higher and farther back, and two planes far up and to the rear. I have often wondered how many of them came home again.

The next two weeks dragged horribly. I had never realized, even as a boy, that a day could be so long. I was taken to a war hospital at Laon, filled to overflowing with wounded from the great battles of May and June. Nevertheless, being an officer, they gave me a little room to myself on the second floor, and there I lay on my cot, unable to move because of my broken arm, staring at the white-washed ceiling and wondering how long the war would last. The operating room was at the other end of the corridor, and the most serious cases were taken there mornings to have their wounds dressed. Their moans and cries, echoing and re-echoing along the corridor, froze my blood. There is a quality scarcely human in the screams of a man crying out in sheer animal terror and pain. Once again, as at the American hospital at Neuilly, war was stripped for me of all its romance and glory. Many a time I wished that politicians, munition makers, breeders and abettors of war of whatever sort, might be forced to make the round of such hospitals so that they might see with their own eyes the horrible suffering they had brought to pass.

The nurses were gentle, patient, devoted women, members of a sisterhood who spent their lives in hospital work. They had never a moment to themselves save for ten minutes in the morning and evening when they assembled for prayers. My nurse was a frail little person, but with the Spartanlike courage and endurance so often found in delicate women. She had the manner and bearing of an aristocrat, and the most menial of tasks, as she performed them, seemed beautiful. Although she had many patients to care for, she found time to come in to see me and to keep wet dressings on my arm, which was still badly swollen. She spoke excellent French and treated me as kindly as though I were one of her own countrymen. I looked forward to her visits, and when they were over I had only mealtime to think of.

Now that I was able to eat at leisure, my appetite returned, lustier than it had ever been. Alas! it was never satisfied. In the morning, at seven, I was brought a single slice of war bread about four inches long, three wide, and very thin. It had been spread with jam, but the jam seemed to have been scraped off again as a thrifty afterthought. That and an excellent cup of broth was my breakfast. At midday, soup and a fairly generous plate of vegetables, but these latter were usually carrots and turnips, which gave only a momentary sense of satisfied hunger. An hour later I would be as ravenous as ever. At 6 p.m. came another cup of broth and bread—two slices this time. I made supper last as long as possible, taking tiny bites and sips; but delay as much as I would, the meal was soon over. Then I would put down my cup regretfully and stare at the ceiling again, watching the evening sunlight creeping up the walls and thinking how far away breakfast was.

It wouldn't have been so bad if I had had something to read. How I regretted that I had not always carried in my Spad two or three thin volumes in view of just such an eventuality as this. It would have been easy to do; but I had never really believed that I should be taken prisoner. I thought of all the books I particularly loved, trying to decide which ones I would have carried, and finally brought the list down to three: *Don Quixote*, the old Icelandic saga, *The Story of Burnt Njal*, and Joseph Conrad's *Nostromo*. Those three books would have made life pleasant even to a prisoner of war. I could have lost myself in them and forgotten how hungry I was. But I had nothing but a small pocket calendar in which I checked off days that seemed longer than a war-time month. One day, however, a wounded German artillery officer came in to see me.

"Just heard there's an American prisoner here," he said. "Thought you might be bored with nothing to read," and he handed me a copy of *Henry Esmond*.

I have not forgotten that kindness and never shall. I read *Henry Esmond* three times, and there was a long list of publisher's announcements of other titles in the back of the volume, which afforded diversion for a day or two longer; but this latter was painted-grape nourishment to a book-hungry *Kriegsgefangener*.

I knew nothing of what was taking place on the front save for scraps of news the doctor, who visited me each morning, let drop. I liked him no better than he liked me. It was plain that it irked him to have anything to do with an enemy of his country. Nevertheless, although he was not so gentle as he might have been and nearly killed me when he set my broken bones, he made an excellent job of it, and my arm has never since given me the least trouble. During his visits, while he changed the bandages on my squashed nose, he would keep up a running comment on the success of the German attacks. "We're across the Marne everywhere between Château-Thierry and Rheims," he would say. Or "We captured an entire American division yesterday, generals and all." I didn't believe him, of course, but I couldn't help fearing that there might be a certain amount of truth in his statements.

One afternoon toward the middle of August, fifteen airmen, all Americans, stood in front of the commandant's office in the prison camp at Karlsruhe, in Baden. We were a disreputable-looking crowd, for many of our uniforms were soiled and torn and travel-stained, splotchy with blood and castor oil. We stood in the same clothing we had been captured in, and marks of the misfortunes which had made us reluctant guests of Germany were written plain on every man's costume. The most fantastic-looking member of our little band was Lieutenant Robert McIntyre of the 91st Pursuit Squadron, who had been shot down in flames on July 15—the same day I myself dropped in German territory. He had had a marvellous escape from death. He too had been flying low at the time of his accident, shooting up infantry, when he was attacked from above, and he had managed to wing-slip to the ground, where he crawled out from the flaming wreckage of his bus with only a few superficial scorchings; but his uniform was all holes and tatters, the funniest sight one could hope to see outside a ragpicker's ball.

We Americans had been assembled at Karlsruhe from various hospitals and prison camps in Western Germany. Since the middle of July I had been travelling from place to place, enjoying something in the nature of a Cook's tour along the Rhine. From the hospital at Laon I had been sent to Saarbrucken, a large industrial town filled with munitions factories, which was a point of great interest to Allied bombing squadrons. They visited the town twelve times during the twelve days I spent there, so that I was not at all sorry to be sent on to Strasbourg. From Strasbourg I went to Mannheim, then southward again to Rastatt, and at last, to my great joy, to Karlsruhe, where I met for the first time other aviator prisoners of war.

The Karlsruhe camp was badly situated from a prisoner point of view. It was clean, airy, and commodious enough, and we had a splendid recreation ground, shaded with neat rows of plane trees; but as it lay in the heart of the city the chances for escape were extremely small. The barracks and recreation ground were enclosed by two high fences, one of barbed wire and one of wood. Guards were stationed at short distances on both sides of the enclosures, and at night the area in the vicinity of the fences was brilliantly lighted, and we were forbidden to approach them on pain of being shot. Therefore, although many of us were continually plotting, no plan we could devise seemed to offer even a faint hope of success.

However, a group of us, all American airmen, devised a plan for tunnelling out, and work was started the same night. But we had no place to hide the dirt successfully, and the conspiracy was discovered within forty-eight hours. The camp guards were hopelessly energetic and alert, and their officers, although they were courteous, and some of them affable men, watched us like hawks. Those of us who were implicated in the tunnelling project were confined to our barrack with guards eating and sleeping in the same room with us. Three days passed in this manner. We were beginning to feel horribly bored when orders came that we were to be sent elsewhere. My name was among the first of those to be read by the officer, and I waited anxiously until he called out, "Lieutenant Robert McIntyre," for we two had become the best of friends, and our hope was that we might have an opportunity to escape together.

Before leaving Karlsruhe we were again carefully searched—our naked bodies and every item of clothing being scrutinized by a lynx-eyed *Feldwebel*—and then paraded on the recreation ground. Five guards in charge of a lieutenant were to accompany us. We watched them go through the impressive ceremony of charging the magazines of their rifles; then the lieutenant said to us: "Gentlemen, I hope that none of you will attempt to escape during this journey to your new camp. If you do, these guards have orders to shoot without warning, and I must inform you that they are all excellent marksmen." We were marched to the railway station and placed in two compartments of a passenger coach with two guards standing in the corridor opposite the doorway of each compartment. Our coach was attached to a passenger train, the other compartments filled with German travellers, and we started on our way.

Before leaving Karlsruhe we had cast lots to choose four men who were to try to escape during the journey. Neither McIntyre nor I drew lucky numbers, but it didn't matter, for not even a ghost of a chance presented itself. It would have been suicide to jump from that train, which travelled at forty to forty-five miles per hour, stopping only at the principal stations. We passed through Pforzheim, Ludwigsburg, Cannstatt, Göppingen, following a general south-easterly course. At Munich we were transferred to another train, and an hour later got down at Landshut, some forty miles north-east of Munich.

The Landshut camp had been set aside for American aviator prisoners only a month or two earlier, and the fifteen or twenty men already there welcomed us boisterously. We were quartered within the grounds of Traus-nitz Castle, which stands on a hill above the Isar River, overlooking the town of Landshut. Unfortunately, we could see nothing of town or river or countryside, for the castle cut off the view to the westward, and on the other three sides we were hemmed in by a high stone wall. Guards were stationed on wooden platforms around this wall, where they walked back and forth in full view of everything that went on in the camp. McIntyre and I were lodged with a dozen other men in an ancient stone farm building in the castle yard, and the rest of the crowd in wooden barracks within the same enclosure.

Then began a life of such dreamy monotony that I look back on it now with pleasure, although at the time we were too restless, too eager for freedom, to enjoy it. The change from the hazardous life of war had been too abrupt. Furthermore, we were all young—the patriarch of the camp in point of years was only twenty-six—and the loss of liberty was hard to bear. But for prisoners our lot was by no means a deplorable one. Being officers, we had nothing to do but eat and sleep and loaf during the long sunny days. We walked round and round our grass-grown enclosure, wearing a dusty path through the turf. We lay in the shade of an ancient pear tree, heads pillowed on arms, looking up into the blue sky, thinking of thé glorious life of adventure we had lost, or sat along a bench by the farmhouse fighting old battles over, finding it hard to convince ourselves that they had really happened; and throughout the day seven bells in the old town struck the quarters and the half hours and the hours, reminders of terrible persistency of the glacierlike movement of time to prisoners of war.

Our food was wholesome and much more plentiful than it had been elsewhere, for here we were within the heart of rich agricultural country where there were plenty of fresh vegetables and even meat upon occasion. And to supplement the prison fare we had food supplied by the splendid American Red Cross through the Prisoners' Relief Committee in Switzerland. Some of us, who had been shunted from place to place since our capture, were not yet in receipt of Red Cross parcels, but other men were, and we all shared alike from the common store. Three prisoners were appointed to act as a Red Cross committee; they distributed the food daily, under the supervision of a German non-commissioned officer who opened tins and boxes before they were passed out to us, examining the contents carefully to see that no contraband was concealed in them. This worried me; I was thinking of my wished-for tin of Pâté des Chasseurs; but as it had not arrived, and might never reach me, I resolved to put all thought of it out of my mind.

Our camp commander was a dignified and rather crusty old major with snow-white hair and a William-the-Second imperial. He had a keen sense of the respect due him, but he was fair and aboveboard in all his dealings with us, and treated us even more generously than men in our position had any reason to expect. I remember his address of "welcome," delivered on the morning after our arrival. We were paraded under the supervision of Herr Capp, our camp sergeant, who translated the major's remarks,

"Gentlemen," he said, "you are prisoners of war. You have been and still are the enemies of my country. You have been fighting battles in the air with the youth of Germany. My son was an aviator too. He is dead. Who knows? One of you may be his slayer. . . ." Here the old fellow's eyes filled with tears, and he had to pause to regain control of his emotion; then he went on: "Even though I knew that to be the case, I should still treat you with the consideration which your situation as prisoners demands. We Germans have long been a military nation. In this as in other wars we are never the enemies of the individual, but only of the nations which you represent, jealous of our ambition, our enterprise, our power.

"You shall have certain liberties here. You shall be free to walk in the prison yard through the daylight hours. Twice monthly you shall have walks in the open country, but only those will be permitted to go who pledge their word not to try to escape during these excursions.

"What I wish particularly to say is this: if you attempt to escape from this camp it will be at the risk of your lives. If any of you, having escaped, are recaptured, you will be placed in solitary confinement, on bread and water, for a period of not less than two weeks, and probably much longer. Your liberties will be granted only so long as you do not abuse them."

The major was as good as his word. One privilege for which I, personally, was extremely grateful was that twice each week we were allowed to be visited by one of the kindliest, most lovable men it has been my fortune to meet anywhere. His name was Dr. Jahn, and he was a professor of modern languages in one of the schools of Landshut. He came to give those of us who wished them lessons in French and German. Most of us studied both languages with him; it was a pleasant and profitable way of employing some of our abundant leisure, and we all liked Dr. Jahn. After our lessons we would sit in the shade of the old pear tree, discussing the war and the issues involved as though we were inhabitants of some other planet, looking on at the struggle from afar, trying to decide who had the right of it or whether there was any right in it at all. An astonishing thing, to me, was that Dr. Jahn was permitted to bring us French and English newspapers, the London *Times* and the Paris *Matin*, which he received regularly by way of Holland. How eagerly we read them, passing them from hand to hand until they were worn out! Some of us believed that such generous and broad-minded treatment might be a subtle form of propaganda designed to give us a favourable impression of our captors. It accomplished that result, certainly, in my case. I could not help contrasting such tolerance with, for example, the intolerance that displayed itself in certain sections of

America where the German language was banished from the schools, German names from streets and shops, German music from concert programmes, and where even German sausage had to be called "liberty sausage."

Dr. Jahn accompanied us on our walks outside the camp. Each man gave his word that he would make no attempt to escape, so we were sent out with only one soldier to guard us lest someone should break his pledge, but no man did. What a delight those excursions were after long confinement within the narrow limits of the camp! We were as happy as schoolboys on a holiday. We sang, we whistled, and in turn were silent, letting the peace and beauty of woods and fields sink deeply into us. And something more than its peace and beauty. Our eyes roamed keenly and critically here and there, noting the lay of the land—the windings of the river, the direction of the roads, the location of villages and chumps of woodland; for while we were pledged not to escape during these walks, we were not pledged to banish all thoughts of escape from our minds.

So the days passed, slowly and monotonously, until it seemed that we had always been prisoners and would never be anything else. We boxed and did Swedish drill for exercise; we studied with Dr. Jahn; we told each other the stories of our lives; but for all our efforts to kill time, it was painfully slow in dying. Escape was, of course, the one topic of absorbing interest to all of us, and we did more than talk of it. During the month of September 15 to October 15 three plans for escape were put into execution and all three frustrated.

There were forty men in the camp at this time. Of this number ten were recovering from wounds or broken bones, which prevented them from trying to get away. The rest of us were divided into escape parties and drew lots for the order in which the attempts were to be made. The first lot, of three, managed to be carried outside the walls in a rubbish cart, but that was the end of their adventures except that, as the major had promised, all three were sent into solitary confinement. The second party, tunnelling out from under the floor of their barrack, lacked competent engineers. Their burrow was too near the surface and caved in under the weight of a wagonload of wood being carried to the castle. The conspirators were not discovered in this case. The third party, of six, cut a hole through the wooden wall of their barrack. The building was backed up close to the stone wall surrounding the camp. One very dark night when rain was falling heavily, the twelve-foot space between the hole and the top of the wall was crossed on a bridge made of army cots fastened together. The bridge was then drawn back, the cots replaced, and the passageway through the end of the barrack carefully concealed without the guards suspecting that anything was wrong; in fact, it was not until the following morning that the men were missed. We thought they had made a clean get-away, but late that evening the bell at the prison gate jangled loudly, and when the guard opened the heavy oak door six very crestfallen men were escorted into the yard by a posse of farmers who had discovered them concealed in a wood ten miles from Landshut. One of them had been shot in the thigh. He was sent to hospital and the others to the promised bread and water in the civil prison in the town of Landshut.

As a result of these attempts, we lost the privilege of country walks, and our shoes were taken from us at night. This latter was the more serious deprivation, for without shoes how were any of us, granted that we succeeded in getting out, to make the long walk to the frontier? The closest practicable point on the Swiss border was more than two hundred miles from Landshut, and the hardiest of us could not hope to make the journey barefoot. The guards too were increased, and a system of night roll calls inaugurated. We were awakened, sometimes at midnight, sometimes at two or three in the morning, to answer to our names, and as luck would have it, at the time when the chance of escape seemed all but hopeless, the fourth party—five men, including McIntyre and myself—were to make the attempt. By general agreement we were compelled to lay our plans and carry them out within two weeks of the day of the lot drawing; otherwise we should lose our turn. This was no more than fair, for others were waiting, as eager as ourselves for a chance at freedom.

We had discussed several plans, but only one of them seemed to offer any hope of success. The members of our party were lodged in the two-storey farm building, an ancient massive structure with thick stone walls plastered over on the outside. We were locked in our quarters at dusk and a guard stationed outside the only door. Our room was on the second floor, and the windows were barred with inch-and-a-quarter iron bars four inches apart and deeply embedded in masonry. Escape by the window was out of the question, for the only tools we had were a penknife and a six-inch spike we had managed to keep hidden despite the frequent searches supervised by Sergeant Capp, our good-natured but extremely efficient *Feldwebel.* We were given table knives and forks during the daytime, but these had to be surrendered at evening roll call, together with our shoes. Escape by means of the roof was also impossible, for our ceiling was plastered over and a hole into the attic would have been detected at once. We decided to remove one of the blocks of stone in the wall. These were, roughly fifteen inches square and twelve inches thick, and the removal of one would give us an opening large enough to crawl through. Then came the most difficult part, for we had to let ourselves down into the prison yard and somehow scale the twelve-foot wall enclosing it without attracting the attention of the guards, nowhere more than twenty paces from the most secluded corner of the camp.

The situation looked anything but promising but the very difficulties were a challenge to our ingenuity, and we made our preparations with the utmost care. I shall not go into the details of the plan, for on the very day we started work something happened which altered them very materially. My long-expected parcel from Mme. de Thouars arrived.

It is possible now, ten years after the event, to set down the facts calmly, but on that fifteenth of October there were three men in the Landshut prison camp who were anything but calm, inwardly. I had told McIntyre of my wished-for Pâté des Chasseurs, and, as a matter of precaution, only one other man, Bob Browning, a chap from Minneapolis, who was chairman of the prisoners' Red Cross committee. It was Browning's duty to receive all parcels and distribute the contents under the watchful eye of Sergeant Capp. At this time we had a reserve supply of stores, for many parcels which had been following us from place to place in Germany were coming in now that we had reached a permanent camp. So, in addition to our regular rations, we drew daily on our Red Cross supplies. A kitchen stove in the farmhouse had been turned over for our use; there we cooked savory stews of peas and beans and bully beef, all provided by a more than generous American Red Cross. We were divided into messes of six men each, and in the morning after roll call the president of each mess went to the storeroom to draw rations for the day. I was president of D mess, and one of the most exciting and anxious moments in my overseas experience came on that October morning when I stood in line with the other mess presidents waiting for a tin of pâté. Browning was as cool as iced watermelon.

Presently he called, "D mess next. What'll it be, Selden, potted meat, bully beef, or sardines? Isn't it great to have a choice? We can afford to be liberal now with all these delayed parcels coming in. Why don't you try the potted meat? Pâté des Chasseurs it's called. Got a nice-looking label."

I tried to be as matter-of-fact as possible. "Thanks," I said; "shoot it along. What else do we draw?"

"Two tins of peas, a pound of rice, half a pound of coffee, and a tin of condensed milk. Shall I open the tins, Capp?"

"Yes," said Sergeant Capp.

I nearly had heart failure then. Capp was always on hand when we drew rations, but as often as not he let Browning pass them out without examination. But as luck would have it, in this case he waited while Browning poured out the rice and coffee on a paper. Then the tins of condensed milk and peas were opened, and he fished round in them with a spoon to make sure that nothing was concealed. Browning delayed in opening the tin of pâté, but the *Feldwebel* waited expectantly, and, when the cover was removed, ordered the contents to be turned out in my mess tin. Then he took a knife and sliced it through twice at right angles. It was as though the knife were going between my ribs. "All right," he said, "take it along."

I felt as limp as a rag, but I got out with my provisions without making any noticeable display of emotion. I thought, of course, that I had drawn the wrong tin, for Mme. de Thouars had said there would be two and that one would contain nothing but the pâté. In fact, I was so sure I had the wrong one that it was not until lunch time, when D mess was demolishing the pâté, that the glorious discovery was made. Two saws for cutting iron were wound up in the bottom of a circular box the size of a quarter in diameter. The upper half of the box was a compass. Another tiny container held three maps, one of all Germany, a second showing the German-Dutch frontier in great detail, and a third the German-Swiss. All three maps, on the thinnest and strongest silk, had been rolled into a capsule shaped box no larger than a fountain-pen cap. In slicing through the pâté, Sergeant Capp had missed striking the compass by a hair's breath. That same night the fourth escape party started work.

XVIII

THE ESCAPE

AS I have said, the Landshut prison camp was extremely well guarded, and three attempts to escape in the space of a month had made our captors more than usually watchful. The night roll calls were particularly annoying. Two and sometimes three times between dark and dawn the lights would be switched on, and every man of us had to sit up in bed and answer to his name. Nevertheless, we got a great deal of work done between times. We had one man constantly on watch near the door from the moment lights were turned off in the evening. The rest of us took turns sawing away at the iron bars of the least conspicuous window. We made rapid progress, and every morning just before daylight we slipped pieces of cardboard into the cuts we had been making, concealing our work so well that only a minute examination would have revealed it.

But getting out of the barrack was only a preliminary and the least difficult part of the escape. Once on the ground we had to scale the twelve-foot wall surrounding the camp, and the guards along it were nowhere more than twenty-five paces apart. Each of them, of course, carried an army rifle, and experience had taught us that they were not reluctant to use them when the need arose. Eager though we all were for freedom, we resolved to take no unnecessary chances.

On the night of October 21 we had all but severed two window bars. Meanwhile we had been hoarding food supplies for the long journey to the Swiss frontier. Luck was with us here. Throughout September and the early part of October we had been searched again and again, and Sergeant Capp believed that he had now discovered everything in the least useful to us for an escape; so these search parties had been discontinued just before the arrival of my tin of pâté, and we were able to secrete a reserve food supply which at first we hid under our mattresses. Then we discovered a loose board in the floor, and to be thoroughly safe we concealed all of our food in the space under this board.

We were in excellent trim, and as the nights were now much longer we believed that we could reach the Swiss border, allowing for detours and accidents of various sorts, in from twelve to fourteen days. On this basis we decided to take the following provisions for each man: two loaves of bread, four tins of bouillon cubes (twelve cubes to a tin), six one-pound packets of chocolate, and a pound of hard biscuits. Acting on advice, I carried, as well, a cake of soft soap and a tin of bacon fat, which proved to be invaluable at the right moment. The bread was a part of our prison-camp rations. The loaves were eight inches in diameter and about four inches thick—a day's rations, in camp, for six men. The other supplies were from our American Red Cross parcels.

As already explained, our shoes were taken from us at evening roll call, and as there was no way of getting possession of them till the following morning, we had to make footwear for the journey. This was a great problem, but we solved it, at last, after a fashion. The only materials available were blankets and bits of cardboard, and with these we made four pairs of shoes for each man. They were flimsy, of course, and we knew that the last pairs would be worn out long before we reached the border; but there was no help for that, and once we were within striking distance of Switzerland we knew that we should get there somehow, shoes or no shoes. Fortunately we made our own beds mornings, and the fact that our blankets had been considerably trimmed away was not observed; nevertheless, we put in an anxious five minutes at morning inspection when the major, followed by Oberleutnant Rheinstrom, walked down the aisle between our cots, looking keenly to right and left.

By October 25 everything was in readiness. Our plan for getting over the wall was this: the other prisoners had contributed enough towels to enable us to make a rope of them. When we had let ourselves out of the barrack, one man was to be boosted to the top of the wall where he was to sit, holding the rope, while the rest of us climbed up hand over hand. This was a dangerously slow method, but we had to adopt it for want of a better. We meant, of course, to wait for a dark night, preferably a rainy one, and an engineer among us had been clever enough to find a means to short-circuit all the lights of the camp. On such a night we had reason to believe that we could get over the wall unobserved, and if it should prove necessary, men in the other barracks were to make a diversion to attract attention away from that part of the camp where we meant to make our break.

On the night of the twenty-sixth the moon was nearly full, and there wasn't a cloud in the sky. We let it pass and spent the next day hoping for rain. Throughout the twenty-seventh, twenty-eighth, and twenty-ninth, the same clear crisp weather continued. We were in despair, and McIntyre was for making a break on the night of the thirtieth no matter what the weather. But after talking matters over we all agreed that it would be worse than foolish to run a needless risk of being shot and having our plans miscarry, and we should be sure to have a cloudy night soon.

October 31 dawned as gloomily as heart could wish. Heavy clouds hung just over the treetops, and a fine rain was falling. Those of us who were to go ate a huge breakfast, and we planned an even heavier dinner, for we wanted to store up as much reserve energy as possible at the start. But we had no more than finished breakfast and the orderlies were washing up the dishes when we were summoned out for roll call. Oberleutnant Rheinstrom was awaiting us with a paper in his hand.

"Interesting news for some of you," he said. "You're going to change hotels. The following officers are to leave Landshut to-day for the prison camp at Villingen: Captain George McLeod, Lieutenant Roger Avery, Lieutenant Robert McIntyre, Lieutenant Charles Selden—" He went on down a list of fifteen men who were to be moved. "Get your things together at once," he added. "There will be a medical inspection, and you will be marched to the Landshut railway station at nine-fifteen."

Never in my life, I think, have I felt more disheartened than at that moment, and McIntyre's face was a study in wretchedness. We were the only members of the escape party who were being sent on, and to have our chance for freedom snatched from us on the very day of the break was the worst possible luck. However, it had its good side, as bad luck often does. We all knew of Villengen, the nearest of all German prison camps to the Swiss border. It was situated in a town in the Black Forest not more than twenty miles from the nearest point of Switzerland.

The moment Oberleutnant Rheinstrom dismissed us we held a hasty conference, and it was unanimously agreed that inasmuch as McIntyre and I were to be deprived of our chance for escape from Landshut, we were to have the first opportunity to make a break from the train if one presented itself during the journey. There was a heated discussion about my compass.

Although it was indubitably mine, it was the only one in the camp at that time, and its possession was essential to the other members of the escape party who were staying behind. I was very reluctant to part with it and so was McIntyre, but the others convinced us that they would have greater need of it at Landshut than we should in a camp so close to Switzerland; so we left it with them. My map of the Swiss frontier I kept, folding it into a thin square and fastening it to the bottom of my foot with a piece of adhesive tape.

At eight-thirty the fifteen of us stripped for inspection in the medical room. Sergeant Capp examined our bodies as well as our clothing, but by the grace of Providence he neglected to look at the bottoms of our feet, so my map was saved. Then we dressed, paraded in front of the commandant's office, and were marched to the station.

It is needless to go into details of the early part of the journey. We changed trains at Munich, and there were put into a passenger coach which was shunted about the Munich railroad yards for a quarter of an hour; then, to our surprise and delight, the coach was attached to the rear end of a freight train and we started in a south-westerly direction, every mile of the journey bringing us nearer to Switzerland. We prisoners occupied only two compartments of the passenger coach. The others were for the use of Bavarian farmers and their wives and children, going from one small town to another. The train moved at a leisurely pace, never faster than twenty miles per hour, and stopped at every station. We reached Ulm, only ninety miles from Switzerland, at three in the afternoon, and after a brief halt were again plodding along, always west and south, toward Villingen.

McIntyre and I were tremendously excited, inwardly, but tried to appear calm. The afternoon wore on; the rain had stopped, but the sky was still overcast and dusk was gathering rapidly. Lamps were lighted in the train. A guard stood in the corridor outside the doorway of our compartment, his rifle leaning against the wall beside him. McIntyre and I sat facing each other next to the window. We had agreed to be ready to go at any time after leaving Ulm, but as the train was still carrying us in the right direction we decided to wait until the last possible moment. The car window had been made fast, but it was a large one offering ample room to dive through. We planned to break the glass with our ration bags; first McIntyre was to dive, then I. The four others in our compartment were to follow if they had the chance. As the event fell out, they were compelled to remain behind.

It was not until after leaving Donaueschingen, a town less than ten miles from Villingen, that the favourable moment came. The train was travelling at about twelve miles per hour. Our guard turned for a moment toward the corridor window, pressing his face against the glass as he peered out into the darkness. McIntyre sprang up and with two quick thrusts of his ration bag smashed the glass beautifully; then he lunged through the opening as though making a dive from the end of a springboard. I glanced over my shoulder and saw the guard turn with a look of blank astonishment on his face. I saw him seize his rifle and start toward me, but at that instant Captain McLeod, who was sitting nearest the door, stuck out his feet and tripped him up. I didn't wait for another glance, and three seconds later I was rolling down the side of a steep embankment.

At the bottom of it I came up against a boulder that knocked the breath out of me, and for a moment or two I lay gasping and gagging and unable to move. I was scratched and bruised and wet through, for I had rolled into a puddle of icy water; but no bones were broken and I had gotten through the broken window with only a scratch on the back of my hand. Immediately after jumping I heard a fusillade of shots fired from the moving train, but it was too dark for the guards to see us, and a moment later the lighted passenger coach disappeared around a bend several hundred yards away. Soon it came into view again: the train was backing to the scene of the escape. By that time I had run across several ploughed fields to the border of a wood I could dimly make out ahead of me. Men with lanterns went up and down the right of way, but it was useless searching for us in the darkness, and after a quarter of an hour they climbed aboard again and the train proceeded on its way.

I went along the border of the wood calling softly for

McIntyre, but there was no answer. It was now almost pitch-dark. I was afraid McIntyre might have been hurt in jumping, so I went cautiously back toward the railroad, stopping at every moment to listen. Suddenly I heard a voice cry, "Halt!" Then several shots were fired in quick succession.

I made for the woods again across the mucky ploughed fields. The voice and the shots had come from a considerable distance—one hundred yards at least—which convinced me it must have been McIntyre, if anyone, who had been seen. Just before reaching the wood I heard someone running heavily in my direction. I decided to chance it, and called out McIntrye's name. "Charlie! Thank the Lord!" a voice replied. I am sure that neither of us ever had such pure joy at a meeting as at that moment. He too had been searching near the railroad when he all but ran into one of the guards left in ambush there. We joined hands so as not to lose each other, and ran along the border of the wood till we came to a narrow opening that proved to be a wood road. This we followed, walking and running by turns, until we were well out of reach of any pursuers.

The railroad between Donaueschingen and Villingen runs almost due north. We had jumped from the left side of the train and had gone off, as nearly as we could judge, at right angles to the railway line. If our reckoning was correct, we were moving in the desired direction—westward. Presently we emerged from the wood. It was a shade less black here, but still it was impossible to see anything but the slope of a hill in front of us. The road mounted this hill. We took to the fields and after a short steep climb came within view of the lights of a village lying in a valley on the other side.

We descended the hill, giving the village a wide berth. The slope was steep and rocky, and several times we started small avalanches of stones that made an awful racket as they clattered down. We had to feel our way, and about half-way down we found something smooth and solid under our feet. It proved to be the roof of an outbuilding of some sort built into the side of the hill. Somewhere beneath us a dog with a deep savage voice started barking loud enough to wake the dead. Some distance away a door was opened and a shaft of lamplight pierced the darkness, revealing a sloping barnyard with a roadway leading out at the right. We crouched down and waited. The man in the doorway shouted at the dog, who stopped barking; then the door was closed again. We felt our way to the edge of the roof and dropped over the side. As luck would have it we landed on a heap of rain-soaked manure, out of reach of the dog, who must have been tethered on the other side of the building. He started his uproar again, and we could hear him tugging at a chain for all he was worth. We ran through the barnyard to the roadway, and just as we did so the farmhouse door opened again and a man came out with a lantern. He was directly in our way, and as we ran past him I gave him a shove which toppled him over on top of his lantern. He yelled as though he were being murdered, and it was plain from the tone of his voice that he was badly frightened. At the bottom of the hill we met the roadway we had left on the other side. Crossing it, we came to a spongy meadow land. The meadow became a quagmire, knee-deep at first, then hip-deep. There were moments when I thought we were lost and would have to stick there, sinking gradually down until we were drowned in mud. This was one of the worst experiences we had during that trying journey, and yet, even in the midst of it the thought came to me; "By Jove! This is adventure—real adventure! We're prisoners of war escaping from Germany, and we're going to escape, too! In a few days we'll be across the Rhine, in Switzerland!" Such an experience was worth all the hardship and anxiety it cost, and miserable though we were, physically, we were conscious of an exhilaration of spirit that was ample compensation for any amount of discomfort. We must have lost an hour in crossing the bog, and when at last we reached solid ground we had used up enough energy to carry us to the border under less trying circumstances.

A detailed account of our adventures from the moment we leaped from the train till the grey of dawn would fill a book as large again as this one. Anyone who has been lost on a pitch-dark night in the Black Forest country will know what sort of adventures they were; and we couldn't, of course, stop at the first farmhouse we stumbled on to ask our way. We had to depend upon instinct to guide us, and, as it happened, instinct led us astray. In the first light of day we came to a crossroads where the guidepost set us right as to our position. We were a mile or two south of the town of Bregenbach. Although we had been continually on the move, with short halts to rest, since seven o'clock, our general direction had been north-west instead of south-west, and we were considerably farther from the Swiss border than we had been at dusk.

It was now necessary to conceal ourselves for the day, and we found a small evergreen wood on the side of the hill above the road, where the trees were so close together that nothing could be seen within the wood. We crawled in and found a little open space in the centre of the thicket that made an ideal hiding place. We were completely hidden from the view of anyone passing on the road, so here we made preparations for the long hours of inactivity ahead of us.

We were plastered with mud from head to foot, and McIntyre had a deep gash on his forehead, received when he had jumped through the car window. We were very weary, of course, but the worst of it was that we were wet through, and with dawn a cold mist rose from the valley chilling us to the bone. Frozen as we were, we removed our clothing and wrung it out as best we could. Then we massaged each other vigorously, greased our feet with soap, and put on dry socks. We each had a spare flannel shirt and a pair of woollen socks which we had managed to keep fairly dry. Each morning throughout the journey we soaped our feet and changed to dry socks, and whatever other discomforts we suffered, we were always able to march.

For the next two hours we were as miserable as it is possible for men to be, for we had neither blankets nor overcoats, and it was impossible to get warm. Tired as we were, we were compelled to do setting-up exercises in our little glade, but as soon as we left off we were as cold as before. At last the mists dispersed and the sun rose in a clear sky. It was wan November sunshine, but a godsend to us. By eleven o'clock we were fairly comfortable; then we lay down on a bed of evergreen branches and fell asleep at once.

When we awoke the shadows had crept far up the eastern slope of the hills across the Brege River, and the air was growing cold again. We got out our map and studied it carefully, laying our route for the coming night. One part of the Swiss border we were particularly anxious to avoid, and that was the small peninsula of land that juts into German territory to the north of Shaffhausen. This peninsula is almost a island in shape, and the northern end of it was temptingly close—not more than twelve miles distant, in fact. But we had learned from other prisoners recaptured on that part of the border that it was very well guarded. Furthermore, owing to the tortuous windings of the dividing line, there was great danger, once you had crossed the frontier, of walking out of Switzerland into Germany again. This had happened to prisoners on several occasions, so

McIntyre and I decided to leave that part of the border well to the east and to strike for the Rhine somewhere in the vicinity of Waldshut or Albruck, thirty miles away.

During the early part of the day we had been too cold and weary to think of food. Now we examined the contents of our ration bags, which we had carried at our belts for greater ease in walking. They were in a sorry mess; bread, biscuits, and chocolate had been soaked with water and mashed into a soggy paste. We sorted things out as well as we could and, although we were not hungry, made a hearty meal, quenching our thirst at a pool of rain water we found near by. Curiously enough, neither of us was at all hungry throughout this journey. Excitement and fatigue seemed to have taken away our appetites.

With the approach of night our sufferings from cold were renewed, but we had agreed never to leave our hiding places, no matter what our discomforts until the evening was well advanced. Several prisoners we knew had been recaptured because they had ventured out too soon after nightfall. So we snuggled together with our arms around each other, rocking back and forth, listening to a clock in Bregenback striking the quarters and never, not even at Landshut, had quarter hours seemed so interminable. People were passing on the road beneath us; we could hear their voices and the rattle of carts, but by nine o'clock all traffic seemed to have stopped. We then made our way to the top of the hill. Taking our bearings from the North star, we crossed a ravine and made for a road which our map told us ran from Bregenbach to Neustadt, a town on the Wutach River and the railroad running east and south from Freiburg.

Once more we lost our way and wandered among small fields surrounded by huge barriers of flints, heaped there, doubtless, by generations of German farmers who had cleared their fields in this fashion. The stones were small and sharp and piled to a height of five or six feet. In fact, these walls were like dikes rather than fences, and overgrown with an especially prickly kind of thorn bush. Barbed-wire entanglements could have been but little more effective as barriers than these dikes covered with thorn trees. It was nearly midnight before we found our road, and when the clocks of Neustadt were striking three we were standing in a stony field above the town, wondering what direction to take next.

Hard experience had taught us that my map had not been prepared with escaping prisoners of war in mind. Many villages, roads, and streams were not marked, and it gave us only a hazy general notion of the windings of the valleys and the heights of the hills. When studying it at Landshut we thought it would be a fairly simple matter to make straight across country to the Rhine and we expected to cover from fifteen to twenty miles in a night. Our first ten hours of cross-country hiking in the Black Forest country convinced us that we should be lucky if we covered five miles in the right direction; but this slow pace was partly due to the fact that we had to use such caution to avoid meeting people. Furthermore, without a compass we were almost as helpless as blind men, for it was only rarely that we were able to check our course by guideposts or the stars; then we found, often, that we had lost much precious time walking farther into Germany instead of out of it.

The Wutach River, which now barred our way to the south, was by no means the insignificant stream it appeared to be on the map. As we proceeded southward, leaving Neustadt well to the right, the valley wall pitched off at an increasingly steep angle. After stepping off into vacancy several times and falling down miniature precipices, we decided to slide down, much to the damage of the seats of our trousers. We came to a wooded slope that was little less than a cliff, and, having let ourselves down by means of saplings, reached the brink of a cañon filled with a mist of broken water. The river was a good fifty feet below, in a straight drop.

Back we climbed the weary way we had come, to search for another way down. At last we stumbled into a road leading down the side of the valley, and at the same moment a man on horseback loomed out of the darkness. The horse shied at sight of us, and the man passed at a quickened pace, without speaking; evidently he was more alarmed than we were. We took to the road, for there was not likely to be anyone else abroad at that hour of the night; but had we met any soldiers our position would have been hopeless—all the way down we had an unscaleable cliff on the left hand and a sheer drop on the right. Upon reaching the bridge we saw that it would be very difficult to ford the river; the current was swift, and, judging by the sound, a large volume of water was rushing through the rocky channel. The bridge lay temptingly before us, but on our side of the river strips of lamplight from the windows of a power station lay across the roadway. We reconnoitred the position and decided to chance the bridge. Creeping close to the wall of the power station, we passed under the windows into the welcome darkness beyond. My heart was going pitapat, for many a prisoner had been recaptured on a bridge. Luck was with us, however; there were no guards as there should have been, and a moment later we were scrambling up the opposite valley wall, well out of danger.

It started raining again, a fine cold drizzle that took its time about wetting us through, but did it perfectly, long before daylight. An hour of steady climbing took us out of the valley to a high plateau covered with tracts of fine old forest and villages and scattered farms. We made detours round the villages, and dawn found us in a wood where we had an increasingly anxious time searching for a suitable hiding place, for the trees were ancient ones and the spaces between them well cleared of undergrowth. At last we found a little thicket that would do, and in the midst of it was a pine tree whose lower branches swept the ground. We crept in under that and made an effective screen of branches all round us. It was well that we did. No sooner had we finished our work than a group of wood-choppers appeared and started felling trees close at hand.

All through the morning they were at work within two two or three hundred yards of us, and one tree crashed into our thicket, so close that we could feel the wind of its fall. I could have chucked a pebble with my thumb and hit the man who came to clear away the branches, but he was intent upon his job, and although he glanced in our direction several times he saw nothing wrong with our pine tree. They all went home at noon, but we didn't dare run the risk of searching for a safer place. They worked farther from us during the afternoon, so that we were able to get a little sleep, only to be aroused by some children gathering bundles of sticks. They had a puppy who ran here and there and finally smelled us out, standing within ten feet of us, barking excitedly. Fortunately the children paid no attention to him, and after five minutes of intense anxiety we were left in peace.

That evening the cold drove us out half an hour before we should have gone. It was another frosty night, and as we had had no opportunity to dry our clothing during the day we were so cold and stiff that it was impossible to wait any longer. We met an old woman carrying a bundle of faggots on her back, but apparently she neither saw nor heard us. After zigzagging down the slope of another steep valley we came to a stream where the water was up to our armpits and the current so swift that we had great difficulty in crossing. The stiff climb that followed warmed us a little, and as we reached the top of the slope we saw a lighted train passing a bit of open country below us. It was a heartening sight, for it enabled us to check up on our position; we knew that we had before us the branch line of the railroad running to Bonndorf.

The country we were now crossing was difficult enough to try the patience of a saint—up hill and down dale, through forests, thickets, and peaty bottom lands, without so much as a quarter of an hour's walking on level ground. We made several errors in direction, and at dawn had covered about eight miles, in a straight line, from our camp of the day before. We found an excellent hiding place for this day—a barn filled with hay in a forest clearing. There were no houses anywhere about; so, having filled our water bottle, we climbed into the loft, burrowed deep down into the hay, and went to sleep as snugly and comfortably as though we were in bed at home.

We awoke late in the afternoon and crawled out of our burrow to have a look around. The barn stood in a wide meadow bordered on all sides by woodland. It looked beautifully secluded, but a clock striking the hour in some church tower warned us that we were not far from a village. We went cautiously down the haymow ladder and found a bin filled with cabbages, a most welcome change of diet from soggy bread and chocolate. We made a good meal of them and requisitioned two more to carry with us. No one disturbed us, and by the time night had fallen we were thoroughly rested and refreshed and started on our way with renewed confidence.

As before, we avoided roads until midnight, except in places where it was impossible to proceed otherwise. Our progress was vertical rather than horizontal, up one hill and down another, and our route might easily have been traced by the barking of dogs we aroused on the way. I have always been a lover of dogs, but those of the Black Forest towns and villages gave us so much trouble that I came to hate them, individually and collectively. Some were savage brutes, and we were fortunate to escape from them with whole skins. One I remember particularly, an enormous animal that looked Gargantuan in the dim starlight. Once he had our scent he came for us with a ferocity there was no mistaking. We carried clubs for just such an emergency, and on this occasion we had to use them with all our strength and skill. We rained blows on his back and head, which only seemed to arouse him the more. At last McIntyre stunned him with a fearful crack on the skull, and we made off without waiting to see whether he wanted any more of it. This battle happened in the small hours of the morning, not far from the town of Hausern, and at the end of it we were so weary that we went but little farther before daylight. Again we hid ourselves on a slope, under an ancient fir tree whose branches touched the ground on all sides. It was a magnificent hiding place from a scenic point of view. Behind us, and to the right, we could see the highest peaks of the Schwarzwald faintly flushed with the light of the hidden sun, and the great trough of the Alb Valley, filled with mist, stretched out before us. That glorious sight warmed us spiritually if not physically. We realized that we had reached the highest point of our journey and now had a long steady descent to the Rhine and freedom.

Incredible as it may seem, we spent five days in covering the fifteen miles from that spot to the Rhine. We were perhaps more cautious than was necessary, but many prisoners had been recaptured because impatience had made them reckless when within striking distance of safety. We meant to reach Switzerland, and had it been necessary we should have wriggled the last fifteen miles on our bellies. It came to something like that toward the end of the journey. Farms and villages were more numerous here, and roads and paths more frequented. In order to be as safe as possible we delayed the hour of setting out at night until eleven o'clock. We were frequently lost, for the country hereabout was a labyrinth of winding valleys and rounded hills, hopelessly confusing in the darkness. On we went, nevertheless, never for a moment doubting that we should reach the border, and not only reach it, but cross it. On the morning of November 10, well before daylight, we crept into a patch of alder and blackberry bushes several acres in extent, and, having concealed ourselves, waited to see what the light would reveal.

Veil after veil of darkness fell away, and at last we saw what was unmistakably a great mountain wall towering into the mist to the south of us. We believed that we were looking at the wall of the valley that still hemmed us in, but crawled through the bushes to the edge of the clearing for a better view. The mist rose by imperceptible degrees, and presently we saw, far away beneath us, a moving white streamer, vanishing, reappearing, changing position constantly. It was a train on the other side of the Rhine.

That day was, of course, the longest as well as the most anxious we had spent thus far. A path ran through the fields near our hiding place, and people were passing all the time. Neither of us slept—we were too keenly excited—but we had a good rest, basking in the sunshine and listening to the conversation of Germans who little realized that two prisoners of war were concealed within twenty-five yards of them. Throughout the day we heard the roar of trains on the German side of the Rhine, and once, peering out through our screen of bushes, we saw half a dozen soldiers march past. They were evidently one of the patrols of the frontier guard.

Toward midnight we removed all our clothing and greased our bodies with the tin of bacon fat we had brought with us from Landshut. Having dressed, we crept to the edge of our clearing and again waited. Now if ever was the time to proceed with the utmost caution. Everything was silent, and we slipped down an embankment and into the bushes on the other side of the road. A little farther down the slope we came to ploughed fields and scattered houses. The fields were enclosed with hedges, making excellent cover, and we crept along these barriers, making right-angled turns, all the time working farther down and away from a village that lay somewhere beneath us on the left hand.

After a half hour of creeping we came to the brink of a railroad cutting and were about to slide down it when we heard the tramp of feet on the right of way. At the same moment we heard the whistle of an approaching train. Peeping over the edge of the embankment, we saw the train pass, and the light from its windows revealed a border patrol standing with their backs toward us, their rifles slung over their shoulders. They marched on down the line, and as soon as they were out of hearing we crossed the railroad and proceeded on hands and knees, stopping at every few yards to listen. A thick mist was rising from the river, concealing everything, but we were sure of our way now with the slope of the land to guide us. Half an hour of creeping brought us to a jumping-off place. We could see nothing, but we heard the most welcome sound in the world—the gentle slapping of little waves on a gravel bank. As we lay there, peering down into the fog, we heard another sound that was anything but welcome—the steady crunching of heavy boots, ten paces in one direction and ten back.

We worked farther along the edge of the embankment. Judging by the sound of the waves we were about fifty feet above the river. Evidently there was a road below with guards stationed at distances of two hundred yards or so. We crept along until we had located three sentry posts, then back to what we judged was midway between two of them. Here we removed all of our clothing except our trousers. We kept our shoes, but unlaced them so that we could kick them off as soon as we reached the river; then we started down.

We were taking a long chance, for it was impossible to judge of the steepness of the descent; but our luck held during this most critical five minutes of the entire journey. The bank fell away at an angle of about forty-five degrees, and there were bushes and saplings to hold to. We descended by inches, feeling carefully for every foothold and handhold. I dislodged a stone that clattered down to the roadway with a sound like thunder; immediately afterward we heard someone approaching.

We lay back among the bushes, scarcely daring to breathe. Turning my head to the right, I saw that the sentry had switched on his flash lamp and was throwing the light up and down the embankment about twenty-five paces from us. He came nearer and in another moment would have unquestionably discovered us, for we were not more than twenty feet above the level of the roadway. Luckily for us, McIntyre had the presence of mind to seize another stone and throw it far along the embankment on the other side of the guard, who heard it bounding down among the bushes, and ran back, calling,

"*Wer da?*" or something to that effect. This gave us time to slide down to the roadway, cross it, and plunge into the water. In three strides I was beyond my depth and struck out into the current, which carried me farther and farther from shore.

I kicked off my shoes the moment I entered the water, and soon realized that I should have to remove my heavy trousers as well, for they were beginning to drag me down. Swimming with one hand, I unbuckled my belt and slipped the trousers to my knees. That was an anxious moment; I had great difficulty in getting them over my feet, and in the process swallowed a pint or two of Rhine water, but once free of them I swam easily. The fog was not so dense on the surface of the water, and I could dimly see the goal I was making for. The water must have been very cold, but in my excitement and elation I scarcely noticed this. However, the moment I touched bottom on the Swiss shore my teeth began to chatter as though they would be rattled out of my head.

I went along the bank shouting for McIntyre, but there was no reply. I had seen him plunge into the river ahead of me, but soon lost him in the darkness. A cold wind from the mountains blowing against my wet body convinced me that I must find shelter of some sort at once, so I struck inland and a few moments later came to a railroad. Not knowing which way to go, I turned to the right, but the rock ballast was so hard on my bare feet that I was forced to take to the fields again.

About two hundred yards farther inland I came to a highway, and ran along it for half a mile or so till I came to a crossroad and a two-story stone house that looked as though it might be an inn of some sort. Everything was dark there, and I hammered on the door for at least ten minutes—it seemed an hour—before rousing anyone; then a be-nightcapped head appeared at an upper window and demanded, "*Was ist los*?" in German-Swiss. I knew enough German to explain my predicament, but I was so cold that I could scarcely speak. However, I managed to make myself understood, and after what seemed another hour of waiting the front door was unbolted by a bearded, kindly-faced man who held a candle in his hand. He gazed at me in astonishment, as well he might, for there I was without a stitch of clothing, wet, muddy, and now so nearly frozen that I could only blurt out unintelligible sounds. But further explanation was needless, and I soon realized that I could not possibly have fallen into better hands. My host led me down a corridor into a bedroom, spotlessly clean. He insisted that I get into bed at once, bedraggled and muddy as I was, and piled another feather bed on top of me. As soon as I could speak I told him about McIntyre, and he immediately sent out one of his sons with a lantern to look for him. Meanwhile he had aroused the rest of his household, and, while his wife was preparing some hot food in the kitchen, he and another of his boys kneaded and rubbed me from head to foot until the blood started to flow again. Then he gave me a large glass of schnapps that sent waves of delicious warmth to the ends of my fingers and toes, and that was followed by a bowl of hot chocolate and homemade bread and butter.

Never will I forget the kindness of that Swiss family. Within half an hour after getting to bed they had me thawed out, and the only thing then wanting to complete happiness was the news that McIntyre was safe. That soon came. The boy who had gone in search of him returned with the word that he was snugly in bed at a house a mile or two down the road. I went to sleep at once and didn't waken till after midday, when I was aroused by someone shaking me by the shoulder. It was McIntyre, dressed in borrowed clothing three sizes too small for him. He was looking down at me with an ironic grin.

"Well," he said, "what do you think has happened? Listen—hear anything?"

Somewhere not far away church bells were ringing furiously.

"The war's over," he went on. "An armistice was signed at eleven o'clock this morning."

I didn't believe him, of course, and turned to my Swiss host who was standing near by, his face wreathed in smiles. He nodded his head vigorously.

"*Ja, ja! Krieg ferig!*" he said.

Three days later we crossed the border into France.

XIX

AFTER THE ARMISTICE

I OPENED my eyes that morning in the same upstairs room at the Héraults' where I had spent my first night in France. It was Christmas morning, and a year had passed since the Christmas I remembered so well at La Noblette. No one was astir as yet; the light was still grey, and a fine dry snow was falling softly outside.

Gordon Forbes was a guest in the Héraults' house with me. His luck had never deserted him; and for a Spad pilot to survive the attacks of 1918 and live to celebrate the Armistice was luck indeed. He still wore the uniform of a French lieutenant, but had been granted a long leave to America, with the privilege of being demobilized at home. Thanks to the friendly offices of Dr. Gros, Forbes and I had our travel orders to sail for America the next day, when we were to board the *Mauretania* at Brest. I was to be demobilized in New York, and it was strangé, almost incredible, to think that in two weeks I should be free to lay aside my uniform for civilian clothes. We had talked everything over. Gordon was to stop in New York to set his affairs in order, and to have plans for a schooner drawn up by a famous naval architect. I would cross the continent at once and wait for Gordon at the ranch, where he would join me as soon as he was free, and stop while our vessel was building at Oakland. Perhaps a wire to my uncle would persuade him to come north. . . .

Thinking happily of what lay ahead and of the joy of seeing my people once more, I was conscious at the same time of a feeling of keen regret at the prospect of leaving France. I loved the country and its people, with many of whom it would be a genuine wrench to part. The Hérault s—what good friends they were! Only last night, Mme. de Thouars had arranged a little Christmas Eve dinner for us, with a tableful of French officers, and young girls whose gay, inconsequent talk brought home all that a soldier must forgo in war. I longed to chat with them, but I found myself brusque and tongue-tied, unused to the company of women, and distrustful of my French—by no means of the drawing-room brand. My account of the arrival of the Pâté des Chasseurs at Landshut, given at Mme. de Thouars's request, brought smiles that were partly on account of my Aviation French, but they were friendly smiles for all that, and I didn't mind.

Early that afternoon, Forbes and I set out to call on Dr. Gros, to say good-bye. We had telephoned in advance, and found him in his drawing-room. The interview had its painful side, to me at least, for it meant parting from a man who had been more than kind to me, who had placed me under obligations I should never forget. I wondered, as I shook his hand, when I should have the good fortune to see him again.

"I'm glad you chaps dropped in," he was saying. "I was hoping you would come to say good-bye, and there's something else. I have a little Christmas present for you." He handed each of usan envelope. "They're the special Service Ribbons and the Certificates the Ministry of War has just conferred upon the members of the Laffayette Flying Corps."

I found a small blue ribbon on a pin—spangled with stars, and bordered with the tricolour; and a very handsome engraved certificate, signed by the Under-Secretary of State for Aeronautics and phrased with a moving beauty no translation could preserve.

"You'll be proud of that paper," said Dr. Gros, "and prouder still as the years go by. The Corps has played its little part in history—perhaps not such a little part after all. You chaps and others like you have served in more than ninety French squadrons along the front, and more than a hundred of you transferred to our Service when America came into the war. Think of it! Out of the six hundred American pilots at the front, one hundred were Lafayette men, and others of you, like Forbes here, were flying and fighting in French uniform till the close. Well, it's over now. Hard to realize, isn't it?"

We parted from Dr. Gros with sincere regret. He stood in his doorway watching us as we walked down the snowy street, and waved his hand as we turned the corner.

We boarded the subway at the Étoile and got off at the Place de la Concorde. This was our last opportunity to enjoy the streets of Paris, never gayer than just after the war. The sun had come out during the morning, and it was a true Christmas day—clear, cold, and sparkling, with snow on the scanty patches of grass. We turned up to the Madeleine, and followed the boulevard past the Café de la Paix and the Opéra. Passing a modest café some distance beyond, I chanced to notice that it was called the Maxéville. A few soldiers, muffled in overcoats, sat on the terrace sipping drinks. Just then a handsome military limousine whizzed up the boulevard and came to a spectacular stop by the kerb. The front door flew open, and I heard someone shouting my name.

"Hey, Selden! Hey! Cut your motor!"

It was Golasse, pale, cheerful, and walking with a cane. Flingot crawled out from behind the wheel and sprang down after him. To say that I was glad to see the pair expresses nothing at all. We shook hands all round, and then Golasse hobbled across the sidewalk, past the men on the cold terrace, and into the warm restaurant beyond. He seemed to be well known in the place. An old waiter came forward with alacrity, smiling at the invalid.

"A *porto* for you, *mon adjudant*—no need of asking, eh? What would these gentlemen like?"

With all the rich vineyards and distilleries of France at

his command, Flingot ordered a litre of *pinard*. "My palate's gone," he remarked, apologetically. "The war's killed my taste for anything but red ink! Selden, do you remember that vinegar we drank—or rather, that I drank—the night I came to Châlons to take you up to Sénard?

"Notice my car?" he went on when the waiter had served us. "A beauty—what? Major Beaumont's a colonel now, on the staff of the Aéronautique, and I'm his chauffeur. What do you think of that? After four years of wire-pulling to get a soft job in the rear, I finally get it when the war's won! Well, I'm not complaining. We'll all have soft jobs from now on." He looked at Forbes. "You and Colonel Beaumont have had the devil's own luck, *mon lieutenant*. Through the whole show, flying every day without a scratch! Not many of 'em in your class. Some didn't like their messes and flew over to try the Kaiser's soup, like Selden here. Others jumped in front of a bullet, like Golasse; but most of 'em are pushing up daisies now. By the way, Selden, how *was* the soup?"

"Delicious! You could suck it through a straw!"

Golasse reached over to feel my ribs.

"H'm!" he observed dryly. "You've got fat on it, anyhow. If I'd known Fritz's tucker was as good as that, I'd have come over to join you. I don't mind saying that I envied you just before I got this leg in the Argonne. I felt as though I'd had about enough. Forbes, you birds who went all the way through are marvels! How did you do it!"

"Luck," said Gordon, with a wry smile. "Believe me, I know how you felt!"

"My worst time was at Villeneuve," said Golasse reminiscently. "*Bon Dieu!* I was half crazy. . . . One night I nearly had a scrap with the best friend I had left. Remember, Selden? You told me I stank. . . Well, so I did! And I said something I shouldn't have said. *Sacrée guerre!* How long ago that seems!"

"How's your leg getting on?" I asked. "I didn't know you'd been wounded."

Golasse stretched out the wounded limb stiffly, for a critical glance. "They tell me it'll be all right one of these days. But I should worry! That American hospital is a dream! Three square meals when I'm there to eat' em, a bed fit for a general, and the prettiest nurses in France! And now that I'm convalescent, they let me out for a whole day whenever I like. My pay's been mounting up, you see, so I can blow myself to a day out now and then. By the way, I met McKail yesterday. He told me that he is sailing for America to-morrow, from Brest."

"Selden and I are going by the same boat," said Forbes.

"No! Is that so? Bad news for me. Well, that's the way it goes, isn't it? We'll all be scattered now—those of us who are left?"

Neither Golasse nor Flingot had much squadron news for me. Weiler had been sent to the rear as an instructor. Of Cartier, Vigneau, old Felix, and the rest, they could tell me nothing. Perhaps they were still with the old outfit, now on the Rhine. Perhaps not. It was sad to reflect that in all probability I should never see any of those good fellows again.

Golasse was nudging his companion. "See that old *sergent de ville* by the door?" he said warningly. "Look out for him! He suspects the truth—that you're joy-riding with some officer's car." Flingot glanced through the window and tossed off a glass of wine, airily.

"*Pouf!*" he exclaimed. "Let him think what he likes. He'd need a microscope to decide that your cap is not an officer's, and when he gets a flash of all those bananas on your chest he'll probably present arms."

I had noticed the old policeman—legendary enemy of all airmen—and now it struck me that Golasse was right: he was looking hard at the car, and turning for an occasional undecided glance in through the window.

"So you fellows are off to the South Seas," remarked Golasse, when Gordon had ordered a third round of drinks. "Well, I hope you enjoy yourselves. As for me, give me the good old Maxéville, with a *porto* on the table, and money to buy more when that one's gone."

"You told me that once before," I said. "A long time ago."

Golasse sipped the last of his port, set down the glass, and smacked his lips.

"Yes—and I'll be saying the same thing fifty years from now."

He took up his stick and rose painfully from his chair. "Time I was getting back to the hospital," he explained "I'll have to say good-bye to you chaps."

He clasped our hands briefly and warmly, and Flingot did the same. We stood outside on the terrace to watch them go. As they crossed the sidewalk the policeman took a step forward and came to a halt at sight of Golasse's decorations, displayed when his overcoat flew open as if by chance. Golasse struggled into the front seat and waved to us. Flingot leaped to his place and started the engine with a roar. The policeman seemed to have arrived at a decision at last and started for them, raising his hand. But he had misjudged his man. Flingot released the clutch, and as the car bounded forward he leaned out of the open window to thumb his nose back at the scandalized *sergent de ville*. The limousine whizzed off, weaving in and out of the traffic at a tremendous pace. The policeman stood at the kerb, his mouth slightly open as the car flashed round the corner and disappeared.

CPSIA information can be obtained at www.ICGtesting.com
Printed in the USA
LVOW11s1955130716

496174LV00001B/155/P